# The
# Innkeeper
# Tales

# The Innkeeper Tales

John L. Herman Jr.

Edited by Clarinda Harriss

HSB Press

2007

The Innkeeper Tales

www.TheInnkeeperTales.com

Edited by Clarinda Harriss

Copyedited and designed by Carmen M. Walsh

Front jacket photo by Jacqueline Slavney
Back jacket photos edited by Jacqueline Slavney

ISBN-13:  978-0-9790204-0-7
ISBN-10:  0-9790204-0-9

Library of Congress Control Number: 2006935526

HSB Press
11615 Greenspring Avenue
Lutherville, MD 21093  USA

Distribution by Itasca Books
www.itascabooks.com

Printed in the United States of America

# Dedications

To Kelly, Colleen, and Shannon,
who mean the world to me ...

To Maggie, Sonny, and Julie,
who add so much to my life ...

And to Clarinda Harriss,
whose many hours of dedication
allowed my voice to be heard.

# Acknowledgments

No book is ever written solely by the author. Swimming inside the author's head are myriad ghosts of past books they read and of people who touched their lives. First off, therefore, I want to acknowledge those early teachers who taught me and encouraged me to read.

Authors disappear from their families when the writing process steals them away for hours, for whole days, as the keyboard calls at all hours to put the words to paper. My wife, Maggie, sacrificed those hours too: not just in my absence during the writing, but by listening to the same stories over and over again as they were assembled.

For this book, I also need to acknowledge a place: a building, along with a staff that makes the building warm and friendly, truly a best friend. The "Inn," the Abacrombie, is a real bed and breakfast and restaurant, which many wonderful guests have visited over the past four years. And so these guests too must be acknowledged for their support and patience as the stories you will read here were told and retold. Without the dialogue between the guests and the Innkeeper, there wouldn't have been a book.

Finally, I want to acknowledge two wonderful people who have enhanced the words I gave them on paper, but more importantly who have become new friends. Clarinda Harriss, the editor, is a literary genius. Her talent, skill, and teaching have been overwhelming in a wonderful way. Her many students, faculty colleagues, and the authors she has worked with can never say enough about her impact on them. The second person is an emerging star in the publishing world. Carmen Walsh has designed a beautiful book for me. The interior text and jacket show the talent she possesses. And her copyediting and proofing proved invaluable to the end product. No author has ever been blessed with two better professionals to encourage this work to completion. May every author have a Clarinda and a Carmen by their side as I have.

# Contents

# The Innkeeper Tales: Prologue

When you stay at a hotel, you eat in the hotel dining room, separated by a proper amount of personal space so you don't have to engage in conversation. Not so at a Bed and Breakfast. Breakfast at a B&B finds you sharing a table with anybody who gets up around the same time as you. Maybe with somebody who isn't a morning person and doesn't engage in conversation anyway; more likely people who chose a B&B over a hotel because they actually like to listen to something a little more interesting than the sound of their own cereal crunching.

As "Herman the Host," the owner of Abacrombie's in downtown Baltimore, I can tell you that just about all this week's guests have become conversationalists. That's because they've been pretty much stuck here. It's early March. In Baltimore, March means (a) the beginning of spring and (b) the chance of a blizzard, often the city's only snowfall of the entire year. A blizzard that shuts down the airport. A blizzard that makes Baltimore's public transportation seem more than a little erratic.

That's why my guests are lucky. My B&B is cozily located in a part of town where you can walk to museums and art galleries, the famous Inner Harbor, the symphony hall, antique shops, trendy clothes and jewelry stores, dozens of bars and restaurants. Hey, my own bar and restaurant's one of them, and among the best, if I do say so myself. So cabin fever is not a problem.

Judging from the group that's here now, though, I'd say cabin fever would not be setting in even if they couldn't get out of the building. For one thing, breakfast here is like most everything else here— better than home! Seven kinds of fresh fruit. Four different cereals. Bagels. Homemade bread. Honey for your tea. Little pots of jam. Danish pastry, maybe a butter crumb cake on a small buffet. No limits on the meat and cheese platter. Free. Free to share with your spouse of many years or your new lover. With your fellow guests. Vacationers—or Baltimore locals too tired or old to drive home after the opera. Gays and lesbians. Students coming to look over the

Maryland Institute College of Art or the Peabody Conservatory of Music. People from all over the globe here to learn about the latest medical research or to study at the world-famous Johns Hopkins University and Hospital. Young people who want to save money by not paying big-city hotel prices. Yankee fans and Red Sox fans when their teams are playing at Camden Yards.

Breakfast is where the stories are told. You won't ever see your new breakfast-mates again, so who cares what you say? You can be anyone you want, even if that is not who you are. The others in the room may be spellbound or bored, but one thing is for certain: people open up to strangers. That goes for even the kind of people I call "Skeptaters"—my own word for "Skeptical Spectators," people who are generally afraid and confused about their place in the world, what they're doing on Planet Earth. The opening up may start with a simple "Why are you here?" "Where are you from?" "What kind of accent is that?" As Herman the Host, I get my opening into the conversations when I serve their coffee and explain how the fancy toaster works. I get to share the stories too. This snowy morning promises to be an exceptional one for breakfast stories. I'm going to pull up a chair at the biggest table. You might want to do that too.

# First Jobs: Enzo's Tale

Enzo had come to Baltimore for a few days to visit family and some old friends he'd grown up with. He'd also hoped to evade the filthy gray snow that litters city streets, and Baltimore temperatures had been in the sixties only a week ago. Ironic—but at least this week's new snow was clean and white. Over his third cup of coffee, Enzo said he felt guilty staying away from his job an extra day, even though the Baltimore blizzard obviously wasn't his fault.

## "How the hell did we get this way?"

We wondered where the work ethic started in any of us. Enzo said he was picking beans before the age of ten for thirty-five cents a bushel. It was a thrill to be a wage earner. But actually the first money Enzo earned was shining shoes at the neighborhood bar at the age of four, with the shoe-shine kit he got for Christmas. No self-respecting drinker could turn down a four-year-old kid willing to shine his shoes while he swilled his beer. And then there was the "helper" job he had with relatives, painting and fixing restaurant equipment.

Or the time Enzo was hired to knock on doors to ask residents if they had received their free gift card from *Look* Magazine or *Ladies' Home Journal*. Since they hadn't (none were ever sent), he would sign them up for a subscription and promise home delivery if enough neighbors signed up too. Few did, but it was worth a buck to the "route manager" who drove the neighborhood if Enzo could talk the homeowners into letting him (the route manager) inside the house to speak to them or, better yet, "close" the prospect.

But the real first job was when it became official. When he actually got a work permit and was really paid on a payroll, one where his hours counted. A job where he had to wear appropriate clothing. In other words, a uniform.

"Pearl diver" was the nickname for Enzo's first official job. Not where you dove under the sea for oysters with pearls. But rather where you sloshed your hands in a deep sink of hot water, washing dishes, pots, and pans. On the day Enzo turned sixteen, he went to the government office and took out a work permit to become employed, sixteen being the minimum age for getting one of these permits. At 5:00 PM, with "working papers" in hand, Enzo reported to Bickford's Restaurant at a busy downtown location to officially begin his life of work. He was proud of the fact that he was official on the first day it was possible to have a permit. Sure, it was his birthday. But who cared about celebrating when there was a chance to make money and be an adult? Parties and friends could wait.

It took three buses and about an hour and a half to get to Bickford's from his suburban home. What did it matter to him? He was officially employed. Six days a week at eight hours a day at $1.10 per hour. Forty-eight glorious hours of pearl diving for the gigantic take-home pay of thirty-nine dollars per week. Minus bus fare of about four dollars weekly, of course. That meant he got thirty-five dollars in real money for sixty-six hours of travel and work each week. Just about fifty cents an hour. His friends said he was nuts. They were still home playing baseball and poker and pitching nickels, dimes, and quarters against the school wall, while he had given up his freedom to go make thirty-five dollars a week. But Enzo was thrilled to be doing it. Now he wasn't a kid any more. Everyone else at the restaurant was supporting himself or his family by working there. Enzo felt just like them. A member of the adult world.

## What a world

Enzo was in for a few shocks. Some workers routinely stole the meat when it was delivered. Some people didn't ring up customers and kept the money. Sometimes dishwashers at other restaurants near Bickford's didn't show up because they were drunk or sick or just couldn't stand to dive for any more pearls. And that misfortune was Heaven to Enzo, because it meant he could get off at 1:00 AM, run the six blocks to the other restaurant, and wash dishes all night until 6:00 AM. Overtime. His first taste of time and a half.

"Wow, I thought to myself, they have to give you extra for working more hours! What a country."

And what an education about people that job was. Especially the night people who came in after the famous "Baltimore Block" bars closed. Strippers, transvestites, drunks. Lonely people. Politicians. Businessmen. Sports figures. News reporters. Everyone came in after a night of howling downtown. For a suburban teenager, it was amazing to see so many different kinds of people. Black and white. Straight, gay, and lesbian. Homeless people with just enough money for a coffee. All kinds of people. And he learned that people are truly all alike. They all want to be happy. To be accepted as they are. There at Bickford's, Enzo got an education a person couldn't get in school for any amount of tuition. An education certainly worth many times the thirty-five dollars a week he was paid.

"So, besides the 'We are Family' thing, what else did you learn from your first real job?" I asked, pouring him a fourth coffee.

Enzo didn't have to think long. To be on time. To understand travel schedules to and from work. To get the dishes done quickly so he could coast during the second half of his shift. He also learned that the government took out taxes. He learned that some people worked harder than others. That some were thieves. That some were bouncing back from a crisis in life. And, of course, that when you worked overtime, you could make time and a half. Why didn't everyone want to work a double shift?

## Graduating to burgers

From dishwashing, Enzo graduated to a fast-food restaurant, making crab cakes, hamburgers, and chicken. It was Enzo's first bout with management. The workers felt they were not being paid enough. Enzo took the lead and offered to speak to the boss for all of them.

"How about a raise for everyone?" Enzo asked the owner.

"How about ten cents more an hour for you and nothing for them?" replied the boss.

Enzo was in an ethical dilemma. Take the dime an hour and tell the others nothing, or refuse his own raise and perhaps quit. Coming from a labor background—his own father was a union shop steward—Enzo chose to repeat his demand: a raise for all, or he would leave.

"Good luck," said the owner.

Enzo learned that sometimes worrying about those "others" could cost you your job. He thought he might have to reconsider that socialist concept in exchange for a more self-serving capitalist philosophy in the future.

## Out there alone

Next Enzo landed a job as a delivery boy for a pharmacy. His duties were to drive the car, making about twenty stops a day. Sometimes, when he brought the prescriptions to people's houses where they lay in misery from a cold, the flu, or other nasty ailment, he even got a tip. Enzo liked this job better than the others. He discovered something about himself: he liked working alone. No one else was in the car with him. And he liked the challenge of delivering the prescriptions quickly so he could get back to the store to stock shelves or watch the pharmacist fill the "scripts."

Howard & Morris Pharmacy dated back to the 1950s. It was unique, especially by today's standards. It sold only drugs and related items. There were no snow shovels or auto supplies, no candy aisles or magazine racks. The two owners felt that filling a prescription should be like getting a haircut. Materials plus labor. Specific materials. Specific labor. Howard & Morris charged customers the cost of the drugs they bought from the drug companies plus two dollars to the pharmacist for filling the prescription. True, they also sold foot pads, powders, band-aids, and enemas, but the real money came from those two-dollar fees. Every nearby retirement home, elderly care facility, old person, and common Joe came to realize they were saving money by getting prescriptions filled there. The place was always jumping with business.

Enzo was learning another bit about business: customer care was vital. Howard & Morris would actually call customers to remind them it was time for a refill. They'd send each customer a statement at the end of the year to show what was spent on strictly medical needs for use when they filed their taxes. These considerations built loyalty. Loyalty meant repeat business. Deservedly, these guys thrived. They opened a chain of stores in the surrounding county.

I interrupted to ask, "Enzo, were you working downtown during the riots that broke out after Martin Luther King was killed? Wasn't there a curfew down there that said you couldn't be out after a certain hour without special permission?"

"Yep," Enzo said. "To tell the truth, it made me feel nervous but important."

Because of the nature of his work, he had been allowed to drive, while many people much older than he was had lost the freedom to leave their homes.

My bringing in a batch of sweet rolls hot from the kitchen somehow gave Enzo the go-ahead to launch into another recollection, one that embarrassed him to tell. Seems there was a daytime driver named Richard at the store. He worked for Howard & Morris full time, had done so for years. Richard was always getting a ticket or banging up the delivery car. The owners were always threatening to fire the guy. One day Richard called the store to say he'd slid on ice, jammed the car against a curb, and the car was stuck there, too damaged to drive. It went into the shop. The front wheel was repaired. The day the car came out of the shop, Enzo drove it. He too slid on the ice and hit the curb. The accident re-damaged the wheel.

"Oh shit! I said to myself. I could still drive the car, but I had to tell the owner the wheel was damaged again."

Enzo phoned his boss with news of the damage. But before he could say he was sorry, the owner blurted, "Richard must have done it again. If we didn't love him so much, he'd be gone. Now what was it you wanted to say, Enzo?"

"Nothing."

Enzo swears he let the owner believe Richard had done it only because he knew it wouldn't cost Richard his job. He confessed his lack of character that week at church, but he learned that situational ethics was a part of adulthood. And to this day he apologizes to Richard—wherever he may be.

## "Who moved my ductwork?"

Enzo's next step was to become a laborer on a construction site. This position led to his first trouble as an overachiever. His dad had gotten him a job on a union work site. Laborers there had a specific job to do: the grunt work. Lift this and take it over there. Go get that and bring it over here. And at lunch, take the order from everybody on the job site and bring the food back on time. And then hide. If you were an overachiever, the other laborers didn't want you to be "high profile." It showed them up. Take a while to find "this" before you bring it here. Don't rush to lift "that" and take it over there.

"Take your sweet time," the guys told Enzo. "We get paid by the hour. Not by how much we do. So doing more is not good. Because then we ain't working enough hours. Get it?"

He didn't get it.

One day a truck arrived at the site with a load of ductwork. Metal pieces of heating and air conditioning systems that would go in the multi-story building, some on each floor. And the laborer was to unload the truck. Period. Just leave the stuff there. But Enzo, the laborer, could read the numbers on the pieces. And the paperwork showing where on the job site each piece belonged. Well, he didn't have anything else to do. So. He picked up each piece, climbed the stairs about fifty times, and took each to the place where it was to be installed. In about two hours, all the ductwork was where it belonged.

And Enzo was in trouble, though he didn't know it. Because "a laborer ain't an expeditor," and he was "taking a job away from a family man by moving the pieces without being told." And doing it in *two hours* was so very wrong. It should have taken all day. For two men. Who now couldn't get paid because the kid had moved the stuff they were supposed to move. Enzo thought he was being promoted when he was asked to report to a different job.

That next day took Enzo to a nine-story sugar plant. New heating was being installed along the baseboards. About a ton of heater covers were being delivered to the job site. A laborer had to unload the truck. So, early in the morning, the truck came and the laborer unloaded them, and the truck left. No one was there but Enzo, the laborer. So ... why not start taking the covers up to the floors where they belonged? And leave each one where it was to be installed? There was nothing else to do, and, after all, he was getting paid. Three days later, all of the covers were placed at their final destinations throughout the job site. And union workers showed up and went nuts.

"Who moved the fucking covers?"

"Who put these fucking covers on our job site?"

Shop stewards were called. A union rep showed up. Enzo proudly proclaimed he was the one who put them up there. Every single one.

And they shut the job down until it could be sorted out. See, he was taking more work away from a union man with a family. By being industrious. By working too hard.

Enzo's father was called. He tried mightily to explain how the kid had screwed up by working too hard. Even though others were furious, his dad was proud of the effort. However, he admitted that perhaps his son should work someplace where he wouldn't be hurting a union man who wanted to "pace himself" on the job site.

How about work in a steel mill? Here he was to simply stand at one end of a platform where an overhead crane would lower a beam. Enzo was to stamp the beam with a mallet and die showing the letter $N$ to indicate which was the "north," or top, of the beam. There was a kid at the other end of the beam marking the number of the piece so it could be identified on the job site. The crane would then lift the piece away and lower another one. Unfortunately, the other kid forgot to keep his hands clear. The beam came down and crushed his right hand. Five days of marking $N$ and seeing a kid's working-hand crushed were enough for Enzo. There had to be a better way to make some money.

## Time and a half

Like stamping cans. More precisely, stamping the prices on cans before loading the grocery shelves. And so a new chapter in his work career took Enzo back to the public: stocking shelves and working the cash register in a supermarket in the real working-class part of town. Where factory workers brought handcarts weekly to buy food. Where kids helped old ladies by carrying their bags for small change. And where overtime was again available.

"Wow," Enzo reminisced. "Work that sixth day and your check jumped. And no one cared how many cans you stocked in a day. Hell, stock the whole back room if you felt like it. It just meant that tomorrow Eugene or Kenny could coast. It was Heaven."

Enzo stayed at that job until the end of college. The job paid so well that when he graduated college and started his first-ever white-collar job, Enzo actually had to take a cut in pay.

"See, the grocery store job was union too," he said.

Like the Howard & Morris Pharmacy, the supermarket Enzo went to work for was a throwback, a tiny place with just three aisles stocked with food and three register lines to check out. It was the smallest store in a chain of fifty-five stores, and it was constantly busy. Enzo learned percentages. He learned that per square foot his store had the highest average dollar of sales per year. Enzo learned that coupons in the paper translated into higher volumes on that product. Business stuff.

And, as on his first job, he learned about employee theft. Seems the butcher would come through his checkout line with a large box of meat. His sales slip would show two hundred dollars. Then the butcher would go up the street to the restaurant that had placed the order, deliver the box, and get paid. Only he would get paid three hundred dollars—the problem being that the store didn't get the money; the butcher did. The store was subsidizing the butcher to the tune of about one hundred dollars a delivery. The store manager caught the guy. Suddenly he was working for another store. The union saved his job, but the butcher was no longer a meat manager and therefore took a cut in pay.

"Lucky he wasn't cutting meat in jail," Enzo laughed.

On that job, Enzo also learned about on-the-job sex. Up till that time, he had figured that talking about it was one thing, but actually doing it was something else. Until the store manager couldn't find Eugene one day, and then the freezer door opened and out popped Eugene and Mary—cold, half dressed, and apparently very satisfied. Unabashed, Eugene thought nothing of discussing the pleasures of Mary with Enzo and other employees.

"And frankly, Mary didn't seem to mind either," Enzo added.

A few of the Abacrombie breakfasters expressed skepticism about Eugene's ability to perform at a temperature that cold.

"Hey, you can't make this stuff up," Enzo assured his audience.

During this time, Enzo was both a full-time college student and a full-time grocery store clerk. He would go to school until noon each day, then head down to the store to punch in by 12:30. Eight hours later, he was off to his girlfriend's house for a quick hello and was home by 11:00. It was a schedule to make a person old before his time, but that was okay. Enzo couldn't grow up fast enough.

Enzo discovered that by taking classes in the summer for two years, in addition to the regular semesters, he could finish one semester early. That's what he did. And after his third year of college, with just one semester left and with that full-time paycheck from the grocery, Enzo and his childhood sweetheart were able to get married. Enzo was what he had always wanted to be: a real adult, just like his dad.

"So—what were all these first jobs about? What did I learn from so many different experiences?" Enzo waxed reflective. He learned about life and himself and what being an adult was all about. He learned responsibility. Being at work on time. Giving an honest day's work for your pay. He told us he believes many kids are deprived of lessons like these because no one makes them work. Or, in reality, no one allows them to work.

"A lot of kids, especially poor kids, inner city kids—I don't care whether they're white, black, Hispanic, or whatever—don't learn to experience that feeling of accomplishment that you get from working. Start people earlier and they'll want to achieve so much more," Enzo declared. "And you know what? I'll bet every person who is successful can tell a story pretty much like the one I just told."

# First Professional Job: Tim's Tale

Most of the breakfasters agreed that they'd been indoctrinated with the idea that a good education was the way to get a good job. Tim piped up that he was a case in point—up to a point.

The state Tim lived in offered college graduates a test to qualify for certain jobs. The test also served as a general application for those jobs. When he first filled out the application, Tim had checked off only the management positions that his business degree prepared him to try. However, Tim's wife worked for the personnel director of one State-job group; she showed Tim's completed application to this director, who took one look and said, "No. Incomplete. All categories that require a college degree should be checked." Tim's wife did that herself before sending the application to be processed. It proved to be a life-changing revision.

Though no management positions were open, other jobs were available. The State had just raised the age of a juvenile from sixteen to eighteen for criminal prosecution, which meant that thousands of young people were now part of Juvenile Services. All charges against sixteen- and seventeen-year-olds were "delinquent" charges, not criminal charges. The department would have to almost double in size to handle the increased number of kids in the system. It needed "Juvenile Counselors" to work with the extra kids, those who up until that year were processed as adults. This need for more counselors, plus getting almost a hundred percent on the test, put Tim at the top of the list. He was called for an interview.

The two men who interviewed Tim were athletes. Both played tennis, football, baseball, and lacrosse. Although short in stature, Tim played soccer, baseball, lacrosse, and tennis, and ran track. Looking back at the interview later, he didn't remember ever discussing crime, juveniles, or how to counsel them, but he'd proved he could become a sports buddy. Tim got the job. Doing what? He had no idea.

## Matters of life or death

On the morning of Tim's first day, Tim's supervisor took him out of a staff meeting to advise him that his first case had arrived from court. Tim had to interview him. The juvenile had just been released that morning from the State Institution for Boys. His grandfather was with him. The boy was being released on "Aftercare," and Tim was the juvenile's counselor. That meant Tim was to oversee the boy's time in the community and "counsel" him to a good life. After getting his name, address, and a little background information, Tim sent the boy home with his grandfather.

The next morning, the supervisor called Tim into the office. Seems Tim's first case didn't go well. When the first juvenile Tim ever "counseled" went home, the boy robbed a house. He was shot on the front porch and killed. Tim's caseload had gone from thirty down to twenty-nine.

"It wasn't the way you were supposed to close cases," Tim acknowledged ruefully.

Families tend to be confused about what a juvenile counselor is really supposed to do. One sixteen-year-old car thief had a father in the merchant marines. The juvenile's dad was gone six months and then home six months. While Dad was away, Junior was assigned Tim as his counselor. A few weeks after the father got home, he called Tim for an appointment at their house. When Tim arrived, the kid was not there. Tim was puzzled. Dad told him he had not been asked there to see the boy.

"I got you to come here," Dad informed Tim, "because the stress in this house is going to affect my boy. I need you to reduce the stress."

Tim waited.

"I want to have sex with my wife. She won't do it. Says she needs a little more time to adjust to me being home. I want sex, and I want it now."

The boy's father expected Tim to "tell her she has to have more sex with me" or the house would continue to be highly charged with the emotion of his pent-up desires; surely this would impact negatively on his son. As astute as Dad seemed to be about how one person's problems affect all members of a household, it wasn't Tim's job to order Mom to give it up.

Fathers learned the system in ways that amazed Tim. One girl was on probation to him for her acts in the community.

"The kind of acts where strange men took her out for a very short date and thanked her with a few dollars," Tim clarified.

Her dad called Tim for a family meeting. As the head of the household, Dad wanted his authority and Tim's authority combined to straighten out the situation at home.

"What situation?" Enzo and I demanded in unison.

The situation, according to Tim, was a family squabble involving the girl, her mother, and her grandmother. The girl worked the park where men sought the comfort of her hand for five dollars. Mom worked the corner at the edge of the park for drivers passing by wanting a twenty-dollar car date. Grandma worked inside the air-conditioned bar on that corner and received forty dollars for her services—out of the broiling sun. Seems the young girl figured out that Mom got more for driving around with men; Mom found the corner too hot and wanted to share the air-conditioned bar with Grandma, who was furious because, even in the dark, the men at the bar preferred her younger daughter, so she was losing clients. Dad's concern was that the bickering over territory was killing the family business. He wanted Tim to tell them to stick to their assigned turf.

"Amazing," Enzo said.

"You can't make this stuff up," Tim assured us.

Tim may have actually saved one kid's life. About eleven one night, Tim answered his phone.

"Are you so-and-so's probation officer?"

"Yes."

"Then get down here to my house, because I have him on my front porch, and I have a gun, and I might just shoot him."

Tim drove fast. Sure enough, there the man and boy were, as described. The kid on probation had the hots for the man's daughter, and the feeling was mutual; so much so the girl's father caught her and the probationer in his car in the driveway doing what can happen on a big back seat. Dad had decided that Tim should order the boy to keep away from his daughter unless he wanted to get shot. Rather than explain the limits of his powers, Tim did order the boy away and also told the girl to forbid him to see her, or she would face court consequences.

"Hey, it was better to lie and get the boy out of there, wasn't it?"

We had to agree it was.

## Long, strange trips

Maybe Tim's most amazing story was about a young car thief who would leave his home in the morning and snatch a car to go to his girlfriend's house, then snatch another so they could joy ride, and finally snatch a third car to go home. By his own count, from Thanksgiving to Christmas, the boy had stolen almost ninety cars. He never got caught. He confided in Tim how he moved about the city and how worried his mom was that a police chase might shorten his life.

The boy was on probation to Tim, but no one had brought any charges for the car thefts. However, he had violated probation by staying out after his imposed curfew. To ease the boy's mother's fears, Tim filed a violation of his probation and put Mom on the stand to testify that he was ten minutes late for curfew. Tim asked the court to find him "delinquent" so his agency could change the boy's probation status. The Juvenile Master halted the proceedings and took Tim into chambers to tongue-lash him for bringing a case to court over a ten-minute curfew violation.

"I implied that there might be more to the story, but that during the phase of determining guilt we couldn't discuss them. However, if the court found the child in violation of his probation and therefore 'delinquent,' in the sentencing phase we could discuss behavior other than what had been testified to by the mother."

Now, this boy was smart. He couldn't believe any judge would send him away for being ten minutes late, so he got on the stand and said, "Yeah, judge, I did violate my probation." The Juvenile Master pronounced the child "delinquent" and asked the kid why he was really there. Since he had not been charged with any crime, no cop had caught him, and he was sure no one could prove he had done the car thefts, the boy bragged to the court about how he had traveled so freely all day every day over the last thirty days. The court thanked the smart boy and promptly sent him away to training school, where he remained until a friend broke him out. They ran away on a spree that left several people dead.

At one point in their travels across several states, the two were in a bar holding everyone hostage as the police surrounded the place. In the chaos, each young man killed a patron. The murder victims had been standing at opposite ends of the bar. Of course the boy and his cohort were caught and sent away for years. But there were still open cases back in his home state, including escape, kidnapping, and assault when he broke out and took his girlfriend along for the ride. And the boy's mother wanted Tim to clear them, so that when her son got out of prison (he was doing life), he wouldn't have to face charges in his home state. The mother mused, how could her boy be charged with killing *two* people? After all, when one person was killed, her son was busy at the other end of the bar killing his own victim. Shouldn't that mean only one murder charge?

"Believe me, you cannot make this stuff up," Tim repeated, shaking his head.

Twenty years later, a woman tracked Tim down to say she was that boy's wife. He was up for parole. Didn't Tim want to help him get out? The boy had changed in prison and was a good man. Tim said no, pointing out that at least no cars were stolen or people killed by her husband while he was away.

Tim stayed in the Juvenile Services job for almost ten years. His best friends are just now retiring from the department. One story the friends tell reflects pain and suffering from the citizen's point of view, countering the thirty-year focus on not blaming "little Johnny" for his acts and certainly not holding him accountable by locking him up.

## Working the system

"Kids in the system know it well," Tim reflected. "It takes many offenses to get you removed from society."

"Little Johnny" was in court for snatching a woman's purse. She testified how scared she was and how forceful Little Johnny was when he ran by her and grabbed her purse, knocking her to the ground. The court found Little Johnny delinquent and ordered him placed in custody of the State Juvenile Services. Court was adjourned. The old woman walked out slowly, at least comforted that she wouldn't have to face Little Johnny for a while.

Ah, but not so fast. Seems the State took Little Johnny across the street from the courthouse and decided that custody meant "intensive probation"—where a counselor would see Little Johnny every day. Not custody as in "jailed and out of the community." The counselor assigned immediately took Little Johnny home to explain the new rules of his "intensive probation." The buses must have been slower than the counselor's car, because by the time the old lady got off her bus, Little Johnny was standing on the corner. She thought he had been put away, and so did the court; but the system knew better than to "punish" kids for their behavior. He would be counseled "intensely" every day. And the world would be safer, wouldn't it?

"But what do you do with your assigned kid every day?" Tim asked us. "There can only be so much talking. So, let's get a budget for 'activities.' You know, ball games and movies; one kid actually took a hot air balloon ride. Imagine this, now," he continued. "Little Billy attends school and stays out of trouble. He sits on the front stoop watching his neighbor Little Johnny, the pocketbook thief, head out to the ballpark. He learns that actions do indeed have consequences. The worst kids get 'intensively counseled' and taken to the circus."

At one point in his ten years with the agency, Tim became the supervisor of the night shift. When a juvenile was brought to a police station and charged with a crime, one of Tim's workers would make a decision about holding the child or letting him go home with an adult. Sometimes there was no choice: no parent or guardian would come to the station to claim their offspring. One mother walked in the station, slapped the kid, and said, "Take him away."

Girls could be as touchy to handle as boys. One night Tim was called in because Wanda was tossing furniture out of the upstairs bedroom of her home. Pushing chests of drawers, lamps, and bedding through the front bedroom window and out onto the street. Something had pissed her off. Her drug-induced state provided her with a wealth of energy. Finally subdued, Wanda was brought to the station, where she vowed not to spend the night in detention. She had a plan.

The girls' detention facility was about twenty miles away, and not too many girls were sent there nightly. Usually a "paddy wagon" was the transport vehicle. It was something like a pickup truck with a box on the back bed with a small window in the rear door.

That night, with Wanda and one other girl loaded in the truck, the driver took off. When he backed up the truck to the detention facility's entrance, the driver noticed the back window had been broken out. Fortunately a wire mesh screen, with one-inch openings at most, was in place so no one could get through the window. The openings proved to be just big enough so the two girls could take off all their clothes and squeeze the garments through the mesh, out onto the roadway, during the ride. The two girls were totally naked when the doors opened. Both shouted that the driver had stopped along the way and had come in the truck and raped them.

The fifty-year-old, almost-retired policeman driving the truck was mortified. He would have to face charges. Fortunately, medical tests showed no apparent rape, and eventually the girls admitted they had made up the rape story so they could go to a hospital and not the detention hall. But Wanda was right. She didn't spend the night in a detention facility. After that night, two police officers had to be in the truck, and at least one had to be female.

"We all know juvenile crime is a major big-city problem," I observed. "Hell, I live in the city that starred in the TV series *Homicide*."

Tim nodded. "I was always frustrated. I knew some of them were just kids making their first mistakes. And yet, a lot of urban crime was committed by young people who didn't fear consequences because they had so many 'second chances' before being taken off the street.

"This kind of crime is also a political football," Tim continued. "Shouldn't we blame society and not the kid? Is it the kid's fault he doesn't have the right support system to keep him on the straight and narrow? And let's not create a career criminal by keeping these kids locked up for long periods of time."

Tim said he remains convinced that most politicians lack the courage to build bigger facilities to house the worst offenders. Once, at an agency meeting, Tim advocated that the worst offenders, those who had been clearly identified by their many arrests, should simply be waived to adult court and sent to jail whether they were fifteen, sixteen, or just days shy of eighteen, when they would officially be "adults."

"While I was on that job, I studied the numbers," Tim recalled. When juveniles were supposed to be in detention awaiting their court date, many were sent back to their families on "home detention." A counselor would visit them at home five, six, even seven times a week until the hearing was to take place. The Juvenile System proudly pronounced a stellar success rate: almost ninety-seven percent of home-detention kids showed up for their scheduled hearings. See? The system worked, right?

"But my numbers showed that a large percentage were being arrested for other charges during their 'home detention.' Obviously at that point the kid was actually in custody. He would be transported to his court date in a locked bus. Of course he would show up," explained Tim. "But the ninety-seven percent figure was all that was talked about."

Tim suggested that a letter of apology be sent to each crime victim during the time the perpetrator was supposed to be locked up but wasn't. Tim's boss pointed out that State rules forbid Tim from discussing his thoughts with the local media and he could lose his job.

"Since I haven't worked in Juvenile Services for over twenty-five years, I feel like it's okay for me to be saying something to you guys. Anyway, I trust you not to rat me out."

Tim added that friends who still work at the agency believe the gag order might still hold true today.

# The Politician: Pete's Tale

Grousing about the city's public transportation, its public works, and the seeming lack thereof this snowy morning—after all, what good did it do to grouse about the blizzard?—the guests started on the subject of politicians. Mostly how disappointed in them they are, no matter where they hailed from. How could Mayor X or Congresswoman Y have turned out to be so bad? They didn't seem so bad before we elected them. What happened?

In the four years my family has operated the Inn, we've listened to hundreds of guests spout their political opinions. A nationally touring comedian was a gay rights activist. The ex-wife of a former Democratic governor gave her slant on the party and its inner circles. Attorneys, social workers, and doctors attending conferences in Baltimore have sounded off on various sociological and medical issues. Scientists have expressed their fear of worldwide spread of disease. Water is of global concern. This breakfast table has heard from AIDS workers. Elementary school teachers and college professors. Presidents of large corporations. All have sat side-by-side in the Inn's breakfast room and, through conversation, sometimes agitated conversation, tried to right the world.

Many very wealthy people stay at our place, including world-famous musicians, artists, and actors as well as doctors with global reputations. These are people who demand a beautiful room, quality service, and excellent food, which of course is what they get at the Abacrombie. So, I ask myself, how come no mayor, congressman, governor, senator, or, to my knowledge, any other elected official has stayed with us in four years? One reason, I suspect, is that they wouldn't want to face their constituents over breakfast.

## Really running

Pete was different. Pete had actually run a campaign himself. I was as intrigued as my guests—maybe even more so—by Pete's breakfast conversation. We weren't so much interested in Pete's politics as we were curious about what it was like to put your name in the hat and really be in the running.

Growing up, Pete said he had been sure that one day he would be the President of the United States. His history books taught him that Presidents were always something else first, so he couldn't just skip ahead to the White House. He would have to start lower. At the time of his actual entry into the political arena, he was twenty-nine years old and in a low-level government job where his function was to help people. He felt it was time for him to represent more people than his job permitted.

Pete decided to run for the House of Delegates in his home state. The job covered the annual ninety-day session of the legislature, which meant it was considered a part-time job; most delegates kept other employment during the balance of the year. At least, it was the first stepping stone to the Rose Garden. He wondered how many other steps it would take before he could sleep in the Lincoln Bed.

In the breakfast room, the listeners concluded from Pete's tale's preamble that he possessed the first attribute of a politician: an ego the size of Mount Rushmore.

"You have to be able to visualize yourself as the winner in your race," Pete told us. It was his credo. "In fact, you have to expect that you'll get elected—why else would you run? Surely others can just look at you, your passionate faith in yourself, and see you as the winner too."

"My ego was up to the task," Pete assured all the breakfasters. They chimed in, agreeing that the thing that would stop them from ever considering a run for office was not a lack of belief in their own ability, but the fact that others would have to validate that ability with a vote.

"And if they didn't, and you lost an election, wouldn't that mean that you might be wrong about yourself?" one of the guests observed.

The thought had never entered Pete's mind. Ego!

Pete felt ready, even though no individual or group came forward to ask Pete to run. No, there was no groundswell of talk about Pete. The press wasn't suggesting his name in any discussion of who could lead the masses out of their messes. Not a single person had ever suggested to Pete he should consider representing them. Pete just knew they needed him. He would run.

## Is there room on Mount Rushmore?

Initiating the process was simple. "All you have to do is fill out an application and put up the filing fee."

And then you're just as legitimate as Clinton, Reagan, either Bush, or, as Pete so unhumbly thought, Abraham Lincoln. Didn't Ole Abe simply put his name in the hat one day long ago? Pete was sure that, with his name on the ballot, his heart full of sincerity, and his head teeming with brilliant analyses of issues, the voters would come running.

"Think maybe you were moving a little too fast, bud?" a guest asked. Pete answered the question by pulling the heart of his tale out by its grass roots.

Pete had five brothers and sisters and supportive parents. He had a loving, concerned wife and daughter. He was a religious man who attended church weekly. They loved him at his job. He could count on dozens of campaign workers just from the people around him.

"Or at least a couple, anyway."

Pete got a guy from work to take his picture. He wanted some handout flyers and cards made to give away on the door-to-door campaign. And lawn signs, my God, he needed those lawn signs to tout his candidacy. Pete found out he could get the signs made fairly cheaply down at the local Mom-and-Pop copy shop. Cheap was good—essential, in fact—because he didn't have any funds in his campaign coffers. At this point, he would have to write his own checks; in view of what he already owed Household Finance Corporation, the checks had better be small.

## Pete knows best ... yeah, right

Pete's father pointed out the first blunder in Pete's run for office. The Mom-and-Pop shop didn't belong to any union. Only the larger printing shops had union workers, meaning that only the larger shops could print that little Union logo down in the corner of his printed material. That was the logo every red-blooded, hard-working American looks for when he picks a candidate. How could you vote for someone who took printing work away from a union man trying to support his family? Who cares that you could save money by using the "little" printer? You were turning your back on the masses to save a few bucks.

"Son," Pete's dad advised, "you better get your stuff reprinted."

Pete, however, clung to his ideal: waste was exactly what was hurting the people. Once in office, he would put an end to the money wasted by getting things printed by costly companies who could supply the correct logo. Score: ego one, politically correct method zero.

Next: chance books and bull roasts. Every politician used both. Sell a raffle ticket, get a couple of dollars for your campaign, and give the winner a basket of booze; he'd be happy enough to vote for you. Hold a roast, raise money, slap a lot of backs.

Hmmm.

To book a hall for a roast would cost more than Pete was planning to spend; he would have to sell a couple hundred tickets to pay for the roast and still have enough left over to make the event worthwhile. That meant risking money he didn't have, just to raise money he needed. Worse, it also meant schmoozing with all those people: making small talk, glad handing, faking laughter—when he really just wanted to take a buck or two out of their pocket for his run for office.

No way.

Pete didn't really like people that much, and he didn't want to end up owing more than his house was worth. He skipped the bull roast and started selling chances for the booze. Back to the Mom-and-Pop shop for chance books. Less-than-brisk sales yielded Pete a few hundred dollars. At least there was some profit, maybe enough to get gas for all the driving back and forth to the non-union print shop. Pete didn't worry. He wasn't running for the office of fundraiser or bull roast planner. He was running in order to change the face of mankind with his political and social energy.

Now, when you have a raffle, you have to have an actual winner, and the winner had to be some complete stranger who had put up the buck to support your candidacy. Possibly because his family had bought most of the chances, Pete's brother, the same brother who had bought the basket of booze at a discount from his favorite watering hole, won the raffle. Not good. Pete kind of assumed he already had his brother's vote. Where were the masses clamoring for Pete's big win and his badly needed reforms?

Pete's ego remained intact, however, and he plowed ahead to the door-to-door phase of his run for office. It is an American tradition, Pete reflected, that if a person pulls your doorknob and says hello to your face, you are duty bound to march to the polls and pull his lever. How could you not vote for a person so close to you that he peered at you through your screen door and begged you to? Why, that close encounter made the candidate and the homeowner practically lifetime friends. Besides, when he won the election, you could tell your friends you shook his hand. You could say you knew him since he was a kid.

Alas, Pete found out what a mailman already knows. There are lots of developments where the doorknobs are too far apart. Walk an hour in any one section and, not counting all the "nobody homes," you could speak to a few dozen people at most. He decided to focus on row houses. That is where the real door-knocking paid off. Fifteen feet between each knob and people could hear you coming from three doors down. After all, they couldn't let you shake "Bob's" hand and not theirs. Some had the door open before you hit the top step. But with eighteen candidates running for delegate, sometimes the steps were crowded. Where did those other candidates come from? Why weren't they walking around the tract home developments in the wide-open-spaces communities? The answer, of course, was that all bright politicians had learned the efficiency of battling in the crowded trenches.

Man the battle stations. Pete's patrol consisted of himself and one volunteer worker, along with a few—a very few—family members. This so-called team planned to blanket key neighborhoods with as many handouts as possible in the limited time allowed. His campaign workers and family would have to spread themselves and their efforts wisely to reach the maximum number of people.

How many walking workers did Pete muster? There was Pete, and there was his office co-worker Mike. That was the walking team. Everyone else was either busy or already felt sure that this campaign was a joke. Undaunted, Pete and Mike went out night after night after work, shaking hands and waving. Almost no one asked a single question, like What do you support? What are you against? "You came to my house and shook my hand. I won't forget you." That's what everybody said. There were eighteen candidate door-knockers that the voters promised not to forget.

## "Where everybody knows your name"

Unable to make a dent through press releases, Pete sought another way to secure name recognition. Familiarity is comforting to the voters. If his father has run, making his name well known, a son or daughter has a better shot than a newcomer, even if that well-known-named offspring is a dolt.

Pete elaborated. "Own a popular bar and everyone knows your name. Your customers may not know you, but they know your name. Do you lack a well-known last name or a corner bar named for one? Then you have to plaster lawn signs over the landscape to get your name recognized."

During the campaigning, one young man running against Pete had an enormous edge in lawn signs. His father had won many years before and had ultimately become a judge. Everyone knew his name. Also, the bar owner—a bar owner/candidate was not just hypothetical here—got a lot of people to put up his signs, though not quite as many as the judge's son. A third candidate had a rich history in the area and a respectable number of lawn signs. These three, holding the most popular names, hooked up to run as a team. In this election, there were to be three candidates elected out of the thirteen running.

Overnight, the signage landscape changed. The number one name, the one that had dominated all other lawn signs, disappeared to the very bottom of the new signs that touted the TEAM, because, unfortunately, the best-known name came last alphabetically. Still, the TEAM had total domination of all lawn signs, and it looked as if the TEAM would sweep. The other ten candidates, like Pete, were all average nobodies running for the first time. All except one. That man's family also had been a winner in the past, in what used to be another district. His district had been brilliantly gerrymandered into Pete's district. And that man knew better than to join a team that might bury his name. These four people were now the favorites. None of this bothered Pete.

"Hey, wasn't I the one with the most sincere heart and the strongest will to win?"

Another way to get ahead, Pete knew, was to court the special interest groups. Like those unions discussed earlier. Forget that he was a no-logo-literature jerk. And what about the teachers? Pete loved education and loved reading; surely when they interviewed him, they would see he was the right man for the job.

What did increasing their pension, adding vacation time, and getting better benefits for management have to do with teaching little Johnny how to spell? Pete didn't fare well in the educators' discussion. He kept wanting to go to classroom issues, including what books and supplies were needed. Didn't he understand that more books might mean less pay?

What was he thinking?

Actually, by that time, he was thinking that the Teachers Association didn't have much to do with education.

Radio commercials were out of the question. Newspapers were too expensive. How could he get the maximum number of people to know his unknown name?

Ever since Pete was a kid his family had gone to Ocean City every summer. And you would lie on the beach and watch the airplanes flying low with the banners behind them: "HARPOON HANNAH'S/EARLY BIRD DINNER 5:00 PM." Or "FLIP FLOPS ON SALE $1.99." Pete had spent almost nothing at the little printing shop, and the basket of booze had come from a discount house; Pete felt good about taking what was left in the kitty to hatch his new idea. He added more money of his own and called the airplane guy in Ocean City.

The pilot agreed to two days' worth of advertising; Pete specified the Saturday and Sunday before the Tuesday election. People would be out and about all weekend, and his name would blaze across the sky. At mid-afternoon, prime sky-watching time.

Pete stood on the front lawn at the appointed hour and was mesmerized to hear the plane's engine nearby. Wham! His name was streaming out behind the plane for all to see and memorize. Brilliant. Who needed lawn signs? Or union logos? Those last-minute door-knockers would be shocked to look up overhead and see the genius-in-the-running covering the whole district in one twenty-minute air sweep. Sunday would put him over the top.

"Repetition makes a reputation, right?" Pete asked us, hypothetically as usual, not waiting for a response. "Forget that just reading a name doesn't mean you know anything about that person. You only need to recognize the name and you'll pull down that lever."

Sunday dawned with a brilliant blue sky. The plane was due up in half an hour. The telephone rang. It was pouring down rain in Ocean City, and the pilot couldn't take off. What? No banner? With just two days to go? How about Monday, the pilot urged, or maybe even on election day? Monday it rained, and Tuesday the same. No airplane. No banner.

"With an election like this, you had to understand strategy."

Pete tried to explain the strategy to us. The voters were going into the booth to elect three candidates. Out of thirteen. If ten people voted, that normally means thirty votes spread out amongst the thirteen. *Unless* you don't vote for three when you go in there. *Unless* you vote for only one. This strategy is called "single shooting."

"Forget the damn three-man team. Just vote for one and not the others. You see, if you vote for all three on the team, you're making it harder for your particular favorite on that team to win, because some voters will split their vote for one team member and then pick two others. By single shooting, you were giving one vote to your choice and no votes for any other." Pete was orating now.

"Is it ethical to get yourself on a team, take over a guy's lawn signs, and then dump the team by advising your particular supporters to 'single shoot' and beat the others?" This time we had no doubt that Pete's question was purely rhetorical.

## "And the winner is ..."

Election night was amazing. Pete's family and friends joined him to watch what would easily be the high point of Pete's life: his first election to public office. The first stepping stone to Washington D.C.

The race for delegates is of extremely low importance in this type of election, ranking barely ahead of the school and road bond issues, so a candidate can't look for early results. You had to watch the sparring for Governor's race, who was being elected Mayor, and who would be the next Senator—as if that were as important as Pete's election to office! Finally the numbers were trickling in. There it was. Pete's name on TV in those little charts that tell you how many votes and what percentage candidates had. The chart stayed up on the TV screen just long enough for Pete to count down ten names to get to his. He had beaten only three people, and they were definitely not the three at the top where it counted.

That was the first millisecond when Pete believed he wouldn't win.

One other unknown candidate in the race was named Whatmough, pronounced "What Mo." As the people watching with Pete saw the chart and looked at the numbers, Pete's dearest and oldest friend proclaimed, "WHAT-MO GAVE YOU WHAT FO!" And it was true.

Pete philosophized, "When the world collapses under you and you get that sinking feeling of failure, you can either crash or realize that you are still alive and still have a chance. I was down, but not out."

Looking back on his campaign, he realized that name recognition was his real failure. He did something about it. He became president of his neighborhood improvement association and vice president of the Northeast Coordinating Council. At last he was really visible. But when the next elections for public office came around, Pete had had enough of politics. He never ran again.

"So who did win?" I asked Pete.

"The guy who finished fourth was Mr. Most Lawn Signs—before teaming up with those others. The winner from the previous election—the one who had been gerrymandered in—was well-known in his part of the district, so he was a top-three vote-getter. Funny thing about that big three-man TEAM, though. They didn't all have the same number of votes. And another thing, when you multiplied the number of votes received by the number of voters, it seemed that many voters had cast a ballot for only one person. Some voters didn't want to make three choices. Or were they 'single shooters'? Whatever, two guys on the TEAM beat out the third guy on the TEAM. Mr. Most Lawn Signs never knew what hit him."

Name recognition, I thought. Isn't that why there is always a Kennedy in Washington?

"There's an epilog to the tale," Pete added. The guy who took the top spot alphabetically on the TEAM lawn signs while running for office, the guy who allegedly proposed that his supporters "single shoot" the ballot and not actually vote for all three people on the TEAM, won. Later he became a State Senator. He was recently indicted for crimes concerning his appointed position in government. His trial is scheduled to begin soon.

# The Rebuilder: Ben's Tale

Although the guest's name was Ben, the card he handed me had but one word in the center: REBUILDER. At the lower right corner was his telephone number. Nothing else was on the card.

"Just what do you rebuild, Ben?" I wanted to know.

Of course my guests and I got the answer in the form of a narrative that delved far back into the teller's past.

As a kid, Ben liked to spend time by himself, working on one project or another, using a small toolbox with real tools—a hammer, some screwdrivers, a folding wooden measuring stick, a small builder's square, some pliers. Santa had brought him this mini-version of his dad's toolbox one Christmas. With his few tools, Ben did typical kid-construction, tree houses—that sort of thing. His favorite was "Ben's Dugout," a neatly excavated hole under the back porch for use by neighborhood kids when they played ball.

"When I got married and bought my first house," Ben recalled, "I enrolled in a workshop at Sears where you could learn how to do home repairs and then buy some Craftsman Tools each week after class."

He tried small household projects, including a bookcase he still cherishes: it was the first time Ben had ever used a router. With each completed project, he gained confidence. The bookshelf led to drop-down stairs from the attic to the hall below. The stairs led to a shimmering wall of smoky mirror tiles in the living room. Tacky? You bet—but what a nice job of cutting the tiles around the fireplace!

Ben always believed that guys who built things around the house were the "Vocational Tech" guys who majored in shop in high school. "Not that I was a snob, but I figured if they could do it, then so could I—all I needed was patience and the right tools."

At that time Ben drove a Buick Riviera, the model with a "bullet back" styled after the earlier Corvette. The car stood out in any crowd, and Ben liked being different. But the car was on its last legs, and there wasn't enough money to go up to the obvious next level, a Cadillac. What was a man to do? One day while reading a golf magazine, Ben's eye lit on an ad showing a great-looking roadster with golf clubs strapped to the back. It was a replica of a 1954 MG-TD built from a kit called "Daytona Migi." The car was awesome. And you built it yourself. Could he do that? The instruction manual cost fifteen bucks. Off through the mail went his check.

"To be honest," Ben told us, "the manual was too simple. You start with a Volkswagen Beetle and lose the body, leaving the floor pan, engine, gas tank, steering, and wheels. Bit by bit, you rebuild the Migi body on top of the VW frame. Somebody, somewhere, had actually done this. I knew I could do it too."

## The kit cometh

Luckily his credit cards had enough room for him to order the kit. It cost almost three thousand dollars, but hey, this was going to be a dream car. Next he scoured the papers for an old Beetle. Back then, there where hundreds of them still floating around. The one he found had a blown engine, but the frame and wheels were in great shape. He plunked down four hundred dollars and towed the car to a VW shop for a rebuilt engine and some brake work, all of which cost less than five hundred dollars. Nine hundred dollars for a drivable car that didn't even look too bad! Of course, as he drove the car into his garage, the neighbors wondered why the Riviera had been scrapped for this old Beetle. Not to worry, Ben told them. Wait until you see what comes next.

The truck containing the kit arrived at lunchtime one weekday afternoon a few days before Christmas. The driver refused to unload the wooden box, which measured about three feet high by three feet across by seven feet long and weighed close to eight hundred pounds. "I'm a driver, not a delivery man," the driver announced.

Laughing, he suggested that Ben get some of the stay-at-home moms to come out and help him take the box off the truck.

But as the driver stood there laughing, Ben noticed that the shipping documents that he had to sign included a checklist for Ben to initial, indicating that he had inspected the parts and found them all in good order. Ben suggested that he simply pop the top off the box and unload the several thousand parts one at a time, inspecting each one to be sure he could sign off on them.

The driver stopped laughing. Together, they built a little ramp and unloaded the box onto Ben's front lawn.

Merry Christmas to Ben from himself! Ben opened the top of the box and peered inside. Shiny blue bumpers! Chrome lights! Turn signals and a dashboard and the wonderful wooden steering wheel he had custom-ordered! Small metal decals of the old MG and the German VW to adorn the front grille! Wires! A windshield! New wire wheel hubcaps!

"My God," Ben murmured to himself, "this really is Christmas."

He now owned a perfectly good Volkswagen, plus he had a box of thousands of large and tiny parts that would transform the old Bug into a brilliant new roadster. If he could figure out how to build it.

For about two days, Ben sorted out the parts. Fenders and welting over here. All electrical items down to the basement. Parts for the seats over there. The seat inclusions were just covers, so he would have to cut wood to make the seat base and fill it with foam before installing the pretty, pure-white, rolled and pleated covers to complete the bench seat. Typically, Ben had jumped off the bridge before checking the height of the water. But others had jumped before him and they were driving Migis—so off to work he went.

First, off came the VW body. After removing the doors and unbolting the body, Ben got two neighbors to help him lift the body off the frame. Ben had them put it on the lawn right at the property line between their properties.

"What are you doing?" the neighbors demanded.

"It's so we can plant some flowers inside and make a nice VW lawn ornament."

They thought Ben was crazy—as always.

Piece by piece, Ben followed the instructions. Part A to Part B and so on and so on and on and on. For days and weeks. Hundreds of hours of attaching this to that. Doors to the frame. Windshield to the frame. Sweet white convertible top to the frame.

Within months, the old VW frame sitting on four jack stands had been transformed into a beautiful Daytona Migi. Ben got his dad to help him weld an extension onto the brake pedal, because in the new version you actually sat in what was originally the back seat of the car. Another outsider helped with the electrical mess. Ben knew his limitations.

A quarter of a year after Christmas came the moment of truth. The garage door was opened for the first time in months, revealing to the world Ben's new car. He cranked the key. The engine started up. Out the door he and his Migi rolled. It worked! Ben the rebuilder had done it! The car was stunning. It was a one-of-a-kind car, and it was all Ben's. The naysayers were wrong again.

Ben was on Cloud Nine. He insisted that his wife and daughter climb in for the inaugural ride, even though it was getting dark and they already had on their pajamas and slippers. Not to worry, Ben assured them: once around the neighborhood and back into the garage. After all, the car didn't even have license plates yet.

About half a mile from the house, smoke started pouring out from under the dash. This wasn't good. They'd better stop before the whole car caught on fire. Funny? His wife and daughter in their nightclothes didn't laugh. Ben ran home and got another car and a tow rope. The new roadster had ended its first trip headed to its home garage on the back end of a tow. But the next day the wiring problem was solved, and the car ran beautifully until he sold it several years later when he needed money for another project.

## A new toy

"Remember the t-shirt that said 'HE WHO DIES WITH THE MOST TOYS WINS'?" Ben asked us. "Well, after I sold my dear little kit-car, I needed to score a big new toy."

Money always being the inhibitor, once again Ben had to be creative. Why not another toy that he would put sweat equity into?

On a Saturday morning, breakfasting with his youngest daughter, Ben scanned the newspaper ads under BOATS FOR SALE. Ben hadn't been on a boat in almost twenty years, but man, they were nice-looking toys.

"You like boats, Lisa?"

"No."

"But you girls seemed to love walking around on them when I took you to the boat shows at the Civic Center."

(Silence from Lisa.)

True, his family had never even gone fishing. They were not outdoor types. They loved the community swimming pool, not the rivers, lakes, or bay. No one clamored for a long-distance trip on the water. But look at these boats for sale—and a lot of them under four thousand dollars. How could you go wrong with that?

Lisa climbed into the car next to Dad (this all happened way before child seats), and off they went. First stop: a twenty-four footer with a trailer—all ready to go. Father and daughter made their way toward the water, winding their way down small streets to find a house at the water's edge with a small boat in the driveway. In fact, the boat was so small it didn't have a cabin. They'd all fry in the sun. Nah, Lisa, not this one.

Next they hit a large shore home with a long dock out into the river. Whoa Nelly, this one was thirty-six feet long with a "flying bridge" (that's an open area on top of the pilothouse with additional controls to drive from above) and a rear door to the tri-cabin, which was actually a sliding glass patio door. You could stand up in the shower. There was a galley with booths that folded down to sleep six. Now we're talking. But how could this guy only want two thousand dollars for this monster?

The answer was simple. Because it was twenty-five years old. Because it was made of wood, not fiberglass. Just above the water line, you could see the wood rotting. And the deck was shot. And the paint was peeling off everywhere. And it sucked gas faster than an airplane. But its twin 454 Buick engines both started right up. The man said he hoped Ben would drive it away immediately. Ben handed over a check. Lisa seemed excited to tell her sisters they were now going to be a boating family, even though her daddy knew absolutely nothing about boats. Or navigation. Or what it meant to own a wooden boat.

Every marina he called refused to rent him a slip. No way. No wooden boats allowed. Huh? Isn't a boat a boat? No, Ben learned, wooden boats leaked and sometimes went under. Finally he found an obscure marina, located at the river's farthest point from the bay, whose manager said Ben and his boat could dock there. For an annual fee of two thousand dollars. Ben had just doubled the cost of his investment.

During the several days it had taken Ben to find a slip, the seller gave Ben a hard time. "When are you getting this thing out of my backyard?" he kept asking. When Ben brought a motley moving-crew consisting of a young nephew and two guys married to his nieces, along with his wife and daughters, the seller was visibly nervous. Did Ben know it was twenty-five miles across the bay to where he was going? Did Ben know how to get there and what the rules of the water were? Ben himself was rather concerned that the bilge pump was running full force, and so was the standby pump, whose hose, hanging out the side, was pouring a steady stream of water. What, Ben worry? Fire up the engines! They headed on up the bay as if they didn't have a care in the world. God watches out for fools, they say. God proved the adage that day.

Plowing through the waves meant the water was rushing up against the rotting wooden hull at considerable force. The standby pump the seller had plugged in at the dock was no longer helping, since it was back on the dock. The regular bilge pump was all they had. No one said anything. But everyone must have been wondering what they were doing out there on the bay with a boat taking on water. Nevertheless, the crew continued sunning themselves on the deck, telling themselves that of course they would make it. They did, too.

The next day the dock master called Ben and said the marina had made a mistake. They didn't like the looks of Ben's boat. He couldn't keep it at the marina after all. Ben agreed to try to find another space.

"You'd better take care of your bilge pump in the meantime," the dock master said. "It almost never shuts off. It'll kill your battery."

Ben headed down to the marina, plugged the pump into the electric outlet on the dock, and went home.

About ten o'clock the next morning, the dock master called Ben to tell him the boat had sunk in the slip. Someone had unplugged the pump, and the boat had filled up with water. When Ben arrived, he saw that the boat had sunk about seven feet. The top deck was almost under water, and the water was about to spill over the sides. The Coast Guard was standing by to contain the gas spill, should one occur, and some major-league pumps were going full blast to raise the boat. After a few hours, it bobbed up like a cork. Ben was told to take his boat and leave immediately. First, though, he had to write a check—for the magic number of two thousand dollars to pay the salvage company for pumping out and raising the boat. Ka-ching. Everything connected with that boat cost two thousand dollars! Two new batteries later, the engines kicked over again. Those engines refused to die.

Upon arrival at the new marina Ben had located, the boat was lifted by a crane onto two cradles waiting on sweet dry land.

"Come see us tomorrow," said the new dock master, "and we'll discuss the next move."

Next morning, Ben heard the sad news. The hull was shot. Completely unsafe. The boat would have to be dismantled. Ben would have to pay to haul away the remains. Ka-ching!

"Unless."

"Unless what?"

"Go see the old guy over there working on his boat. Let him take a look at yours."

The old guy looked Ben over slowly.

"Got any guts?" the old man asked. "Got any skills at all for working on a boat? Are you willing to work hard for months to save this thing? Because, if not, just junk it."

Hell yes, Ben had guts. Look what the fool had just done.

"Don't confuse stupidity with guts," responded the old man.

But he outlined a plan. The hull could be wrapped in new plywood. Every inch to the bottom of the keel. And after a new wooden base was in place, then Ben could fiberglass the entire hull up to the deck line. It would take months of hard work, but the boat could be saved.

The dock master agreed to let Ben try, and for the next six months Ben was a boat builder. Alone. The old man supervised. He watched but didn't participate, advised but did no lifting. "Not bad" was the most encouraging comment Ben could muster. In time, though, the boat started looking pretty good. The old boat wasn't going to die on Ben's watch.

From the bottom of the keel to the top of the flying bridge was a distance of over fifteen feet. At thirty-six feet long, the boat was bigger than some houses. Ben installed electricity to keep the music going and a refrigerator to store food. It was like a summer house perched on stilts. Just climb up the ladder and hoist yourself over the side. You could even take a nap in the cabin if you wanted.

But the dock master wanted to see progress. New parts were needed now that you could see the props and stems. The great shower you could stand up in had quit being functional years ago. The toilet had to be replaced. Those fold-down benches that converted to a bed would have broken through under even a child's weight.

Nevertheless, as long as his charge card didn't bounce at the boat supply store, Ben was going to be a seaman. The charges were approved; the deck was re-covered, and the bunks in the fore-section rebuilt. A new hatch cover was installed. The windshield got new wiper motors. Damn, she was starting to look good!

Since it would take months to actually get out on the water, Ben enrolled his family in boating classes to make up for the nautical knowledge he had none of. Navigation, boating safety, all you needed to know to cruise the bay safely. Alas, Ben discovered something while his family attended classes, something he needed to realize sooner. No one but him wanted a boat. The boat was just a thing that would keep them from the pool and their friends. Ben sought to change the family negativity by scheduling a picnic on the boat while it was in dry dock being repaired. Let the wife and kids climb on board and eat some chicken and be together and have a blast.

## Family fun

"Doesn't this thing have air conditioning?"

"What do you mean, we can't use the toilet yet?"

"There's no place to swim here!"

No more picnics. Just wait until they launch the boat, Ben told himself, and all will be better.

With the last of the fiberglass in place and the final paint dry, Ben received congratulations from other boat owners who had watched the process over the previous months. They were impressed and said so. But would she float? She did. Finally *The Admiral* could be put in her own slip. ("The Admiral" was his family's nickname for his father, a reference to his earlier Navy days—at far below the rank of Admiral.)

"Hey, everybody, let's go boating!"

"Sorry, Dad, there's a swim meet at the pool. And the cousins will all be there. Maybe another time."

Ben's family made a total of three voyages out onto the bay during the first year of ownership. Dock fees were due again. And the first winter had done what winter does to all boats. Didn't Ben just scrape and paint this thing last year?

Jim blurted out, "Jesus, Ben, how much did it cost to go out for a couple of hours?"

Ben calculated that with the purchase price, slip fees, repairs, supplies, and gas, the tab was about two thousand dollars a trip.

Time to unload the boat.

Ben was having a house built at the time. By professional contractors. When the "Punch List" guy walked the final inspection with Ben, he noticed a picture of *The Admiral* hanging on Ben's office wall.

"What a beauty," the guy declared. "My dad and I would kill for a boat like that."

The man's father owned a shore home on a river with a forty-foot dock out back. Ben leapt at the opportunity.

"Let's go see the boat," he said.

Both engines fired right up. The boat looked like a beauty to the punch-list man. Ben made him an offer he couldn't refuse.

"Will you take the boat for nothing?"

Ben explained that he would be saving the upcoming slip fee renewal as well as other costs for normal upkeep.

The next day was Ben's greatest day of boat ownership: it was his *last* day of boat ownership. As soon as the title was transferred, the boat left the docks headed for a new home. And Ben hasn't been on a boat since.

# Up in the Air, Junior Birdman: Tuck's Tale

"Hey, Herman, what're the chances of getting out of Baltimore any time soon?" Enzo wanted to know.

I phoned the airport and found out that ice still had BWI locked down. My phone call somehow got my guests onto the subject of flying—mostly telling tiny tales of inconveniences and snafus. But my guest Tuck warned the breakfasters his tale was a good bit longer. It began when he was finishing college.

## Tidings of discomfort, oh boy

While visiting his parents' home about a week before Christmas, the telephone rang. His dad took the call, then came into the living room and laughingly said, "They want you." The caller was the draft board. And the message was that he had two weeks to report for his Army physical. But ... he protested, his class didn't graduate until next June.

"Yes," said the caller, "but you finished college early. You have lost your deferment."

What? This wasn't in the plan. Tuck had taken extra classes and finished a semester early so he could get started in business. Although the first-ever draft numbers had been drawn and his birth date made him number twenty, he didn't think the draft applied to him until after his class graduated.

Wham. Vietnam was bubbling over. His brother had already been there. And he didn't want any part of it. But what could he do? His older sister's husband had an idea. Join the Air National Guard. He knew a pilot friend who could see if there was a vacancy. Without any strings being pulled, the Air National Guard granted him an interview. The upshot was that, because he had a college degree and perfect health and eyesight, he could try for a pilot's slot that was open. He could do that, or he could be a soldier heading to Asia. And so, without ever having been in an airplane, Tuck signed up to be a pilot.

"Jets. Sweet mother. Supersonic-white-rocket-like-the-astronauts-flew jets. Jets that looked like little bugs on the ground and climbed to the skies at unbelievable speed," Tuck rhapsodized. "I was hot to go."

But not right away. First there was Officer's Preparatory Academy. OPA. Knoxville, Tennessee. Without time to understand what happened to the launch of a business career, he waited for OPA and then several more months for USAF Pilot Training School.

Once dubbed an Officer and a Gentleman by proclamation, and after about six weeks of extensive training, he was ready. But there were lessons learned in those few weeks that have lasted a lifetime.

"Resistance to change. It's got to be one of the strongest human traits. We love our routines. All of them. And we don't like people messing with them. But being a soldier means change all the time," Tuck reflected. "War isn't routine. And our training was designed to make us understand how to be a leader and see how all people resist change."

After twenty days or so of following the exact same daily routine, Tuck's fellow trainees were abruptly awakened an hour early and sent out to march before breakfast. Then they were fed a different diet. And had their classes with new teachers. And were treated quite differently.

"Although the entire program was stressful, we'd become used to the routine. We had mental meltdowns at the changes.

"About two that afternoon, our regular teacher entered the room. He immediately told us to hold onto that feeling of anger, hostility, and confusion we were all experiencing. He told us the routines had been changed to give us that feeling, to show us how people resist change."

Each of those men learned to understand that anything can change at any moment. And that they can either spend their energy resisting the change or spend it adapting to a basic reality: many times, things do change.

For Tuck, it was a life lesson. He told us that, to this day, people wonder how one minute he can be showing a particular emotion and, with a phone ring or a door knock, immediately transform. When the roof leaks, or the car gets wrecked, or his child doesn't act as he thinks the child should, he doesn't panic or give in to the resistance to change we all feel.

"You can understand why you feel that resistance, and you can recognize it and think past that feeling and go forward. Because you can't change the fact that something has changed. You can only control your response to the change. Not that you become cold and unfeeling. It's just that you understand the need to move ahead, while most people languish in the battle against the change."

"Where did you do your air training, Tuck?" I was trying to prompt him to get him out of "Lessons" mode and back into "Tale" mode.

"Where in the hell is Phoenix, Arizona?"

That's what Tuck asked himself when he got his assignment. He had been an East Coast boy all his life. But pilot training was at Williams Air Force Base near Phoenix. From his Guard unit, he knew one guy there. So he sent money ahead, and his friend signed him up for an apartment. A nice one. Two bedrooms. A swimming pool. Arriving a day before Thanksgiving, Tuck learned that the pool was a necessity. It was eighty degrees that day in Phoenix, a far cry from the forty degrees he'd left behind.

The deal was this. Pass and get your wings, or flunk out and report to the Army. Motivation! Pass and go back to a Guard unit where no one shot at you. Fail out and bullets would be flying over your head as you marched through the jungle. Eighty guys started the class. Seventy were Air Force, and ten were Air National Guard. The Guard guys all had the same thing over their heads. All ten Guard guys got their wings. Only thirty of the Air Force guys completed the training. It wasn't easy.

Tuck described his first day.

"We climbed on a bus heading to Eloy. The middle of nowhere. A small field with small single-engine planes. T-41s: starter Cessna aircraft to teach the basics of flying.

"It was very dark at 4:30 in the morning when we went to get the bus. And it was quiet on the ride down. We didn't know each other. Why talk to a stranger? But there was some heavy thinking on that bus. When it stopped at Eloy, two guys raised their hands and said, 'I quit ... I don't want to fly.'"

Two down. Before they even got into the cockpit.

## "Flying the ride"

Although he couldn't remember much about learning to fly, Tuck remembered being sick on almost every ride. So sick he worried about flunking out and learning to dodge bullets for real. So he sucked it up, and off to fly jets he went. T-37s. Subsonic jets. Sweet old jets that were loud and scary.

The first ride is a "Dollar Ride" where the flight instructor shows you what the plane can do. While it is meant to impress you, it also is designed to make you sick. Hell, he didn't need much help to get sick. Lots of lunches lost. Many sick bags used. Tuck was not the only one with the problem. One guy actually pissed his pants and the seat of the jet. While the ground crew was used to puke, urine was another matter. The guy was hauled out of class when he got back and told to go clean the cockpit.

Tuck's first ride alone was frequently described as "aerobatics." Not that he was trying trick maneuvers on purpose. He just wasn't ready to fly yet. Nevertheless, after that first solo, it was on to the jets for Tuck.

"You're in the Army now" constantly played in Tuck's head while he kept throwing up during his daily lessons. Generally, by the time the lesson was almost over and it was time to land the plane, Tuck was too woozy to see straight. Finally came a day when the instructor landed the plane and said the situation couldn't go on much longer. Tuck was seeing the flight surgeon so often others joked that he was "going to see Dad again." And finally he "pinked" a ride. Failed to perform. Incomplete mission. Unable to function in his job.

Tuck could almost hear reveille being played at boot camp. He had to see the Major. The Major was his last chance. Could he get over the throwing up and learn to fly? Could he ever learn to stay in control? Tuck needed help. It wasn't a lack of brains. He was doing great in class. He simply couldn't keep from getting sick in the air. Could the Major help him figure out what to do?

The Major could.

"Fly the ride, son, just fly the ride in your head."

The Major was right on the money. Getting sick was about nerves, not inner ears. Getting sick was about worry, not physical skill. Getting sick was about not knowing what was coming next, about not being in control. And so the Major gave him a technique that perhaps changed his life more than anything else he ever learned. "Fly the ride." Sit in a chair alone in a room. Study the flight plan for that day. Spend ten minutes with your eyes closed and fly the ride in your mind. Taxi … take off … turn right … Go through the entire ride in your mind. Every maneuver. Then land the plane, and it's over. That way, when you are really flying, you already have experienced the ride. You know what comes next. You can anticipate what to do. You can be in control again.

And it worked. The next day, Tuck soloed in a jet. He did very well in flight school after that.

Tuck told us he still "flies the ride" in everyday life. Years later, he was in a business meeting full of lawyers, bankers, and business owners. He was negotiating a tough deal. Lots of opposition from all sides. As tempers flared, he had a sound argument for or against any proposal made. In the end, he got all he wanted in the deal. At the postmortem, one of his competitors said, "You must be one of the smartest guys I have ever met. How could you have the right answer to block us every time we made a proposal?"

The answer was simple. For two hours before the meeting, Tuck "flew the ride," going over every possible scenario the other side could come up with. In silence and alone, he prepared the appropriate answer. As each offer came out during the meeting, he instantly responded with the self-assurance of knowing he had thought it all out. To others, he appeared completely spontaneous. But Tuck knew he owed the Major for teaching him to fly the ride.

## Flyboys and friends

Sensing Tuck was slipping out of "Tale" mode again, while showing no sign of ending, I asked him about people he'd met during the course of his armed forces experience.

"In the service, you meet people that stay with you for a lifetime. Some as real friends who are frequently in touch and others who remain only as memories. A guy named Claude was both kinds. Quite a character."

Claude's last name was Smith. On the first day of flight school, with all the boys sitting in an auditorium, the Captain up front announced, "I'm going to call your name, and when I do, you are to rise and say your full name followed by your wife's maiden name and then sit down."

When the roll call got to Claude, he stood firmly and shouted, "Claude Smith, Smith, sir," then sat down.

"No. No. No. Do it again."

Again Claude stood firmly. This time he shouted a little louder:

"Claude Smith, Smith, sir!" and sat down.

"What's wrong with you? Stand and give your first name, your last name, and your wife's maiden name!" bellowed the Captain. For the third time, Claude stood. Now he almost screamed, "Claude Smith, Smith, sir!"

Since Claude had married a woman named Linda Smith, of course he was doing the routine correctly. But with his deep Southern drawl, it just didn't sound right. Everyone in that room was wondering who this weirdo was.

Claude was, among other things, a true-blooded patriot. He felt that anyone who lived in America should bleed red, white, and blue. Years after he and Tuck met, Claude, who by then was working at a company Tuck ran, happened to be in Tuck's office watching a baseball game broadcast from Toronto. As the Canadian National Anthem was played, Tuck's assistant said she thought the Canadian anthem was more beautiful than America's. The veins popped out on Claude's neck. He snapped that perhaps she should move to Canada immediately if she was going to go around denigrating his country's national anthem.

A handful of other guys who rose and declaimed the required names at that opening day assembly lived on in Tuck's memory. The boys had all been issued their gear the day before. They were wearing flight suits for the first time that day. And official hats, shoes, and aviator-style sunglasses. Real *Top Gun* outfits, for sure.

"Are there any questions about your gear?" asked the Captain.

A hand went up. A boy stood and asked, "Are our aeronautical chronometers waterproof?"

"What?" The Captain squinted at him. "Might you possibly want to know if your watches are waterproof?"

The word "asshole" did not escape anybody's lips, but it loomed in Tuck's mind and probably a few others'.

Another guy bragged of having an antique Harley at his apartment. He didn't mention that it was in a basket behind the door in a million pieces, unassembled. Yet another proclaimed that he came to pilot training to learn how to fly jets only because his father owned a fleet in Texas and wanted his son trained by the best before getting into one of his private planes.

One had flown copters in Nam. Low-flying copters that engaged in combat. This guy's agenda was simple. In his one-man fixed-wing aircraft, he had been able to do some damage. But if he could fly a jet with lots of big bombs, he could do a lot greater damage. "Fly and fight, shoot and kill" was his mantra.

"This guy had major anger issues," Tuck told us. An example was what he did the day his wife left him for the dentist she worked for. A note on the refrigerator announcing her departure triggered a response. The guy pushed the fridge off the third-floor balcony of his apartment and down onto the pavement, because he didn't want the note in his house any longer.

"A great temperament to trust with bombs, wouldn't you say?" Tuck voiced what we'd all been thinking.

## Surviving survival training

When flight school was over, Tuck still had survival training to endure. The first of the survival schools he attended was located near Spokane, Washington. Here pilots in training spent sixteen days learning what to do if they were shot down in Vietnam. Apparently being in Nam and being shot down were real possibilities. The Air Force took this training very seriously.

Tuck described it this way.

"You entered what was mocked up to be a prisoner camp. Manned by real Vietnamese personnel for maximum effect. At the beginning, you were huddled in a fenced yard with others. Digging a ditch that could have been your grave. Learning to think about the consequences of being caught if you were shot down. Being interrogated by supposed enemy captors who knew stuff about you from high school you didn't think was possible.

"The day you started this survival school, you knew it was just a training exercise. Several sleepless days later, under intense questioning from a foreign man in his foreign accent, you started to feel it was real."

The exercises were intended to let the pilots try out different techniques for refusing to answer questions. Tuck remembered pretending he had gone nuts in his cell. He kept muttering, "The rats are going to eat me" over and over again to the interrogator. This ploy seemed to work. They put Tuck back in his cell. Alone, sans rats.

As the trainees were moved about the "camp," they had a bag tied over their heads. By then, they were naked except for the bag.

"You were fed daily but were not allowed to talk to anybody else; hell, you didn't even know if anyone else was around. But sometimes they would gather a few of you at once and take you to a wall where there were small cages you had to climb into. You were scrunched into the cage. On your knees and head tucked down. The music they played was 'Sky Pilot' from back home. By now you really believed you were overseas. You waited for the song to end. It did, but no one opened the cage. Then you heard the ticking of a timer. By now your legs were cramped and you were stifling hot. What the hell is this? They can't keep us this way much longer. The bell from the timer went off. Whew, now the doors would surely be opened."

Nothing.

It took only a few more minutes before one guy lost it. He screamed "Let me out of here" at the top of his lungs. That guy was speaking for everyone.

"When they let us out, the bag was still on our head, and we were led back to our individual cell to ponder that it might be better to never get shot down."

The next phase for the trainees was a many-mile walk over rough terrain with their flight packs on their backs. This simulated that they had ejected safely from the plane, but were now behind enemy lines.

"You had a map and a few bits of survival gear from your seat pack. You also had a buddy: your navigator on board the plane was with you. The two of you had four days to get to safety without getting caught."

In the rainy season of the always-wet Northwest, that is. Constant rain and temperatures just above freezing.

Day One of walking was bad. Day Two, the freezing rain soaked through Tuck's skin. He was tired and cold and getting sick. The third morning, Tuck wanted to quit. He had had enough. His body was shivering uncontrollably.

Tuck's partner started to worry. Brad huddled close to Tuck to try to warm him. Tuck's shivering was getting stronger. He was shaking like a twig in a hailstorm, and he was deathly pale. It was time to call for help. Tuck and Brad knew there were monitors on the course; Brad signaled for one to come get them.

When the truck pulled up, Brad was relieved. By now, Tuck's body was out of control in its useless efforts to get warm. The monitors responded to Tuck's condition immediately and put him in the truck. Tuck banged against the sides of the truck, actually making the truck sway: that's how badly he was shaking. The monitors took him to a shelter, placed him under a hot shower, and began warming his insides with hot coffee. Tuck had hypothermia. A week before, one student had died during training. These monitors were not going to lose another one. Within a few hours, Tuck started coming around. His body was warm again, and his spirits almost back to normal.

The monitors then said something that stunned both him and Brad.

"Quit now and you'll have to start this part of the training from the beginning. Or get out of the shelter now and finish the hike."

Tuck was weak but not crazy. And his buddy Brad said he wouldn't let either one of them start over. When they left the monitors, Brad was carrying all of the gear, and he did so the rest of that third day. Without Brad's efforts, a very nasty few days would have started all over again for Tuck. The fourth day, Tuck was feeling a lot better: he could see the light at the end of the tunnel. Brad and Tuck finished together. Land survival school was almost over.

To finish this program, the Air Force brought in the wife of a POW. Her husband was a pilot captured in Vietnam. He was still being held.

"Please, please, please remember what you learned here."

She was certain that her husband had a better chance of surviving because he had completed this training. Chilling and memorable to this day.

## Trial by water

Next up, water survival. While flying across the country from the West Coast to Florida, Tuck's thinking had changed. He had always taken his training seriously—but he had just been very ill. He wasn't happy about that hypothermia incident. A tea drinker before the hot coffee was poured down his throat, Tuck has never tasted coffee again since that day.

Still, Tuck assumed that water survival at Homestead Air Force Base would be a piece of cake.

Right.

"They make you wear black socks over tennis shoes for the training, because when they put you in the water, they don't want the barracudas biting your feet. They put you in a harness on a flatbed boat. From that point, you're hooked up to a tow rope. You're dragging behind a very high-powered speedboat that's starting to pull away fast."

"Just run along the flatbed boat a few feet, and you'll pop right up like a cork into the air," the trainers said.

"Sounds like fun. Don't people pay money to parasail at resorts?" Tuck asked himself. "This is not just free—we were getting paid to do it out over the ocean!" With a seat pack beneath us, like the one in our jet airplane, loaded with an inflatable raft, and some fishing gear, and pills to make the water palatable.

"Hell, except for the barracudas, what did we have to worry about?"

Tuck found several answers to that question.

"Once you were as high as the tow rope would send you, they signaled you from the speedboat to disconnect the tow rope. Just unhook the sucker from your chest, and you're flying on your own. Parachuting, actually, from what seemed like a very high perch. With the tow rope gone, the boat would take off toward the horizon. They'd be back to get you in several hours. With any luck, you'd be sitting in your raft trying to catch lunch with your neat little fishing gear."

Bye, guys, thought Tuck. Don't forget me out here.

"The next part of the exercise was to return to Earth, that is, to the ocean, as if you had actually ejected from your plane. You checked your chute and then released your seat pack under you. All your gear would come out, and, with the ropes tied to it, you would reel it in when you dispatched your chute after you landed in the water."

But Tuck was in trouble. The ropes were not tied to his stuff. As he swirled in his chute down to the oncoming water, he saw his raft and gear fall to the ocean, not attached to him at all. There would be a big splash when he hit. And he had to lose the chute so it wouldn't drag him under. And then he had to pull in the raft and climb aboard. But the raft had sunk, and he had no rope to pull it back. Tuck bobbed in the water like a little cork. But he didn't move his feet too much, because he didn't want to be a barracuda snack.

Fortunately the guys in the boat were watching through binoculars. When they finished laughing, they turned the boat around to come back and get him. Tuck spent the rest of that day in the speedboat traveling about, picking up the others who had spent a few hours in their rafts. At least it wasn't his fault the equipment failed. Tuck didn't have to repeat this part of training.

With water-survival training behind him, Tuck was heading home. He thought that meant back to his wife in their hometown. He had been on active duty with the Air Force for over a year. It was time to return to his waiting wife and parents.

Wait, not so fast. Tuck was going to be assigned as a "FAC." This means "Forward Air Controller," the air guy in charge at a battle site. The FAC was the commander in the sky talking to the troops on the ground and the big bombers zooming in overhead.

What Tuck would fly was an O2. This aircraft had a propeller in the front and one in the back. Nothing normal for Tuck!

## Forward, Air Controllers!

"The minute you looked at the plane you knew people would make fun of it. The salute these pilots gave each other was like this: they'd put one hand on their forehead and one behind their head and twirl their thumbs like propellers. Really goofy."

Goofy or not, this job required a bit of expertise besides flying. The FAC was the "on scene commander." Leadership was expected, and knowledge of types of bombs was a must. The FAC would call back to an air base from his perch a few hundred feet above the action and decide what armament the jets awaiting his instructions ought to bring in. Those guys on the ground depended on the FAC to identify their exact position. They didn't want the bombs dropped on their heads. So Tuck was sent to advanced training to learn how to be an FAC in the O2.

That school was also in Florida, at Eglin Air Force Base. It would require a few more months. Tuck's wife was permitted to live there with him. Tuck and his wife had never lived in a trailer before.

The other eight men at the training session outranked Tuck by several levels. On Day One, Tuck became the coffee runner for the class. By Day Two, however, Tuck had asserted himself, reminding them that they were all FACs; they could go get their own coffee. The others shrugged and decided to treat the kid as an equal.

"In training, you learned each player's position. You had to know each position from the troops manning the ground to the jets waiting nearby. You even had to know what the enemy was doing at the time you were flying circles over their heads. Some of the enemy were climbing trees and getting close enough to shoot you with a handgun," Tuck recollected.

"But it rained a lot that winter in Florida. And you couldn't fly a training sortie in that weather. So you sat, or went home to the trailer and did nothing."

Well, not really *nothing*. Tuck's first child was conceived during one of those rainy days.

The men spent six weeks waiting for it to stop raining. They'd been getting in almost no flights, yet they couldn't go home until training was complete. There seemed to be no end in sight.

"You flew over fields and fired smoke rockets at pretend targets on the ground. When the weather let you. One trainer got too close to the field. When the craft was pulled up quickly, the G-forces caused the wings to fall off the plane. It crashed. Two guys died. The planes they were using were old and had already been to Vietnam for many flights."

A command decision was made. Everyone was moved to another air base, where the training that had been stalled for six weeks was completed in about six days. The trainees flew twice a day to log the number of sorties demanded by the syllabus. Finally it was over. Tuck could go back home to be a Guard pilot.

## Seeing (through) the sights

As the first of his guard unit ever to attend the advanced FAC training, Tuck was named to lead a four-ship-formation training ride once back at the unit. He led a bombing run to the area where they could shoot live rockets at mock targets. On the site, Tuck picked out a ship at one end of the island.

"Let's hit the deckhouse at the north end of the boat," he called to the others.

They snickered.

"Why are you laughing?" asked Tuck.

"The deckhouse?" they replied. "We'll be lucky if we even hit the ship."

On the first pass, each man launched a rocket that harmlessly splashed in the water near the intended target. Then Tuck let his first rocket go. It blew off the deckhouse, having struck exactly where it was supposed to. The laughter of the others changed to gasps.

"Do that again," they asked by radio.

"On the next passes," Tuck recalled, "they all got close to their targets, but no cigar."

Tuck, meanwhile, kept hitting right where he intended.

"One guy had a premature ejaculation," Tuck observed, then chuckled at our startled glances.

"No, the guy didn't shoot his load in his pants. This guy launched a rocket as he pulled off the target and sent the live round wandering down the bay far away from the safe zone. Luckily, it didn't hit any fishermen or sporting boaters."

Out of rockets, the four-man formation headed back to the base. As the pilots climbed out of their cockpits, Tuck walked over to the other planes. There he discovered why they hadn't been able to hit the broad side of a barn with their shots. The planes had sophisticated sights in place on the dashboard, but each pilot had pushed them aside and had drawn a black grease pencil cross on the windscreen to use as a guide. Kind of like holding two fingers in front of your face and squinting at it to focus on a target. No one had ever taught the pilots how to use the sights. Tuck's knowledge was a benefit of his being the first in his group to attend advanced training.

## "This man is crazy; give him a bomber!"

The mixture of Tuck with his "comrades at arms" during his Guard duty was pretty much oil and water. Tuck said he realized, looking back, that he had never fit in. He had joined the Guard because he didn't want to go to war. The other guys were there because they wanted to be there. Some actually hoped they *would* go to war. Tuck didn't play well with the others in that particular sandbox. Tuck had no intention of ever killing anyone. He thought war was a waste of life. Yes, you should kill someone trying to kill you, or your wife or your family. An intruder. But what if one side just went home in a war? Who would the other side kill? Tuck bided his time, expecting to complete his required term and leave quietly.

A gas shortage hit before Tuck's time was up. The Guard unit was getting cuts in the number of slots for pilots. There were fifty-five pilots in the unit, and there was only enough fuel to keep fifty of them flying a complete schedule. Five guys would have to go. Tuck went straight to the Commander and volunteered out. The others wanted to stay. Some were near retirement. Why cut them?

Tuck got an answer to that question. Because the Air Force had just spent over one million dollars training Tuck. He was an asset they wanted a return on. Tuck argued that all the pilots had been trained; getting rid of him was no more wasteful than cutting someone else.

The purity of his logic unnerved the brass. They ordered him to go to a psychiatrist at Andrews Air Base near Washington. The cover of the records he carried with him was marked, "FOR EVALUATION TO CONSIDER PUTTING THIS CANDIDATE ON WORLDWIDE ACTIVE DUTY." Maybe they thought they could scare Tuck into withdrawing his request to get out. Fortunately, the doc liked Tuck. He saw Tuck as an honest young man fulfilling his country's obligation to serve. He felt he had no reason not to recommend that Tuck be discharged honorably.

At that point, none of the other pilots were in touch with Tuck. He had been excused from showing up for duty as soon as he made his request to leave the service. The brass must not have wanted this malcontent Tuck to stir up other young pilots. So, though Tuck was honorably discharged, it appeared to his "comrades" that he had disappeared without a trace.

Tuck had honorably fulfilled his obligation to his country without firing a shot in anger. A year or so after he left the Guard, Tuck ran into a pilot from his unit at the mall. "When did you get out of jail?" the other guy asked.

"What are you talking about?"

"When you suddenly weren't around anymore, we thought you got in trouble and landed in prison."

Apparently the brass didn't squelch that rumor. It was useful. It made other young guys think twice before they made any waves. There was always the possibility you could end up like Tuck!

# Remembering That First Car: Tony's Tale

The streets had been clogged with graying snow for several days now. Some of the Inn's guests had made extended reservations anyway; some remained just to enjoy the odd calm of the blizzard's early aftermath. They'd been getting more comfortable after listening to the musings of others. Made them open up. Tony was one who stayed quiet at first. Then he started to talk, gesturing often at the cars that were marooned in drifts just outside Abacrombie's windows. Ben's tale seemed to have awakened the sleeping story in Tony.

## Stylin'

When Tony hit his fifties, he couldn't get over his perception that people under forty just didn't care what they drove. Style didn't seem to matter to them. Colors were all bland. Everything looked the same. Could you really tell a Camry from a Malibu at first glance? Did they make Camaros any more? Sitting there at the Abacrombie "big table," Tony quietly embarked on a quest, wandering back in time, trying to remember each and every car he owned. He made a list. Surely it would tell him something about himself.

Tony learned to drive in his mother's 1964 Chevy Bel Air. While his father wanted the fully loaded Impala, his parents stuck with the lower priced version.

"The really important car in the family was my father's 1957 red and white Chevy Bel Air two-door hardtop. That car was spotless. But I'm getting ahead of my story."

## Getting blessed by the Ps and the DMV

Although he had begged to drive as soon as he turned sixteen, his parents would have none of that. Throughout his junior year in high school, Tony drove them nuts.

"C'mon," he cried, "wouldn't it be easier for you all if I could drive?"

It took months to wear them down.

Soon it would be prom night. The Department of Motor Vehicles mailed him his learner's permit just in time: a person had to have it for fifteen days before being tested for the real license. And the fifteenth day was the day of his prom. Tony made no other plans for prom transportation. He was driving himself and his girl to the prom. Such confidence! Dad took him out to practice, and his mother was happy to let him have the wheel when she went for errands. His uncle taught him to parallel park. On the fifteenth day, Tony was ready.

The Department of Motor Vehicles was about twenty miles from his house. Tony's older sister Joan had agreed to take him to the main office for his test. They arrived early in the morning. Tony's plan to get this thing over with quickly hit a snag: his records were thirty miles away in the county office, an office that happened to be closed that day.

Surely something could be done? The clerk directed Tony and Joan to a copy of his records held in yet another remote office, one located about forty-five miles away. That office closed at noon. It was by now around 10:00 AM.

"To the car, Batman!" cried Tony. His sister wasn't amused. She hadn't figured on driving over a hundred miles that day to try to get her little brother his license.

"But isn't that what sisters are for? Bailing brothers out of a jam?"

(Luckily there were no female guests in the breakfast room to hear Tony raise that rhetorical question, albeit the question of a sixteen-year-old boy.)

A little after 11:00 AM, the pair pulled into Main Street, Tinytown, USA. Two people were working in the office of the DMV, which was closing in less than one hour. Sure, there was time for one more test that day.

At the main large-city Motor Vehicles office, where Tony had started that day, a driving course was laid out for the test. There were red lights, places for you to show you could do a turnaround, crosswalks to stop at, and the dreaded parallel parking area where many a driver's test came to a dead stop. Not in Tinytown. Main Street itself was the test. Don't hit a farmer, and you were halfway to your license.

Tony's sister watched from the sidewalk as the car headed down the street and around the block. She was still there two minutes later when Tony approached the parallel parking area. A space big enough for two cars was marked by two peach baskets with a broom sticking out the top of each. Tony was elated; one reason why Tony picked his sister to take him to get tested was that her car was a Chevy Corvair Monza, about half the size of a normal car of that era. He could park that baby for sure.

As Tony pulled up to the front peach basket, he seemed a little close. Oh well, too late for any maneuvering now. He placed the car in reverse and started to back into the space. He felt the basket rubbing against the front fender, and for a moment a picture of his dad driving him to the prom flashed before his eyes.

"Keep going," Tony thought. "Just get that baby into the space, and all will be well."

He could see his sister cringing on the sidewalk. As the car glided backwards, the basket began moving; he could see the broom starting to flutter. But he was almost back in the space now. Tony kept his foot on the gas real low and just eased on back. The basket toppled. The broom lay on the front fender of the car. The car was in the space, but if that broom had been a person, that individual would have been sprawled out across the hood of the little car. His sister had covered her eyes by now. Surely it was over for that day with no license in sight.

But this was Tinytown, where Hearts are Big. The guy giving the test said Tony didn't do "all that bad." He couldn't expect a little guy like Tony to see the basket over the dashboard when it was lower than the hood of the car. And besides, he had merely brushed it. He didn't really run it over. Tony and the test administrator went into the office. Joan was wondering how to console her little brother when Tony emerged, triumphant, license in hand.

That night, Tony drove downtown to his junior prom. He was terrified to be out driving alone. (He told us he could still feel the terror today, sitting here, nursing his coffee and bagel at the Abacrombie.)

Soon Tony actually got to drive the all-important '57 Chevy.

"If anybody else here in this room is a car buff, you're thinking it was awesome, aren't you? Smooth as silk. Beautiful lines. A classic. When you see one today, don't you just wish you had one?" Tony laughed. "Let's explore the truth."

The tires were big enough for an airplane. The wheel took twenty turns to go around a corner. Twenty hard-pulling turns—there was no power steering, and the car was heavy. Air conditioning? None. Crank down the windows, no push buttons. Sure, now it's a classic. But in 1967, it was a ten-year-old Chevy. Not especially desirable, and nothing like those little Beetles that suddenly were everywhere. Beetle ads, my God, the ads. Google some old VW ads sometime, and see what marketing really was. Hall of Fame ads that made you want to own one. But who could afford almost two thousand dollars for a new car? Not Tony or his dad. So. What about a used Bug?

For extra money, Tony worked with his father on the weekends, doing maintenance and paint jobs. One Saturday, the old Chevy kept missing a beat. The engine wasn't firing smoothly any more. The body was still perfect, but its "mind" was heading south. Tony's dad had actually considered a rebuilt engine from "Monkey Ward." A rebuilt could be put on a ninety-day charge card for about three hundred dollars.

## Movin' on up

Tony supplied an alternative to giving the Chevy a brain transplant. That Saturday, going to the local hardware store for supplies, Tony hopped the curb with the car, pulling the exhaust pipes off of both of the twin mufflers. His father claimed he could hear the Chevy coming from a quarter of a mile away.

"Do you have any idea what a dual exhaust would cost on that car? A car that already had a sick engine?" his father groaned.

Father and son knocked off work immediately. They headed down Belair Road (coincidentally, the street's actual name) in what was to be their last ride in the Bel Air car and pulled across the street from a used car lot where his father had seen a dear little green 1962 Beetle. What a beauty. Turning radius of half the Chevy. Gas mileage to dream of, even though gas was less than twenty-five cents a gallon at that time. And you could park those things anywhere. Who needed a snappy-looking 1957 red and white Chevy when you could have that green Bug? Tony's dad made him park the car across the street. No reason for the dealer to hear how loud the car was with that broken exhaust.

So, Mr. Used Car Dealer, what will you give us in trade-in on this one thousand dollar used Bug? The man looked across the street and offered seventy-five dollars.

Tony's dad was ecstatic. Gone were the made-in-the-USA days, hello import. A classic easily worth twenty thousand today was traded for a car that didn't bring two thousand, new.

## Wheeling and dealing

Of course, Tony wanted complete independence, not a share of Mom and Dad's ride. But a car of his own was out of the question. Eighteen years old, having just graduated from high school, and with his first summer job under his belt, Tony convinced his father that, with college on the horizon, he needed some wheels.

*Two* wheels were what he got. Specifically, a small, shiny red scooter called a Vespa, with a 90cc engine. Top speed of fifty miles an hour. Ninety miles to the gallon of gas (mixed with a little oil). While his mother was not happy, she didn't fight it. Tony was on his own, transportation-wise. Completely on his own: his girlfriend's parents forbade her to ride on it, so he scootered to her house, and then they walked wherever they wanted to go. But Tony had his first wheels, and he loved them.

The Vespa had a little flaw: the steering locked, but the engine could still be started. Every workday, someone would come and get Tony with the news that neighborhood kids had started the scooter, even though they couldn't drive it anywhere. Tony learned to shut off the gas so the engine wouldn't be running all day.

Rain, snow, freezing weather: they didn't matter to Tony. He drove the scooter every day for a year. He fell a few times, and he was wet often, and he was cold almost all the time. Time? Time to move up. Mom, however, wouldn't allow him to own a car. One day, however, an accident cured her resistance. Tony and his Vespa hit a car, from the rear, that had stopped at a green light for no apparent reason; Tony went flying over the handlebars and onto the trunk of the woman's car. He was not hurt, but the scooter was bent like a big letter V. He pried its injured body apart a little, enough to drive it home in the one gear that worked. Mom was seriously concerned.

"Let's look at some cars," she said.

## Tony gets Bugged

For four hundred bucks, Tony found a Blue VW convertible. Rust everywhere. Top all ragged, windshield cracked, tires bald, paint bad. It was his dream car.

Mom drove him to get it and said no. No! Tony actually cried. What good is it to have your own money and be eighteen and not be able to make adult decisions? Here he was, about to enter his second year of college, and Mom was still calling the shots. Dad intervened. It was Tony's hard-earned money. And Tony never got into trouble. Whatever rift occurred between his mother and father over the issue of Tony's car didn't matter to Tony. What mattered is that Tony got the car.

He spray-painted the car himself with jet black primer. Did a little body work to smooth out the dents. Got the windshield repaired.

To Tony, the car was a beauty. He drove it proudly for about a year, at which time he realized that the dull black paint just didn't cut it. He wanted to be noticed, and not for a bad home paint job. The color that struck his fancy was "Poppy Red," really closer to orange. The Poppy Red car was stunning.

"You could see it coming for a mile, sober or drunk," Tony laughed.

Speaking of "drunk" segued Tony into the next incident. As Tony drove down Harford Road at thirty miles an hour, a car turned left immediately in his path. Tony crushed into the side of the car, pushing it across the intersection and up onto the sidewalk. Tony's beloved VW was a wreck, smashed in up to the windshield, with the fresh Poppy Red now smeared with ugly tan paint from the car he had hit. Both fenders were bent into the tires, making them useless. His VW looked like a goner. The other driver sat in his car unfazed. What had happened? The driver was so drunk he didn't know he had been in an accident. But he was shocked sober enough to blurt out that he had just left a hospital for treatment of alcoholism, and this accident would send him to jail. If only Tony would drive him home, he would write a check for Tony's car, and all would be well.

"No one was hurt," Tony said. "Why should the guy go to jail? I drove him home, and his wife gave me a check for the four hundred dollars I paid for the Beetle."

The next day, Tony pulled the broken fenders from the Bug's body and took off the hood. With spare tires attached, lo and behold, the car started up and drove just fine. No hood, no fenders, no lights, no bumpers, but a drivable Bug on which he had just been given a full repayment of his four-hundred-dollar investment. He removed the hood and jumped up and down on it in his backyard. Same with the fenders. New lights would soon be installed.

"Hey, everything was all wrinkled in front, but the car moved, and the bumper wasn't so bad after a little home repair."

To mark the occasion of the accident, Tony sprayed the damaged hood black and drew a bull's-eye in orange paint where he had slammed the other guy. He drove the car for another year that way. Why not? He had his money back, and God knows the Bug was unique-looking. He bought his girlfriend an engagement ring with the four hundred dollars.

Unfortunately, though the Bug's engine was still good, its body had quit. Damage from the accident left it unsafe to drive. Tony's dad still had that little green Bug they bought when the Chevy died, and Dad's Bug was a vice versa: it looked great but had a worn-out engine. For two hundred dollars, a Bug shop switched the good engine from Tony's wreck with the bad engine in the little green Bug. Voila. Tony had a "new car"; it kept going for another year.

A 1972 yellow Beetle convertible was Tony's first-ever new car. "Man, it was stylin'!"

Tony took a long drive down Mexico way from Phoenix, where he had bought the car, and washed the dust off the windshield with that newfangled automatic washer system. When he got a flat tire, he found out how the pressure was obtained to squirt the juice on the windshield. It came from the hose connected to the spare tire, which was now flat from spraying the dusty windshield so much. First new car, first flat. Spare tire flat from too much dust. Who was the engineer on that system?

## Wheel reduction

Next came a motorcycle. A Kawasaki 500cc Mach III.

"That bike did over a hundred miles an hour, easy, and I tried it one day way out on Harford Road. Not too bright. If I'd hit so much as a small stone, the bike would have sent me to the next life."

The 500 was chrome and green and beautiful. It even had an alarm system attached to the back license-plate holder. If somebody tried to move the bike, the alarm would sound. One morning, up at seven after a late poker game the night before, Tony looked outside: his Kawasaki was gone. What happened to the alarm? And what about his dog, who slept in the front bay window and surely must have watched the thieves take off with the motorcycle?

The police who came to take a report laughed when Tony asked how often bikes like that were recovered. Never, was the answer he feared and heard. That bike was his Elvis. It had left the building.

Tony had insurance for an accident, whether he got hit or hit someone else, but theft insurance was another matter. He would have to eat the loss of the bike. Ouch. Plus he was going to miss riding the damn thing. To soothe his pain, Tony bought a cheaper 400cc version that Kawasaki came out with in 1978. It looked like the early Triumph bikes. No frills, though. Kick start, fenders painted rather than chrome; but it was still a motorcycle. And big enough, considering its vintage.

"That bike has less than ten thousand miles on it—and it's still sitting in my barn out back," Tony admitted.

## Looking mah-velous

Next, an interim car got stuck into Tony's vehicle history, a Mercury Cougar. Not Tony's style. He soon sold it to a local weathercaster who bought it for his elderly mother.

"My business buddies chided me about my vehicles. Said that to be successful you have to look successful. But who knew what looked successful? I didn't."

Maybe a bullet-back 1972 Riviera, maroon with a black vinyl top and a great eight-track player? Tony loved this car. As a softball player in an inner city league, Tony's black friends were impressed with his "short," their nickname for a car. One guy peered in the open window and said, "Who do you have on that eight track, Tony, Robert Goulet?" Tony hit the eject button and out popped his tape of George Benson, one of the greatest black (or white) jazz guitar players who has ever lived. The guys hooted loudly over that discovery. The hot Riviera lasted three years. When it hit 135,000 miles on the odometer, it also hit the very top of the car pile at the local junkyard. Although Tony actually drove it into the junkyard, there wasn't much left in it.

It saddened Tony for months to drive by the yard and still see the now-crumpled car perched atop the heap. Finally, one day it was gone. Tony felt better.

Next in Tony's automotive life came a demonstrator, a car that the dealership let people drive to see if they wanted that model. The "demo" was a brown Ford station wagon. Tony cringed when he looked at it, but the price was right. Being raised as a Chevy guy, buying a Ford, and a blah one at that, made him feel like a traitor. That car didn't last long.

But soon two cars came at once! A brand-new 1986 Dodge Caravan for his wife (he had by now married the happy recipient of the insurance-money ring) and a beautiful long 1982 Cadillac Sedan DeVille for Tony. The Caddy was awesome. Blue inside and out. Plush velour seats. Everything push-button, just like the Riviera that had died a while back. This was truly stylin'. Why not add vanity plates that pronounced the name of his business? Tony was, after all, on his way up in the world. Funny thing: although the Caravan was new and cost over thirteen thousand dollars, the Caddy was bought used at an auction for just four thousand. Yet the Dodge said "Run-of-the-mill family man," and the Caddy said, "Look at me! I am SO freaking successful!"

"Or so I thought," added Tony. "I later found out most people thought it made 36-year-old Tony look like a 60-year-old fart."

The first Caddy gave way to a 1976 Cadillac convertible. Tony didn't mind going backwards in years. He liked the older stuff, and this was the last year Cadillac made a convertible. He bought the '76 from a retired dentist and found a great shop to restore the old car. New carpet and top. Paint stripped to the metal and several coats of the original soft yellow color applied. This huge Caddy was the Queen Mary of cars. But the Queen probably got better gas mileage.

Tony was in an up-and-down financial situation during those years. Any gob of cash that came his way during an "up" period seemed to be a message: "Buy a car." But the downside—the financial downslide—was also his reality. One day, with the rent due on his house, he found the money cupboard bare.

"One thing you got to understand," Tony declared, "is that I was never late paying my bills. Sure, I could run up charge cards like Michael Jackson, but I didn't want bad credit, so I always paid the bills on time."

This time, however, there was nowhere to turn for money. He advertised the Caddy in the paper and let her go for a huge loss on his investment. The landlord got the money on time. Tony's family got to eat. But this was one instance when it hurt him to the bone to see a car go. There were real tears over the sale of his baby. He promised himself he would never again get into a situation where he'd have to part with something so dear. But things got worse, and the next car was a disastrous old Datsun, "which doesn't deserve more than a mention," according to Tony.

The place where Tony worked saw great things in him. They knew from the old yellow Caddy that Tony believed he had style. Both the business owners that Tony worked for had nice cars, one a Caddy and one a Jag. By now Tony was making those boys some money, so they wanted to reward him. They would lease a car for Tony.

"Just pick out whatever you want," they said.

Tony pimped out a 1988 blue Cadillac reminiscent of his old 1978 version. The Rolls Royce–style grille Tony added made the vehicle one of a kind. It boasted the softest leather interior ever made. Tony was back on top of his car world. Over six hundred dollars a month to lease that baby, but Tony wasn't paying for it. Sad to say, when Tony left that company just one year later, he inherited the payments.

During the charmed year when Tony had no payments to make, he became nostalgic. His friend had a 1958 Chevy that needed to be restored, and Tony took the car to his house, looking forward to the adventure. Tony and his friend never started the project, however, and, after taking up space in the driveway for many months, the car was traded for a copier for Tony's business.

Lease payments on the Cadillac were choking Tony to death. Finally the four-year period was up. He figured he would simply flip the lease into a purchase agreement and keep on going at lower payments until the car was his. Tony was wrong. He had gone several thousand miles over his allotment. At the end of the lease, when all monies came due, including the mileage overage, it cost Tony almost two thousand dollars just to turn the car back in. Time for another used car.

By now it was the early nineties, but Tony still loved the looks of the 1984 Seville. The model with the sweet rear trunk lid done in Continental style.

"So, you bought one," Tim prompted.

"Hell yes," laughed Tony.

While going through a divorce, Tony was dating his future second wife, Carmen. She told him it embarrassed her to get in the gaudy wine-colored Caddy. Shouldn't he consider driving a more stylish car? A Jaguar, perhaps?

The Jaguar looked terrific. Chocolate brown, with a moon roof and classic Jag wheels—ooh la la! It had over one hundred thousand miles on it and spent more time in the shop than on the road. But Carmen thought it looked just right. Oh, the money wasted on that Jag.

## Have truck, will haul

Tony and Carmen liked to go to auctions and buy old furniture to refurbish. For that, they needed a truck. And since the Jag was never available to drive (the mechanic needed it at the shop), Tony bought a "Shaggin' Wagon," a big Chevy van with god-awful brown shag carpet on the floors, walls, and ceiling. They could haul furniture, all right, but they didn't want to be caught dead in that thing. Fortunately the engine blew up in less than a month, and the shag era ended quickly.

"While we were riding past a local church one day, my wife-to-be noticed a fifteen-passenger van out front with a FOR SALE sign on its windshield. The truck was twenty years old, but it had only fifty-two thousand miles on it. There were four bench seats behind two bucket seats in front. Sliding side doors. That baby was huge!

"I was constantly grateful that the van was previously owned by a church," Tony told us, "because that meant a lot of prayers had been said by church members en route to outings and whatever." He added soberly: "God was surely present to oversee all its occupants. How else can you explain that one late night one of my daughters rolled the van over two, three times, and it got crushed like a tin can, but she got thrown through the windshield and came out without a scratch?"

Once again needing a truck to haul furniture, Tony happened to notice an old, small-town gas station with a big 1978 Chevy van parked on the side. With rusted-out sides and floors, the van was used by the county school system and had low mileage. For seven hundred dollars, Tony was back in business. Some sheet metal work, a brake job, a tune-up, and Tony had his new auction hauler. Tony applied a coat of green Rustoleum, using a brush, of course.

"I loved that old ride. It's still part of my fleet today."

## Bugging the next generation

When Tony's daughter Linda was only ten, she announced that she wanted to drive a VW convertible when she turned sixteen. A Beetle Bug. The trouble was that she said this in 1992, and they had stopped selling Bugs like that in 1979. What's a father to do? Go find an old Beetle convertible and sit on it, of course.

A doctor was still driving the little silver Bug when Tony found it. The car was a mess, but it was still running. The hood was damaged and hanging off the hinges, the top had holes big enough to put your hand through, and the bumpers were all mangled. But it ran. And Linda pointed out that even the clock worked. She beamed.

"How can a dad ever beat the feeling you get when you make your child smile? You couldn't drive the car on the street the way it was, but hey, I had six years to restore it."

So the car went into Tony's garage.

During this time, Tony was going through his divorce. He had moved into a tiny thousand-square-foot house that had a screened-in porch behind a picture window in the dining room. A large sliding door from inside made the porch feel like another inside room. Therefore Tony did the obvious, manly, logical thing. He knocked down the corner wall and installed a garage door on the porch.

"Then I could just drive the car into the porch. And I could sit at the table in the dining room and stare at my car, which was now inside the house. Just like that private eye on TV—what was his name?—who drove his T-Bird into his house."

Tony continued, "Let me tell you about the ride from Linda's house to her father's new digs. No hood—the top had been stripped off down to a bare metal frame—and of course there were no license plates. But we had to go only a couple of miles. Over back roads."

Tony and Linda drove together. Clara, Tony's other daughter, would be following Dad, riding with his third daughter, Lisa.

"The car hadn't been driven in years. Who knew if it would make it? But no guts, no glory, right?"

"Right, Tony," I said dutifully.

All went well for the first mile. Then Dad was passed by a policeman going the other way. Knowing that the cop would turn around, Tony headed down a side street and found a cul-de-sac to hide in, losing Clara along the way. They saw the policeman prowling the next street over, but they were never discovered. Linda was mortified. Would they go to jail if they were caught? ("Daddy, I'm just a kid!")

As they finished the adventurous ride to their father's house, the girls were shocked to see a new door opening into the porch. Oh my God. Dad was driving the Beetle right into the house. And there in the house, the Beetle sat for a year or so.

The next stop for the old Bug was the barn at Tony's new house. The car matched the barn; both were falling apart. The barn would have to be restored before the car could be, but it might fall down on the car before either could be saved. Linda was coming up on sixteen. Get a move on, Dad, Tony told himself.

With the barn finally complete, dry, and safe, the car, soon to be his daughter's gift, could have Tony's complete attention. Up on jack stands sat the old girl. Everything was ripped off of the car. Seats were gone. Floors had rusted through to the street below. Hood dented all over. And Tony discovered that the frame parts for the top were worthless. But Volkswagens never die unless you let them. If you checked out the Internet, you could buy every part for every year a Bug was made. Every nut, bolt, screw, top frame part, and more. Jazzy new seat covers. Metal pan inserts to replace floors long gone. Even a tray to keep the battery from falling through the rusted-out section under the seat where the battery lived. New wiring, no problem. The Bug would live again.

Tony and his daughter debated the color scheme over and over, finally choosing a tan interior, tan top, and black body. Tony would do all the work. He had mastered the art of painting with Rustoleum from working on the truck; to make the Bug more rugged, he painted it with a brush in High Gloss Black. But the car didn't seem to have pizzazz. Tony was a thinker. He strolled through Home Depot and pondered. What made old cars more stylish?

Aha! Wood! He would build the car into a Woody. There were flooring planks in oak that looked just right. Tony brought enough home to give them a try. The doors and side panels in front of the fenders were almost flat and had great lines when you contrasted the sides against the round fenders. About the time he had the first side covered in wood planks, Tony's wife came out to the barn for a visit. "Wood! Who puts wood on a car?" she shouted.

Then she realized it looked just like her grandfather's old Woody and smiled.

With both sides complete up to the window-line side molding, the car was beginning to look awesome. The final touch was the handmade wooden bumpers to replace the rusted, mangled chrome ones original to the car. With a fresh coat of stain on the oak panels, the car looked like something from the 1930s. An old custom-upholstery man said he could replace the top, including the frame. Voila, the car was complete. One of a kind. Beautiful. And Linda was almost sixteen.

The maiden voyage was to show off the car at his wife's antique store. It was only six miles from home. One mile up busy Ridge Road, the left front wheel flew off the car.

"Guess those lugs were never tightened," Tony acknowledged.

He stopped the car in the grass just off the road. Father and daughter watched the wheel just keep rolling. It rolled a long way—didn't stop until it hit a house. They both laughed like crazy.

Tony said he would run home to get a wrench to fix the wheel. Linda would sit and wait quietly at the car. No one had to know this had happened; Tony's limited skills as a mechanic didn't need to be fodder for future family jokes. Once the wheel was tightened, they headed for the antique shop.

"Mum's the word, right?" Tony whispered.

"Did any more wheels fall off?" was the chorus greeting them when they headed inside.

Seems Linda had a cell phone and got bored waiting for her father to get back with the wrench.

"We still smile as we pass the house where the wheel came to a stop," Tony chuckled.

The day was finally arriving when his daughter would turn sixteen. But Tony couldn't bear to let her drive the Woody. It was too unique for everyday use. The Woody would have to live in the barn and wait for special days to go outside. The wood would fade or crack, and the damn thing was just too cute to be out in traffic all the time. So Dad bought Linda a VW Cabriolet convertible for her sixteenth birthday.

"And boy, was that a good thing," Tony recalled.

Just two months after Linda got her license, she ran a stop sign and totaled the Cabriolet. The air bag saved her from any injury. Thank God she wasn't in the no-air-bag Woody.

## Gotta have it

The money situation was getting a little better for Tony in those days, and he still liked the old stuff. Looking through the paper, he spotted a 1973 Chevy Caprice classic convertible for sale. Only nine thousand of those had ever been made. Although Carmen and Tony had more cars and trucks than two people could drive, she accompanied him to the brand-new tract home of the seller, a man in his early thirties. The man's wife fed their one-year-old in the high chair in the kitchen. The Caprice took up the entire garage. Bumper against one wall to bumper against the garage door. It barely fit inside. What a beauty!

"Why sell this homage to oil-guzzlers? When it looks to be in showroom condition?" Tony wanted to know.

And for just five thousand dollars? The baby's cry was the tip-off. The man's wife bluntly said, "We are in over our heads, and that car has to go." She jerked her head toward her husband, saying, "He can get *his* toys back when the kids are grown."

As Tony backed the car out of the garage and put the top down for the ride home, the seller cried like a baby. He stood on the driveway taking pictures as Tony pulled away. His last words to Tony were, "Please, don't drive the car near my house. Seeing it would make me too sad."

It reminded Tony of the day he lost his Caddy long ago. Tony still cherishes the man's well-loved toy today.

On another beautiful blue-sky day, Tony and Carmen (now his wife), driving in the country, spied on somebody's front lawn a little roadster that had been converted from a VW. It had the green body of an MG-TD and the frame and engine of an old VW. Carmen looked great driving the car!

Cars were now coming out their ears. This one had no heat, bad windshield wipers, and doors that leaked when it rained: not very practical, but very cool looking. Carmen's antique store was located in a mall with big glass windows, so you could see all the merchandise from the open space out front. Tony parked the little roadster right there in the front window. This way the men walking by would come in with their wives.

Sexist thinking, wasn't it? But sure enough, hundreds of men came into the store to gaze into the little roadster. None of them bought it, though. The buyer was, in fact, a woman who said she was giving it to herself for Christmas.

By 1996, the old Dodge Caravan from 1986 was shot. Although it seems that most men hate to admit they drive a minivan, Tony didn't mind at all. Minivans grew popular for a reason. They were the most practical vehicle made. Plenty of storage space and great comfort features, and with accessories they could look a little sporty. Tony had reached the point where he could go into a dealership and pay cash. He got a minivan with all the bells and whistles. While he may have wanted a new Cadillac, and he could have afforded one, practicality won out.

Three days after Tony bought the minivan, he left for a two-day business trip. While he was away, his wife went to an auction and bought a dining room set for the store. Like Tony, she could be impatient. She didn't like driving the old furniture in a rented hauling van, and Tony would be gone for another day, so she took out the seats of that Caravan and rolled them under the carport roof so she could pick up the dining room set. When Tony got home that night he noticed the seats sitting out. Then he saw the Caravan—full of a table, sideboard, and chairs, which fit neatly in the open space created by the lack of seats. Ivy covers those seats where they remain today on the edge of the carport ten years later. And Carmen has never given up the keys to her green hauling machine.

## Tony drives Time in reverse

Tony recalled the milestone of turning fifty. What could he do to mark the occasion? What about another car? No, a pickup truck. Better yet, a 1949 pickup truck the same age as he was. Scouring a copy of *Hemmings Motor News,* he came upon a 1949 Chevy three-quarter-ton pickup.

"It had been driven daily in Nebraska by a sweet little old lady. No kidding! She took my offer of twenty-five hundred dollars."

She and Tony hired a man to haul the truck from Nebraska to Tony's home. A few small repairs later, Tony had an inspected, licensed, wonderful old truck to make runs to the dump with the debris from his hobby, which was working on his own house as well as several investment properties he had purchased.

"I've got new hub caps, interior parts, and an ooga horn waiting for the day I get around to restoring the old truck," Tony declared. "For now, she sits proudly at my place, and I drive her a few times each month to keep her fresh."

Not wanting to wear out the old '49 before she could be restored, Tony bought a much-used pickup to do the grunt work of trash and debris hauling. It was a blue 1991 Chevy Silverado.

"Must've been bad karma. Someone made a left turn in front of me and got T-boned by my truck into the parking lot of a local store. Like the accident that killed my first car, this one killed the pickup. I wasn't hurt, but I sure was pissed."

It was clearly the other guy's fault, but how could he replace that truck for the twenty-five hundred dollars he had paid? Surely the insurance would pay him very little. Next day he was shocked to learn differently.

"Let's see," said the insurance adjuster on the long-distance call, "your truck had power windows and doors, didn't it?" (Sure. They didn't always work, but Tony kept quiet.)

"And you had the extended cab. And the eight-foot bed. Your truck was fully loaded. Would you take sixty-five hundred dollars as settlement?"

Happy Birthday to Tony. (The accident had occurred on his birthday.) The wrecked truck had over two hundred fifty thousand miles on it, and the adjuster wanted to give Tony almost three times what he had paid for it. His first wreck got him an engagement ring, and this one was going to get him a better truck.

The replacement truck Tony got was a 1988 GMC pickup, fully loaded. It was purchased on the day its former owner retired from the truck factory where he worked; he had driven it gently and cared for it like a child. It should have been in a museum, not a driveway.

"Months later, after paying the full asking price for the truck, I sent the seller one hundred dollars and a note. I told the guy it was the best used car or truck I'd ever bought, and the man should take his wife out to dinner on me for taking such good care of it all those years."

Five years after his wife commandeered the '96 Caravan, Tony bought another one. A brand-new Chrysler Town and Country. Knowing he would sell his business soon, Tony thought this might be the last big vehicle he'd purchase for cash. He wanted to slow down. The heated seats stopped working after a year. Sometimes the windows don't go up or down. And the car has been recalled twice.

Maybe he shouldn't have gotten a new one. The old stuff seems to be holding up just fine.

# Why Do We Collect Things?: Burt's Tale

Burt sat at the breakfast table and listened as other guests talked about their love of collecting things. All sorts of things. Tuck, Enzo, Tim, Jeff, each person (including me) spoke of starting one collection or another as children and accumulating lots of stuff.

"Stuff we affixed immense value to, when in reality it was stuff anybody could get, and in quantity," interjected Rick. "Try to sell those Beanie Babies today and see what you get for them!"

Burt learned early that you should go after the good stuff. As a kid, he had a friend whose father collected coins. And, as Burt gazed at the bright silver pieces, the man kept saying, "Always buy the best of something, even if you can't buy much. You'll be much happier later if you do." Back then, of course, Burt didn't have a big capital reserve to put this advice into practice.

Burt's first love was baseball. His dad took him and his brother to Memorial Stadium on many a summer day to watch Willie Miranda, his dad's favorite player. Willie was a no-hit, all-glove, worker-type ballplayer, sort of like Burt's worker-type dad.

Baltimore's favorite baseball-playing son, Brooks Robinson, was one of Burt's heroes. Brooksie was going to be at a local car parts store one day, autographing his book, *Third Base Is My Home*. For Burt, walking away from that table was like sex for the first time.

Another great collectible came Burt's way at the awards ceremony at the end of Little League season, where a major leaguer typically presented the trophies and then signed a few autographs. Burt couldn't remember if Gus Triandos had been his favorite player before the awards dinner or became his favorite player when he signed that dirty baseball Burt brought along that night. In any case, Gus etched himself into Burt's memory forever the day he hit a home run to win a no-hitter pitched by Hoyt Wilhelm on Boy Scouts Day at the ballpark.

There was one thing Burt loved as much as he loved baseball: reading. Books about real people were his favorites. How did so-and-so become famous? How did they get to be good at what they did? Burt noticed they didn't write many biographies about nobodies. He set out to link his two loves by collecting baseball books. Given his limited budget, he decided to confine his collection to books about Hall of Fame baseball players.

A cousin gave him an early Lou Gehrig book, *The Pride of the Yankees.* Someone else came through with a book about Babe Ruth. At age twelve, Burt actually visited the Hall of Fame and was hooked. There were names in the Hall he had never heard of. So much reading to do! The public library was a godsend, especially because it sold old inventory at year's end to make way for new books. Ten cents bought him a Ty Cobb book. Another dime brought home *Maybe I'll Pitch Forever,* by Satchel Paige, and then there was the day he bought *Koufax,* by Sandy Koufax, from the Hamilton Public Library.

"In 1964, on my fifteenth birthday, I was bragging to my girlfriend that Koufax was the greatest pitcher ever, and I informed her that Koufax would pitch a no-hitter that very night to celebrate my birthday. And guess what: Philadelphia lost three to nothing on Sandy Koufax's third career no-hitter," gloated Burt. "If it wasn't already obvious to my girl that I was a baseball genius, it was then!"

"Of course, it might've been that Koufax was just really that good," murmured Tony.

Books took Burt to new worlds and taught him much more than he could observe from his hometown. Names of great restaurants in New York: Toots Shore's, Twenty-One, The Brown Derby. Places the ballplayers went in Los Angeles. What did the Chicago Chop House really sound like during dinner rush? And the hotels! They seemed like plush palaces that one day Burt might see.

Relatives added new books to the collection. Books bought at full retail price, not copies from the library that had been read by a lot of other people. Books whose spines had never been broken. To Burt, these new books were like religious icons to be displayed on a shelf and never touched. "Some of them are now thirty years old and unread," he said.

As Burt got older and started working, he was able to make new investments in books. Always treasuring the Brooks Robinson tome because of the autograph, Burt started looking for other autographed books. Geez, he discovered something amazing. Bookstores carried copies of autographed books left over from signing sessions from authors on promo tours. Not just baseball books; all kinds of books. Biographies of people other than sports figures. Bios of business folk, like the *The Dodges,* autographed by Joan Potter Elwart, one of the authors; it was about the auto family fortunes and misfortunes, and it was fascinating. Books on celebrities and politicians. A book by Eugene Cernan, the last man (so far) to walk on the moon.

Burt's world was expanding. He had over one hundred books in his Hall of Fame collection and now dozens of other autographed books on a variety of subjects. And then he was truly humbled. One of his friends saw the interest Burt had in books and took him to his parents' home to show Burt what a real book collector could do. The friend's father was a Phi Beta Kappa who had been a book reviewer for most of his life. The family lived in an old Victorian house in a wonderful part of the city where time stopped moving in the 1940s.

"You could film a movie there today and transport the audience back to postwar time with wide porches and flower baskets hanging in the breeze. You could almost smell the lemonade, walking up those front steps," Burt recalled.

Inside the front door, Burt stopped dead in his tracks. Every wall he could see was lined with bookshelves. Books were everywhere. Not hundreds of books, but thousands of books. Even going up the wide staircase. At least ten thousand volumes in all. Now this guy was *really* a collector. Burt knew he had a lot of work to do.

"You should have seen them all," Burt said. "Books on every subject, from every era. They blew me away."

This book collector was a gentle man who saw right away that Burt had a genuine love for the written words and the effort it took for an author to write them. After just a few minutes of conversation, the man knew about Burt's love of baseball. Instantly the man picked up a bright green-covered book, a history of the Baltimore Orioles. The man then signed the book for Burt, because that reviewer, and avid collector, had actually written it. What a treasure.

In ensuing months, the collector sent Burt many books to fill out Burt's collection. Baseball books and biographies—and a fairly new subject matter for Burt, corporate biographies—piled up in Burt's home waiting to be read.

"Reading those books gave me new perspectives," Burt said. "They gave me a kind of courage and confidence I would never have gotten just walking through life. If only more kids would just read and read and read—oh, what they could learn."

Well into adulthood, Burt continued his pursuit of new volumes to add to his collection. "But common sense and a couple of moves from one house to another thinned the herd, so to speak."

Five hundred volumes became seven hundred, and then a move would occur. Did he really need that Philip Roth novel? Is anyone going to care if he doesn't keep the Elia Kazan? Books Burt could stand to part with went back to where many had come from: the annual sales of used books run by alums to raise money for their various colleges.

"Hey, at least I read some of them before they made the round trip from sale table to my home and back to the sale table." None of those he donated had been signed. He could never part with a signed copy.

By now Burt had two things going for him as a collector. He started to make enough money to buy nice books, and his job made him travel all over the country, giving him access to small bookstores in remote towns across America. "This was before the Internet, where you can find anything now."

The hunt for a treasure matched the pleasure of finding something on a shelf just waiting for Burt to come pluck it. The collection became more refined.

At one estate sale he attended, a book written and signed by President Harry Truman came up on the auction block. One of Burt's daughters, Clara, sat next to him. The place was quiet. Bidders whispered as if they were at a major golf tournament. The hush was broken by Clara's loud cheers as her father placed the winning bid.

"She practically did an end zone dance! Hey, we had just scored a touchdown!" Burt gloated. "We left the auction floor in a hurry so the place could return to the cathedral atmosphere it seemed to need. Outside, we whooped it up as if we were both kids. Who cared what it cost? A President had actually written the book and signed it! Move over Hall of Famers; a new category's moving in."

Surely, if this book existed, there must be other books by Presidents out there. *Autographed* other books. There were. Burt's interest in history and the Presidents went back to his early childhood. Until age twelve, when he toyed with the idea of becoming a priest in the Catholic church, Burt believed he would become the President of the United States. The hunt was on.

As of the date of his visit to the Abacrombie, Burt had become neither. But Burt's travels took him to places where the former Presidents were born and where some had located their Presidential libraries. Some of the adjoining gift shops sold books—autographed books if you had the money, and by then Burt did.

Auctions of estates near where former Presidents lived, or retired, became fertile ground not just for books, but for beautiful signed photographs Presidents had given to friends and neighbors. The picture Burt found of Ike and his wife, Mamie, rocking on their front porch at their Gettysburg farm was priceless to Burt. There they sit smiling, years after Ike had served his country as an Army hero and then as President.

Burt unearthed more Presidential pictures. In a tiny antique shop between Atlanta and Birmingham, Burt found a stoic Woodrow Wilson pictured sitting at his desk in Washington, the photo neatly signed at the bottom. There he also found a Herbert Hoover picture with a personal message addressed to the first owner of the photo. And soon, signed documents joined books and pictures as part of the collection. The Presidential collection started to surpass the baseball collection, at least in stature if not in volume. The pride of Burt's collection was an eleven-volume set of Ralph Waldo Emerson's works published in 1887 and given to Mrs. Grover Cleveland for Christmas in 1925, with a notation by Cleveland inside each book's cover. Burt adorned the walls of his home office with photos, ship documents, letters, note cards, and trinkets all signed by former Presidents. Among the trinkets was the bat signed by George Bush, next to the ball signed by his son, George W., when he owned the Texas Rangers.

Soon the collection demanded more space. Burt constructed "Burt's Presidential Library" in the barn behind the house to store his collection and share it with those who visited.

"I certainly hope my grandkids will enjoy what I've put together for them," said Burt. "But someday, when I stop adding to it, I may turn it over to a school library."

With the Internet came an explosion of merchandise available to collectors: bats, balls, and gloves; documents and uniforms; everything you ever wanted. God bless eBay; at first, it seemed to make adding to the collection something he was never going to stop. "But beware the perpetrators of fraudulent stuff," Burt cautioned. "Check stuff out. Did Roger Maris really sign that bat? Are you sure Mickey Mantle put his name on that ball?"

As Internet rare book sales escalated, older collectors became mortified and disenchanted by the cheaters. Even if Jackie Robinson really signed that magazine article about his fight against racial discrimination as a ballplayer, the many frauds created doubt about what was real and what was fake.

"Listen, even collectors know that a lot of early baseballs were signed by clubhouse boys who were paid a buck by a star to sign a case of balls. But now you have guys buying old books from the library, tearing out the blank pages, and then penning notes and autographs from players who died decades ago. Hey the paper was from the 1920s—but who knows when it was actually signed, or who signed it?"

Burt never bought another sports-related item after the late 1990s spawned shops with memorabilia everywhere. Since Burt had made all of his purchases in good faith, even he didn't know what might be fake; he parted with most of the items acquired over the Internet at any price he could get. He kept only those things found in his days of roaming antique stores and shops.

Burt is in his late fifties now, and as he wrapped up the story of his life as a collector, other guests asked him to tally what a lifetime of searching had amounted to, other than myriad books.

"Well," Burt said, "there are at least two hundred old wooden bats, many signed, and several dozens of gloves from the first hundred years of baseball, and photos of at least a hundred Hall of Famers, all signed. There are contracts from some players. There's a catcher's mask, some uniform items, an old set of bases, and many old baseball banks, bobbleheads, and even a pinball machine from the sixties with ramps to hit a home run and electric lights that make the player run the bases if you get a hit."

He thought a while and continued. The Presidential items included playing cards from Air Force I and Air Force II. There were plates from the White House. Funeral announcements for Presidents who died, like the signed Rose Kennedy piece issued when the country buried her son Jack. And so much more. But Burt knows it is time in his life to reverse the trend. Stop adding and soon start selling or giving the stuff away.

And Burt does have a plan.

There are four grandchildren now, and more will come. As they get old enough, Burt intends to introduce them to collecting. From the reverse side. He will take them to auctions when parts of the collections are sold. Let the kids see how stuff is moved from one person's pile to another person's pile. Who knows? This may instill an interest in collecting. Or becoming a dealer. Or maybe an auctioneer.

Because the thing Burt has learned over the last fifty years of collecting is simple. Money can buy any item. But merely owning something doesn't give you the pleasure of finding the treasure, and adding to the collection piece by piece. Someone offered Burt a complete set of Presidential signatures. Boom. Write one check and own them all. That dealer just didn't get it. Buying the complete set would not fulfill a real collector's passion nearly as much as hunting each signature down one at a time.

"The value of collecting things—anything—is in the pursuit," Burt reflected. "Too bad it takes so long to learn that."

# The Wax Man: Danny's Tale

## Part I. The Flash

Danny was seated at one end of the table. I was at the other end. You could call either end the "head of the table." Danny was so quiet down there at his end I suspected he wasn't listening. He seemed lost in his own thoughts. When he did start to speak, his voice was so low we could hardly hear him. And his story sounded low-key too—at first.

A while back, Danny owned a gas station on a busy highway. The old-fashioned type of gas station with just three islands of pumps and two service bays for working on cars. When he bought the gas station from the previous owner, he did so because he thought it would be an ideal spot for a muffler shop. People in that area were working-class. Cars were old. And back then, mufflers didn't last as long as they do today.

"I wasn't really a gas station kind of guy," Danny told us. "I actually sold muffler franchises for a company out of New York." The franchise consisted of a kit including a bending machine, an inventory of pipes and mufflers, and some promotional literature to allow a car-related business to suddenly become a muffler shop. Gas stations bought the franchises. Auto repair shops did too, and paint shops. Almost anyone with service bays and not enough work to keep them full were candidates to buy the muffler franchise package. A brightly illuminated sign told all the world they could bring their cars in and get a new tailpipe and muffler for less than the major franchises would charge.

"See, this was a sideline to other business. If you brought in four to six cars a week, it meant extra money for the business, and the cost was less than twenty thousand dollars for everything," Danny explained.

In most cases, the gas stations were owned by the major oil companies. They, in turn, leased the space to others who would operate the sites, under the condition, of course, that they sold that oil company's gas and oil products.

"So when you see an Exxon or Mobil or Sunoco or BP station, the real estate is probably owned by the oil company and the business being run there is owned by the operator."

## Suit meets overalls

Danny wandered into the small station. A large man named George identified himself as the owner. George, nicknamed "the Fat Man," was a gentle, kind guy who had grown tired of the daily grind and wanted out of the old routines. Waking up every day by 5:00 AM to pump gas had lost its allure for George years ago. His girth made it uncomfortable to work on cars anymore. The bays sat idle and were the cleanest in any gas station in the city. Pump gas, pay his rent to the big oil company, and watch the world go by. His feet hurt. His legs cramped. But mostly he was just tired of paperwork and people. George wanted out. Just plain out. For the cost of his inventory and gas, he would give up the lease.

There stood Danny in his Joseph Banks suit staring at George in his green Dickey work clothes. Both men thought they were getting the best of the other. For less than thirty thousand dollars, the men exchanged lives. George had more cash than ever before in his life, and Danny was off to mandatory classes to learn from the big oil company how to pump gas.

George had agreed to stay on for a few weeks to help the businessman become a working man. George was amazed when he watched how Danny responded to the first customer seeking the $9.95 oil, lube, and filter hawked on the new sign out front. Just the fact that Danny got the car on the lift and up in the air without it falling off was stunning to George. As Danny unscrewed the oil plug on the bottom of the drip pan, George was further impressed. There stood Danny under the car in his bright white shirt and crisp new ball cap sporting the company logo. George was shocked that a college graduate with business skills and an ability to make more money than he himself ever had was about to work under a car—just as he,

George, had done for years. Maybe George should give the young guy some credit.

That's when George noticed the hot black oil running down Danny's arm. As the screw let loose from the drip pan, Danny didn't move quickly enough, and the crisp clean shirt was ruined in less than ten seconds. George couldn't stop laughing.

"Hey, college boy," he shouted, "is that how they taught you to do it at school? Catch the hot oil on your shirt so it won't drip on the floor?"

George and Danny bonded at that moment. George had learned in that second what Danny already knew: in some ways, the street-smart George was much brighter than the college boy. Danny let George teach him.

"Why not install a coffee machine," said Danny, "and give the early bird customers free coffee with a fill-up? And why not fill the empty candy machine with Tastykakes to snack on with the coffee?"

George just smiled. "Sure, college boy, why not."

So Danny spent about a hundred bucks to put the coffee brewer out, ready for the next morning. Then he loaded the new treats into the vending machine. The blinking-light sign Danny put out front announced free coffee starting at 6:00 AM, and Danny was there early to get the coffee hot. George couldn't miss this either, so he actually beat Danny to the station.

And then, the proverbial rude awakening. Overnight, mice had helped themselves to the cakes in the machine. Each package had been ripped open and chewed on by the little bastards who obviously lived there. Danny never saw a man laugh so hard in his life. George was beside himself to see the college boy had been beaten by resident rodents.

How funny was George? In the next day's mail came a card addressed to Danny. It was a thank-you note from Mickey Mouse. He raved about the cakes, but had a request: "Could you get some with peanut butter next time?" George busted another gut watching Danny read the card. How dumb could the college guy be?

But the college boy won a few rounds also. Certain sodas would sell well. Danny had a vending machine installed outside, so even overnight customers wandering by could spend money at the place. Danny took George to the discount store where cans of soda were twenty-five cents apiece. Since the machine charged fifty cents, the college boy would make a one hundred percent profit.

They were selling about one hundred cans a day, twenty-five bucks of pure profit. Then Danny noticed that George was always drinking a Tab soda; he had one in his hand every minute of the day. And then the college boy saw that half the sodas sold from the machine were Tab. That's right, the Fat Man was spending almost twenty dollars a day drinking soda. And the college boy had given George a key to the machine so it would always be full.

"This proved two things," Danny laughed. "One, George was very honest. And two, he was drinking way too much Tab."

## Thinking bigger

As the days rolled by, George continued hanging around. He had the money from the sale, but he didn't have anything else to do. And he was starting to like the college boy, because Danny wasn't afraid to get dirty or work hard. But George liked to sleep in, now that he could, so Danny needed a morning worker.

A truck was sitting at the pump one morning when Danny arrived. The driver was a kid about nineteen who asked if there were any job openings. The boy hailed from West Virginia; he called himself a "shade tree mechanic," meaning that he had some clunkers he'd rebuilt sitting in his yard back home.

The next day this shade tree mechanic arrived at 6:00 AM to begin work. As he parked his truck on the side of the station, Danny noticed a young woman sitting in the passenger seat. Not wanting to pry, Danny said nothing. The new kid pumped gas. The girl sat in the truck. As the day got hotter, Danny finally asked about the girl.

"That's my wife," said the kid. "She ain't no bother sitting in the truck."

But why, Danny asked, did she want to sit there all day in the hot sun watching her husband work?

The kid said, "I can't leave her home. My uncle lives there too, and he'll be dickin' her all day if I do."

Simple as that. She said she was happy in the truck, and her husband felt safer not having his wife where his uncle could use her as a plaything.

Soon the girl was pumping gas for Danny while the kid changed oil and worked on cars. He did turn out to be a good mechanic. But on a weekend trip back home to West Virginia, the kid got arrested for assault and didn't return to the station. His wife was courteous enough to report to Danny that her husband wasn't coming back. And oh yeah, she couldn't work there any more either, because her husband's uncle liked having her home with him all day.

Predictably, Tim (or was it Enzo?) reminded the other listeners that stories like this have to be true, because (chorus) "You can't make this stuff up."

Danny and his wife had a little girl during that time. When she was born, he placed a large notice on the blinking sign in the driveway: IT'S A GIRL, YAHOO! Several customers wanted to know what kind of name Yahoo was.

Though Danny had other interests at this time, he wanted the muffler franchise to work. He learned how to take straight two-inch sticks of pipe and, following a microfiche diagram, bend the pipe a certain number of degrees, then rotate the pipe in the machine and make another bend. After a few minutes, the straight pipe would be the exhaust pipe or tailpipe to fit the car on the lift. A few bolts and pipe hangers later, and whammo, another Lifetime Warranty Muffler installed.

George couldn't understand how you could give a Lifetime Warranty on something you knew would wear out. Well, at that time, an insurance company played the odds. You purchased a small policy on every car serviced. The insurance company would pay the station to replace the muffler or pipes if necessary. They were gambling that the car owner would have gotten rid of the car, moved away, or lost his certificate before it ever became necessary to put out money on replacements.

Many surprises awaited Danny in this new venture. Even in those days, gas was costly. Especially for people who had little or no money. Sometimes they wanted to trade things for gas. A spare tire, some tools, cartons of cigarettes. Or things like a peek at a tattoo of a rabbit jumping into his rabbit hole—a tattoo located down the pants of some fetching lass, or so said the lad who pumped her five dollars' worth for free. He swore the peek was worth it. Only problem, Danny told him, was that he, the proprietor, didn't get the peek; the worker did.

"So what?" said the worker, "I peeked enough for everyone."

Danny had inherited a worker from George who had been at the station for years, an old guy named Frank. Frank's job was to operate the full-service pumps, but he helped women at the self-service pumps for free. Frank was told time and again that it defeated the purpose of getting the customer to pay full-service price if Frank was willing to provide the service for the lower self-service prices. Frank just waved off the boss, saying he was merely being helpful and adding that the girls came to the station just to see him. George laughed again and told Danny he should watch Frank more closely out at the self-service pumps.

Seems a lady would pull up at the pump and Frank would say, "Sit still, honey, let me get that for you."

He would then open her gas door hatch and discover that the cap was missing. Hey, she shouldn't be driving the car without a cap! Frank would then say he thought he had one that would fit right over there in the trunk of his car. She could have the cap for two dollars. She'd be elated. Of course she wanted the two-dollar cap from Frank's trunk, and wouldn't you know it? It fit perfectly. Of course it did! Frank had put it in his pocket the last time she got gas; he had been waiting for her return to sell it back to her. Do that five times a day and you make an extra ten bucks. And if you don't hit the same lady too often, she never catches you. Danny emptied Frank's trunk and killed that side business.

## Danny's bright idea

The gas station business is unusual in many ways. You could have nine pumps, as Danny did, and be losing money on some of them. That's right, you could be selling gas at a lower price than it cost you, because the guy across the street would lower his unleaded regular, and then you would have to match him. On some pumps, you would make about a dime on a gallon pumped, and on some with full service (most of which are no longer around), you could make almost thirty cents. In all, you were lucky to average five to seven cents a gallon for all the gas you pumped. On Danny's one hundred thousand gallons a month, he might have made five thousand dollars of profit. And that was before the rent, the insurance, the electric bill, the cost of labor, advertising, and everything else needed to run the business.

Danny knew he had to make the service bays productive. Mufflers were the answer. First, two cars a week, then two cars a day, and soon about fifteen to twenty cars a week were getting full exhaust pipes, mufflers, and tailpipes installed. Ka-ching, ka-ching. The money was starting to come in.

Who noticed it first? The big oil company, that's who. The rent when Danny took over the station was four hundred dollars a month. And the station was pumping about eighty thousand gallons a month of gas for the big oil company. Through advertising and specials, Danny had increased the volume to over one hundred thousand gallons a month. The area rep came around to see what was up. They loved Danny and the way he had created such a high-volume spot so quickly. And look at those service bays full of cars all day! Oil changes, exhaust systems, tune-ups, click, click, click. So, although

Danny had increased their revenue considerably over George's sales volumes, Big Oil Boys wanted some of Danny's pocket.

They raised the rent to five times what George had been paying. That's right, it went from four hundred a month to two thousand a month. And the only thing Danny could do about it was not sign the new lease. And leave. He started looking for another spot to try his money-making concept. But he wanted to leave out the Big Oil Boys in his next attempt. He stalled signing a new lease until he found a new spot and a buyer willing to pay him three times what he had given George just one year earlier. As soon as the buyer gave him a non-refundable deposit, Danny signed the lease, assigned it to his new buyer, and then went on to try the muffler franchise on a non-Big-Oil-Boys site.

## Details, details

Danny found a detail shop with three bays for sale in a high-volume traffic area. The lease on the property was fixed and couldn't be raised for years. Perfect. But what was a "detail shop" anyway? Danny found out that detail shops hand-clean and wax your car. They use cotton swabs to get the dirt out of every crevice. They vacuum the French fries out from between the seats. They use high-speed buffers and polishers to get down to the shine and leave the car looking better than it has in years.

A detail shop is where the trade-ins go, so your somewhat tired car shows up on the lot looking better than you ever had it looking. This detail shop was profitably doing about ten cars a day. You could pay a fixed fee to the workers to keep them from taking too long on each car, and they would each turn out three cars in less than eight hours. No Big Oil Boys to hit you up for a rent increase and no complicated pipes to bend or warranties to worry about. So long, muffler world; hello, detail world! Of course, Danny wasn't thinking about one shop. If one shop makes money, then one thousand make *a lot* of money. And Danny's prior experiences with franchises told him they'd be great to sell.

The shop had five car dealers nearby who provided a steady stream of trade-ins to clean. And the neighborhood was full of customers with high-end cars and not enough time to keep them sparkling.

Another idea struck Danny. The front of the property where the shop was located had previously been a used car lot, so why not put out a few cars and make some money there too? George, the Fat Man, became his partner. They used their last-name initials to begin L&H Auto Sales. Unfortunately, it was soon to be known as Laurel and Hardy Auto Sales.

For alas, Danny and George were horrible at this new game. Examples of their non-prowess abounded. Like the time at an auction when George stood on one side and Danny stood on the other as a car rolled up to the block. George made a motion to Danny that inspired Danny to make a bid. George kept gesturing madly; Danny assured him with a smile that he would keep bidding. By now, George was waving his hands to get Danny's attention, but the auctioneer had banged down the gavel on Danny's high bid of four hundred dollars.

Danny was elated. The car had to be worth two thousand. How did they get it so cheap? George made his way through the crowd and laughingly asked Danny if he would please go around to the other side of the car, the side Danny couldn't see while he was bidding. The side that was smashed in from headlight to taillight, making the four-hundred-dollar purchase worth about one hundred. Other than a lot of laughs, they got nothing out of the car business until they rented the lot to someone else.

And now, back to the detail shop. Low-skilled labor, a little unsophisticated equipment, some polishes and waxes, and whammo, any place could become a detail shop. Danny wanted to make this first location a showplace and then duplicate the effort at other sites.

Every employee got a uniform. Every hat got a logo. Distinctive signs went up. Printed brochures boasting the benefits of the shop with color pictures of shiny cars and happy customers went out to area car dealers. The ball was rolling. And the shop made money. You could detail cars all day or all night. Dealers started to call from miles away. A quick trip to the Motor Vehicle Administration to acquire two "transport plates" allowed the shop to pick up cars without license plates and move them around. Danny could pick up cars anywhere and take them back when the detailing work was finished. The dealers loved it. More and more were calling.

## Danny's even brighter idea

There were soon too many cars for one location. Quickly a second shop was opened, and George became "management." Then a third was started inside a major car dealership selling Cadillacs. New services were added to the list, like rust-proofing, undercoating, and fabric protection for the seats and carpets. With radio commercials on the most popular morning show, retail customers willing to pay double what a dealer would pay came calling. Ah, business was good. With three spots humming, it was time to "franchise" the business.

You need a good package to become a good franchise company. Legal documents had to be filed in each state where franchises would be sold. You had to have strong marketing materials and a concept you could show would work.

"And since I was going to sell at least one thousand franchises, why not become the products distributor as well?"

So it was off to the manufacturers to see who would "private-label" waxes, cleaners, compounds, rust-proofing, undercoating, products like that.

Danny pitched the companies, and, with professional packaging in place, another business within the business was born. The first truck was outfitted with racks inside, and a rolling store of everything necessary to detail a car or prep a new car for delivery, including buffers, polishers, and so on, was loaded on the truck. Even if a dealer wouldn't give Danny all of his cars to detail, they could buy products off the truck and money would roll in that way. And if you didn't want a detail shop franchise, why not buy a territory to sell exclusively the products brought out by the company?

"That takes money. Let's talk about that," I interjected. I'd had a little experience with this kind of operation myself.

First was the legal barrier, Danny said. From an "earlier life," Danny knew one of the founding members of the International Franchise Association, based at that time in Chicago. Pitching the idea to his former mentor, Danny wasn't soliciting money, but rather a contact. A key contact. An attorney with clout in the franchise industry who would take Danny and his three fledgling shops seriously and produce the necessary franchise documents. The attorney met with Danny and said his firm would handle the deal for a nominal initial fee.

"The so-called 'nominal' fee was more money than I had, and there were no real assets to leverage. With three shops open and almost no value in equipment, the whole thing was still just an idea."

But they could private-label their products through a major manufacturer. And the three shops were making money. And the business could be set up almost anywhere. You didn't have to be a rocket scientist to run a shop or sell the products.

## Now, how to get those bright ideas funded?

"The problem is, bankers don't lend money on ideas. They need hard assets to go against if you're not paying them back," Danny continued. "People make this mistake all the time. They think a bank should fund their ideas. But think about it. If the idea fails, the guy with the idea loses only time and energy. The bank loses cold hard cash."

"Yeah," I agreed. "That's why there are venture capitalists around who might take a greater risk than the bank—for a piece of the action."

"Or you could go to your uncle, or a neighbor, or your parents. Of course they'll just hock their entire retirement to see Junior make it in business," Enzo put in.

"Not if they're smart, they won't!"

To get the seed money, Danny decided to sell the original location, take that cash, get the franchise documents done, and then start selling shops. The new owner was not given name rights; instead, he could operate under a sublease from Danny and allow Danny to use the shop as a "showplace" to lure others, once the franchises could be sold. But again, that takes money.

Fate always plays a hand in success and failure. The buyer Danny found for the original location turned out to be a sweet little grandmother who said she wanted a business that would provide cash flow without needing her daily on-site help. She had been a customer of Danny's, and she believed his concept was great. Her son living in Colorado wanted to see it for himself before his mother plunked down a chunk of her life savings. Fate! Her son was a stockbroker selling small companies just emerging in what is called the "pink sheets," otherwise known as over-the-counter penny stocks. The son said he loved the "cachet" of the deal and "wanted to honcho taking us public, to raise the money we needed to expand."

## Stinky fish, IPOs, and the SEC

Now this guy was very bright and had contacts in the business, but he had never really "taken anyone public" before. He asked Danny to read some "red herrings" written for other stock offerings. Danny swiftly discovered that a "red herring" in investment-speak was not a stinky fish intended to throw a sniffing hound off-trail (or its metaphoric kin), but rather a preliminary registration statement that has to be filed with the Security and Exchange Commission describing a new issue of stock or IPO and the prospects of the issuing company. There is no price or issue size stated in the red herring, and you can update it as many times as you care to before it is finalized as a prospectus.

"Why is it called a red herring? Is there something shady about it?" Tim asked.

"No. Funny thing—it's called that only because there's a part printed in red. A very important part, especially in my story—it states that the company isn't trying to sell shares before the SEC okays registration."

Most businesses hire a lawyer to draw up their red herrings. Not Danny.

"What was I going to pay a lawyer with?"

Danny spent several days constructing a red herring for the company. It told the whole story about the business: how it would sell franchises and also territories with trucks rolling in every city. And wouldn't that put the name on every street? And wouldn't that make everyone want to buy the stock? They were practically billionaires already.

But even if the SEC were willing to accept Danny's work, investors would want to see a lawyer's name on the paperwork in order to take it seriously. Yes, the red herring had to be filed by an attorney. And now Danny was back at that place where he needed money. The new buyer's son had an idea. Just send out fifty letters outlining what you wanted to do. Send them to people on your Christmas card list. Ask for one thousand dollars in exchange for some stock at five cents a share, stock in what would surely become something bigger than McDonald's. Hope for close to fifty thousand dollars. With that amount, you could pay the lawyer to file those papers with the SEC and raise all the money you needed.

Danny began getting checks a week later. Those fifty letters, sent out to common, everyday people, not big sophisticated investors, created something that worked like a chain letter. Seventy-three people responded, and a sum of more than one hundred thousand dollars was raised.

"I called the woman's son in Colorado and said, okay, what do we do now?"

The son freaked out. Danny and the letters had been *too* successful. The SEC wouldn't like the idea of so many "close insiders," some who didn't have any personal connection with anyone else involved. He sent Danny to an attorney in Virginia, a Harvard graduate who specialized in filing with the SEC those documents necessary to go public. With the money raised, the lawyer's retainer was paid and the document written by Danny met approval to file.

Danny set off to Washington alone. He couldn't afford to have the attorney come. The SEC man whom he met with was less than wonderful for Danny's morale—telling Danny that only a few such filings were approved annually, and fewer still actually met the criteria to "go public." They would respond in a few weeks.

Honest man that he was, Danny had included every detail about raising the roughly one hundred thousand dollars from the seventy-three initial investors in his filing. The SEC man asked for a meeting. A big problem: something about having too many initial shareholders and that perhaps Danny's company had violated some rules here. However, the SEC rep offered a solution.

"We could be approved to sell shares and go public so long as we first advised the initial investors that we had overstepped our bounds and therefore would offer to pay back anyone's money who wanted out," Danny said. "Of course I wrote that letter and sent it out, and of course this letter had the exact opposite effect of what was supposed to be its intention."

"You're not getting my stock back," screamed one guy.

"What kind of scam is this, trying to squeeze the little guy out now, when we're so close?" cried another man.

Remember, these were ordinary people hoping they had bought a winning lottery ticket.

"Face it," said Danny to the Abacrombie audience. "Just from what you heard so far, don't you wish you were in on the ground floor?"

Bottom line: not one person wanted his or her money back.

## Pink sheets and those bright yellow signs

With that obstacle out of the way, Danny was cleared to sell stock at five cents a share until a certain level was reached. If enough stock could be sold, the Initial Public Offering could begin trading in the "pink sheets." Five cents a share. It couldn't miss. They were on the radio every day. The bright yellow signs were cute. The cars sure were shiny when they left the shops. What's a thousand dollars? Boom. Seven hundred people wanted in. And the lady's son who helped Danny get this far was coming home to be the first Chief Financial Officer of the new franchisor company that couldn't miss.

The company needed a bank in New York to be the clearinghouse for the stock. The Harvard lawyer called a friend. Next, it needed a firm to be a "market maker" for the stock. Someplace to buy and sell the shares once they were public. Danny was flying. But not without a lot of help from others, including his brother, his old partner George, and a small staff squeezed into the basement storage room of a local drugstore. The hats, shirts, coffee mugs, and products with jazzy labels made them look huge, not like the tiny, asset-poor company made up of hardworking folks with a good idea that it really was. Kind of like the dot-coms many years later. Danny was always ahead of his time.

Fate. Again. Danny's brother owned some land in a resort town and wanted to build a house. It required putting a crane on the vacant lot next door for use in setting the prefab house on its foundation. Danny's brother called the guy who owned the lot and invited him to lunch at a place next door to Danny's business to ask him about the crane. The guy turned out to be a vice president of a local stock firm. A sophisticated investor, the kind Danny's company didn't have.

"How much is the stock?"

"Five cents."

"What will the initial asking price be?"

"Twenty-five cents."

"Here's a check for fifty thousand dollars. I want one million shares."

Danny put the check in the desk drawer and went home dazed.

## Thinking really, really big (make that "huge")

Bright and early the next morning, before the banks had even opened, Danny heard a familiar voice. It was the guy who had written the big check the day before. He was back. Surely to retrieve his check, Danny assumed. But no, the guy had gone home and told his kids what he ran into; they immediately authorized him to buy forty thousand dollars' worth of additional stock on their behalf. Why should Dad be the only one to make all that money? Danny had received ninety thousand dollars from a total stranger and his kids in less than twenty-four hours after they first heard about the deal. Did people really do that? People who included the vice president of a local stock firm?

Now, with nearly the amount needed to complete this phase, Danny and his brother decided to do some public relations. Why not call the newspapers and tell them what was going on in that little basement office?

The local paper sent someone out to interview the brothers. Find out who they were and what they were doing. A beautiful color picture graced the upper half of the front page of the business section the following Sunday morning. The brothers were standing in front of their locations, which were now approved to "trade publicly" beginning the next business day. Fate again. It was Labor Day weekend. The stock would begin trading on Tuesday. Why is that significant? Because a hundred people called Danny's home and office on Sunday and Monday trying to buy stock. That's called "demand." Two days' worth of demand. And time for the TV stations to see the article and send out a film crew to interview the entrepreneurs who would soon be taking Wall Street by storm.

The stock opened at twenty-five cents a share. Five times the price that the initial investors had paid. The investment guy and his family now owned four hundred fifty thousand dollars of stock. True, as an insider, he couldn't sell for many months. But not to worry. The stock was going up. Since one hundred people were already willing to buy stock, the market makers had a field day inching up the price.

"What're market makers?" Tim wanted to know.

"They're the few legitimate fledgling stock firms that agree to 'make a market' for a new offering by buying and selling the as-yet unknown company."

By lunch time, the price had risen to fifty cents a share. The cameraman from a TV station had to shoot sideways while he laid the camera on a desk so he could call his broker to buy some stock. Jed Clampett from "The Beverly Hillbillies" hadn't struck a geyser this big. With all three channels reporting the offering over the six o'clock news, the next day the stock hit one dollar a share. Holy Mother. The $90,000 family of investors now owned stock worth $1.8 million. In one day. That guy stopped by the office to show Danny a picture of the sailboat he intended to buy from this investment.

Four firms in New York were ecstatic. They were "making the spread" on every share sold of twenty-five cents or so; and, as they churned the stock to every sweet little blue-haired grandmother in the country, the merry-go-round was off and running. Danny was beyond ecstatic. He was awed. He was almost in shock.

"What the fuck is 'making the spread'?" cried Tony, "and how come I never got in on deals like this?"

Danny explained. For this type of stock, you sold at one price and bought at a higher price. While it cost a dollar to buy, you could sell for only about seventy-five cents. Hence the "market maker" made twenty-five cents' worth of "spread" on a transaction.

The breakfasters digested all this in silence.

## Part II. The Crash

"Now pay attention, breakfast buddies." Danny looked each one of us in the eye, slowly, in turn. We obeyed. "Once the IPO— remember, that's the Initial Public Offering—is sold out, the company does not get any more money."

"*What?*"

Danny explained that the money goes from the buyer to the seller, with the trader taking a big piece as commission. Nothing goes to the company any more. So, if four million dollars of stock changes hands in a week, the brokers handling the sale make money, the seller gets his profit or loss, and the buyer gets his stock, hoping it just keeps going up and up. At that point, though, the company gets zip. Look at it this way: the initial money raised was what was actually in the company's bank account—that amount minus sales commissions, legal fees, clearinghouse charges, printing costs, all that.

What was left was not enough for the company to survive.

"That's right, America. A wildly successful offering completed, and we were still broke."

Danny then realized he was halfway to a Ph.D. in the world of stocks. Only halfway.

"Pay attention," he demanded again, this time unnecessarily. "Stockbrokers like news. Positive news. Any positive news helps hawk the stock."

## "Buy now before it's too late"

With every new franchise agreement and every new truck carrying products out on the road, the "boys in the boiler room" would bang the telephones and tell their clients this stock issue was a winner. This one was going to make them rich. But they'd have to buy now before it was too late.

There was even a newspaper that touted penny stocks. Wouldn't you know it? Fate showed up again. The publisher lived in the same city as Danny and had a weekly show on cable television to show investors how to play the long shots listed in the pink sheets and advise them about what companies might be hot. Danny was more than willing to be interviewed. He liked the limelight. More exposure meant more calls about the company, and they would mean faster growth. A prominent newswoman conducted the weekly interviews. (Many years later, Danny ran into her in a restaurant, and they reminisced about those memorable penny stock days.)

"People accept public exposure as confirmation that all is well," Danny mused. "They can't lie on TV, can they? Or in the papers? Or in magazines?" Anyway, Danny never lied to them. All *was* well.

"What a genius I was. On the local business weekly radio program, I handled the interview like a pro."

And in fact, he really was becoming a seasoned professional. Smooth. The host of the local show praised the management of the company and assured the public they could trust this one. Surely this would keep the stock price up and get us all the warrants exercised.

## A warrant for the arrest of ...

Now, every share of stock came with a "warrant." The warrant was to buy additional shares of stock at twenty-five cents a share. Not bad, as the stock was trading for a dollar. This warrant stock would be the additional money needed to grow the company. But the period when you could exercise your warrant was months away. The company started selling franchises. Franchises for detail shops. Franchises for truck routes for the products.

Oh, and about those products, the waxes and compounds and rust-proofing and undercoating and other such products. They were submitted to *Popular Mechanics* magazine for review and were promptly named "automotive products of the year" in the spring issue dedicated to car care.

Danny traveled to Dallas and appeared on a morning talk show to hype the company. And then there was that TV show in Florida, where the local news inserted a two-minute piece on auto detailing, which featured Danny showing the products. The items were displayed on the hood of Danny's rental car, parked in the borrowed service bay of a local transmission shop, but when it showed on TV, it looked like a franchise in the viewer's town. The piece was picked up over the wires and shown in cities across the country, creating demand for the stock, which kept selling at a premium. Big bucks for the market makers. One national magazine dubbed Danny "the Sheik of Shine."

But money was still tight. Danny stopped taking his paycheck. He started putting his own money back into the company. He didn't need his private airplane—a plane he had bought with his own funds, not company funds—as much as the company needed advertising; bye-bye, airplane. No more paychecks, no more airplane, and soon no more Cadillac. But all would be well, wouldn't it?

It was time for the first-ever shareholders meeting. The Harvard lawyer came to town. The stockbroker turned CFO was ready for the crowd. On the way to the meeting, Danny asked them both what would happen there. In unison, both the lawyer and the stockbroker said, "I don't know. I've never been to a shareholder meeting before."

Say what? These guys were pros. It was their field. How was it possible that they didn't know what was going to happen?

"None of the companies we worked for ever made it this far before."

Huh?

"That's what you get for a discount price," said Danny. "Discount advice."

But so what. The company *had* made it that far. And Danny would dazzle them with the facts of their newly publicly trading company.

## So tight it hurt

As the early months rolled by, money became excruciatingly tight. It cost fifty thousand dollars to stock a store, handle the opening ad blitz, and get off the ground—so selling a few franchises wouldn't cut it. The trucks carrying products were also starting to move, but they cost a lot to set up, since some franchisees needed financial help getting trucks and equipment.

Luckily the time had come to cash in the stock warrants. The stock was selling for about a dollar, and you could buy a share for twenty-five cents for each warrant you owned.

Oops.

The warrant people were all being contacted by the market makers, who were telling them that it would soon be time to cash in on the company's success by exercising their warrants. Just send the market maker your quarters, and they'll send you your stock. The hope was that the stock firms collecting the warrants money would gather up the hundreds of thousands of dollars from the warrants exercised and give that money to the company in exchange for the new stock being issued.

But—did anyone notice the stock price dropping? Down to fifty cents if you were selling. Then forty, thirty, and soon twenty cents a share. All at the time people were sending in those quarters for new shares. Wow, how did the stock hit just ten cents so quickly? Oh well. Once the warrant money came in, the company would grow and all would be well. But where was the warrant money? After all, if you sent your quarters directly to Danny's company, the company simply issued the new shares through its clearinghouse in New York, and you got your stock, and the company got the money.

But no. The shareholders didn't send their money to the company. They sent it to the broker who called them to remind them of the great deal they were getting at twenty-five cents. And that is why hundreds of thousands of dollars didn't arrive at the company.

"You see," Danny continued, "the brokers would have sent the money to the company for new stock if the shares were trading above twenty-five cents. But the brokers could buy stock from sellers taking ten cents and send those shares to the people wanting their warrant stock. A share is a share is a share, apparently. So no one was swindled out of their stock. Everyone who sent the warrant money got new shares. But not from the company. The stock was coming from sellers who saw the price plunging. The profits from the sale went to the brokers, not the company."

That didn't make Danny a broker—but it did make Danny's company broke. It was time to pass the hat for more money again.

By this time, Danny had a Board of Directors made up of early stockholders, a vice president at the local bank, the Harvard lawyer, and an old friend from another, larger bank out of town. Danny explained to them all that had transpired. There just wasn't any more money left. The concept had clearly been a winner, but the capital structure of the company trying to make it work just wasn't strong enough.

Danny described for them how he had sold the airplane he loved so much and used the money for advertising. How the Cadillac was gone. How he hadn't taken a paycheck for the last ten months. He told them that, even if he sold his house, there wouldn't be enough to make the plan work. In short, after plowing back into the company all he had, Danny now felt it was all right to ask others for more money.

"Close the doors," they responded.

What?

"Now."

*What?* After Danny spent the last six months trying to get the warrant money, and after exhausting his personal assets, and after going back to Wall Street to restructure the deal? *Now* they said to close, when before they had said to keep trying?

True, all of them were shareholders, and all of them had hoped the company would make it over the hump. Letting Danny pour every ounce of his net worth back into the company was their last gasp. But why did they let Danny go broke trying? Why didn't they tell him to close before he reinvested everything he had?

"Because," as one director told him, "we figured you're young and smart, and you'll make it back again somehow. But now that you are totally broke, we have no choice but to close."

Wow.

"You'd think shutting down a publicly trading company would be easy," Danny said, after a few long moments' silence. "Think again."

## End of the road

Danny called the SEC and suggested that the stock stop trading. The SEC replied that all filings were current, and as long as the company disclosed how bad things were, people in America could continue betting on a turnaround. But Danny didn't take that answer to be good enough. People buying the stock after that Board meeting had no chance of seeing a return. One guy did, however, make a bundle, Danny added. This individual had called his broker the last week they were operating and ordered the stock purchase. His broker didn't know the company was in the "pink sheets." There was a NASDAQ company with a similar name. One week later, when Danny's company had ceased to exist, the lucky friend found out his broker's error had made him a tidy profit instead of a total loss.

The end came with some fanfare. The first annual meeting was scheduled at a large hotel for later that week. By now there were over seven hundred shareholders, most of whom were watching the rise and quick fall of their stock with great interest. It was literally a penny stock now. *If* you were a seller. That guy with the ninety thousand was now down to about twenty thousand, a large drop from the 1.8 million he peaked at, and far from enough for the sailboat.

Danny stood at the podium and looked out at the hundreds of faces. Over there was the radio guy who interviewed him. Over there was the reporter from the local paper. But everywhere were the faces of the little guys. Just regular people betting on the lottery and waiting to hear how much they had won. Was there going to be a stock split? Any chance at a dividend? They had come to the meeting to see how they were doing. Not even the staff from the office knew until the last minute what Danny would say.

"As of nine o'clock tomorrow morning, the company is officially closed. There will be no future in it for anyone. The three-year run is over. Despite so many good things happening, there just isn't enough money to keep the company going."

Danny ended by saying he would then take their questions. He didn't just walk off the stage. He stood there for over an hour and answered every shocked shareholder's questions the best he could. And when they were stunned and silent and had no more to ask, he said goodnight and left the platform.

Danny spoke to no one that evening and waited until he was alone to cry. Nobody needed to see his pain. He had led them from a promising idea up the mountain, almost to the peak where the riches were, only to roll backwards to the bottom of the hill.

The reaction had been swift and devastating. The crowd who had gladly played follow-the-leader when they thought they would find gold had thrown verbal tomatoes at Danny. The tone of the audience was one of sudden and complete distrust. What had the company done with all that money they'd raised? How could the stock price climb to twenty times what the insiders paid and still leave the company broke?

At Abacrombie, all the listeners were silently wondering the same things.

"Fundamentals," Danny said. "People don't understand business fundamentals. They buy the hype, but don't understand the substance. Like, why was the company valued at over ten million dollars when the asset base of the company was less than one hundred thousand dollars? Why would anybody not understand that when a stock goes up it doesn't mean the company has more cash? And how could anybody not understand that even if you sign an agreement to open nineteen new centers in freaking New York City, you couldn't do it without over one million dollars of product to go in there?"

That is what "undercapitalized" means, he explained. The company didn't have enough cash to grow, and the basic shareholder structure was unattractive to new investors who wouldn't put their money in just to prop up seven hundred small shareholders clinging to a good idea.

"The individual stores still made money. Many of them lasted for years after the parent company failed," Danny added. "Investors are so naïve—this is just another example," he went on. "They wanted to know if we were broke, how come there were still locations operating. Simple. Because they had purchased franchises and were not part of the parent company."

The franchises were all given the name of the product manufacturer and continued to buy the products directly after the doors to Danny's company were closed.

A few days after that final public meeting, Danny went to the office for one last time. There in the last day's mail was a brief note.

"Thank you," said the writer. "Thank you for taking all of the little guys on the ride of a lifetime."

## And after the ride

For almost two years, they thought they would be zillionaires, and even though the venture was over, this one writer realized that Danny had done his best.

It was true. Danny had indeed done all he could. Now his life was in shambles. He was broke. He was separated from his wife and kids.

He was unemployed. The shock of his total failure was crashing in on him.

"I spent five days alone in my apartment," he reflected. "The apartment I was about to be evicted from."

How could such a noble effort end in such horrific fashion? What would he do now to support his family? It had been a year since he cashed a paycheck. And his assets had all been sold and reinvested in the company, even as it sank like the *Titanic*. He just wanted to crawl into the proverbial hole and disappear. His ability to rebound from past bumps in the road had never been this severely challenged. Everyone questioned his integrity. Where did the money go? How could such a great idea not make it? He had never felt this low. By now the lights had been cut off in his wife's house. She would have to sell the house and move in order to have enough money to keep going. The cars would go too.

The first day in his apartment, he sat devastated. Numb. What could he possibly do now? How would his kids eat? The second day, visitors stopped to see if he was all right. George stopped by, and so did the wife from whom he was separated, and so did the woman he was dating, even though she had lost money in the venture when her company couldn't be paid for the products that had been delivered. Not one was allowed to come inside. At the door, Danny assured each that he would be fine; now, however, he needed to be left alone. Somehow he couldn't get alone enough. How could failure be so painful?

Danny thought about three possibilities. Why not give up completely? Why not start doing drugs, which seemed to make others feel better? Or maybe alcohol? His dad and brother were alcoholics, and they seemed to be okay. Or maybe he should just turn his attention to the pure physical pleasures of chasing women. That might help ease the pain by providing some instant gratification. The third day, he actually wrestled with those options. Hell, why not combine all three?

That day, George brought a paper and left it at the door. "C'mon, Boss, let's go have some breakfast," the Fat Man called through the door.

"No thanks, but leave the paper."

Danny contemplated the short term and the long. He had been a success, and now he was a failure. Success sure felt better than failure. And he decided by the fourth day to forego the pleasures of drugs, alcohol, or women and find another way to be successful.

"That took some big balls," Enzo observed.

Yes, it was a huge leap to get from the depths of that devastating failure to the possibility that he could ever be successful again.

"And that, my dear guests, is what separates the doers from the watchers," I put in.

Danny wasn't trying to succeed for others. He was trying to succeed for himself. For that tingly feeling some people get from accomplishment, any accomplishment. Somehow he would crawl back up the ladder. But first he had to focus on level one: securing a place to stay and putting some food on the table.

While the stress of business had forced Danny and his wife to separate, the failure brought them back together. On the fifth day alone in his apartment, Danny made himself a commitment. Take a job, get a house, feed his wife and kids. Don't try to be a big shot any more. Just play it safe and don't punish them with another failure. His wife sold her house, giving them a small cushion. They rented a modest little home together.

On that fifth day alone in his apartment, while reading the paper that George had left for him, Danny spotted an ad for a job.

Meanwhile, of course, the press wanted answers. Danny finally opened his door to a reporter, who investigated and wrote a story telling the truth about the last two years. And about the fact that, even in America, some companies fail.

And so, just six days after the last stock meeting was over, Danny went on his first job interview in years. "Hey, aren't you that guy we just saw in the papers?" were the first words Danny heard at the interview. Fortunately, the outfit hired him anyway. Once again, he was working for somebody else.

Danny stayed low-key for some time. It was almost a year before he would venture out to friends and family. Little did they know how much he hurt inside. After all, he was the big-shot tycoon who had taken a company public, and he'd driven that big Cadillac, and don't forget the airplane and the few million dollars in stock. All the toys he'd had. Some thought the humbling experience was good for him. Danny himself often described it as a "character builder."

"But frankly, no one needs that much character."

Almost twenty years later, Danny said he still can sit quietly and know exactly where that pain was.

# A Darker Side: Mike's Tale

Mike shifted in his seat and cleared his throat a couple of times. Abruptly he turned to Danny. "Finally," he said. "Finally."

"Finally what?" Danny wanted to know.

"Finally, after all this rambling about building stuff and buying stuff, somebody has the guts to talk about something a little darker. Coming from someplace where it hurts."

"People love to spill the beans about accomplishments. Of course. Who wants to talk about things that make them uncomfortable?" I interjected hastily. "Things like that make whoever's listening uncomfortable too."

The guests had seemed cheerful and relaxed up till halfway through Danny's story, and I didn't want that mood to change. The damn snow was falling again, and, now that another breakfast had been devoured, people were hinting that I should get some lunch going. If there's one thing men like as much as hearing themselves talk, it's eating. Good for me. Good for innkeeping in general. But Danny's story had cast a shadow over the joviality. Now Mike threatened to darken that shadow.

Mike was a quiet man, but not oppressively so; he'd applauded Enzo's work history, thanked Tuck for serving however unwillingly in the Air Force, laughed with the would-be politician about his oversize cojones. Now, he told us, he felt it was time to speak up. To share a dark tale he'd needed to tell for a long time. To face a demon from the past.

"Go for it, Mike," Benny chimed in. "You have something to say, so say it."

I decided this would be a good time to take a roll call of lunch orders and head back to the kitchen. The men scattered about the room squirmed in their chairs. Mike was going to confess to a murder, maybe? I heard a collective sigh. Soon the chair shuffling quieted down, and Mike seized the imaginary microphone. This was his tale.

## Your basic "good Scout"

"I was a Cub Scout; then, as a young man, a Boy Scout. Merit badges aplenty. Good citizen training and all that jazz. I'll admit that the first time my mother left me at the school in our neighborhood for Cub Scout Leadership Skills Day, I whimpered as she pulled out of the parking lot. Why did she dump me here alone with all these strangers? "Man up, little boy"—that was the message of the day. We were now in the custody of adults who wore the same uniforms we did. They were in charge. You had to listen and learn.

"Some of these people were awesome. Mrs. P. was my first den mother, and she knew how to do everything. Including making each cadet feel important. We did crafts, read books aloud, carved things out of wood. It was wonderful. Each week someone was made the leader of the group. You knew from what the former leaders had done what was good and what pissed kids off. You learned 'be firm but fair.' 'Don't be a whiner.' 'Make decisions.'

## Kid Heaven

"On to the Boy Scouts. Holy shit, camping out. Sleeping on the ground in a tent. The Scout leaders slept in cabins, but the Scouts always slept in tents. First time camping was amazing. It wasn't my brother next to me like at home. It was my friend from school, a guy I looked up to. We called him 'Chow.' He was bigger than most of the other kids, seemed more mature. He told me he had a crush on Linda at school. Linda was the first girl in our class to develop breasts. I thought he must be some kind of a god if she let him be her boyfriend. He swore he would be the first boy to kiss her. And feel her up.

"Fresh air and man-to-man, well, boy-to-boy conversation. City boys out in the countryside. Open spaces everywhere. Incredible activities. Shooting with bow and arrows. Hiking, making a compass that actually worked. Using a map, learning about the stars at night. The leaders were mesmerizing. They knew it all.

"Scouting had to be important. Real important. My dad skipped going to his second job one weekend so he could come to camp as a volunteer parent. Amazing! He skipped work to be there! He didn't skip work even when the family went on vacation. Whatever was going on in scouting must mean a lot.

## When coaches were kings

"In a small community like ours, the Scout leaders often coached Little League and Peewee football as well. Two men who were in charge of the Scouts ran the baseball and football teams for twelve-year-olds. Everyone loved those guys. Both were bachelors and gave their time to help the kids they themselves didn't have. They raked the fields and put their own money up for uniforms or baseballs or helmets if the kitty was short. Our teams were the best-equipped and best-coached in the area. When I was playing football, we won the league, and when we went to baseball with the same core of players, we won that too. The coaches had special jackets made with our team logos and "CHAMPIONS" emblazoned across the front, so other kids would see right away how special we were.

"In between seasons, these leaders took kids to basketball games, or movies, or just out to eat at the new fast-food places springing up all around town. One of them bought a boat and took all the kids out for rides. Heaven. Next came trips away from home. Why not see a game in a nearby city? But that meant leaving early to spend the day in that city. So why not just spend Friday night at one of their houses so everybody could leave early the next day? These guys were the greatest. Parents loved them for their service to their kids.

"When you were picked to go on a trip, you lost your mind with excitement. The anticipation of being able to go on a trip with the coach was incredible. He picked *you*. You would be the one to see the sights, the game, or the boat. Even your own brother was jealous because it seemed for that moment you were the teacher's pet. You were getting something the other kids craved.

## Darkness fell

Mike paused. He looked past our faces to the face of the antique clock on the breakfast room mantel and fixed his eyes there. If he'd been looking at us, he'd have seen we were doing pretty much the same thing. I think everybody could see what was coming.

"The first time I slept at the coach's house, I woke up to his hand placing my hand on his penis.

"What the hell is going on here? I pretended to be asleep. My God, this can't be happening. Why is he doing this to me? He wrapped his own hand around my penis and started stroking. Please God, make the house explode, or make the roof fall in. Someone please help me.

"No one did. No one else was there. My world shattered. Twelve years old and my first orgasm was with a man over thirty touching me, making me touch him. Please let me die, God. That's all I could think of. I never looked at him, and neither of us spoke. He just finished and went to sleep. I went into shock. Nothing had ever prepared that little twelve-year-old, me, to know how to handle a thing like this.

"Yes, I knew what a wet dream was, and I decided that maybe that's what had happened. Or if it was real, it could not have been intentional. It was a mistake. At breakfast, the coach said nothing. He smiled and talked of the great day we would have visiting the big city. I wanted someone to kill me. It didn't happen. It couldn't have happened. It must have been my imagination.

"My parents were excited to hear about my trip when the coach dropped me off. He told them he had a surprise. He wanted to take me to the Baseball Hall of Fame the next week. Just him and me. We would see the land of one thousand lakes as well as baseball's greatest shrine on a whirlwind tour.

## It couldn't be happening

"Why was everyone so happy to hear him say that? I wondered. How could they let me go with him again? This can't be happening, I told myself. It can't be. But it was.

"Who could I tell? I felt ashamed. My fingers had touched his penis. I had helped him climax. I was going to Hell for sure. No one could ever know about this. I had to get away from this guy. Fast. How could I ever go on that trip?

"My best friend had slept in bed with the other coach. Maybe he knew something. And another guy on the team said that this other coach had tried to touch him at night, but, the boy said, 'I told him, Whoa, baby, no way.' Of course I felt a thousand times worse. That kid had rolled over and told the coach to stop, and he did. When my friend asked if the coach I spent the night with had tried anything, I totally denied it. No fucking way would I let a man touch me!

"'Well, you're going away with him for a few days, and I bet he tries something. You better hold on to your side of the bed real tight and don't let him roll you over.'

"Ah, in the nick of time, advice from someone I respected. Hold on tight and don't roll over. Yeah, like I wouldn't fall asleep for three days? Please God, let the world end before this trip begins. That's all I could think. Believe me, no one said anything about child abuse back then. There were no classes at school to teach you to shout and run away. Your coaches and Scout leaders were the pinnacle of society, people who got plaques annually for their good works. Parents didn't know these guys were diddling their sons. It wasn't the parents' fault. But it wasn't the kids' fault either. I thought this evil had been visited on me because I had let God down so much already. Maybe it was *my* fault, I thought.

"Day One of the trip. The man was so pleasant. (I can't and won't say his name. He's a non-person. He doesn't even deserve to have a name.) We stopped for lunch, saw beautiful places, had a nice dinner, and then headed for the motel. Please swallow me up, dear God. Don't let it happen again.

"It did. No matter that I held on to my side of the bed with all my strength—he just tugged me over and said, 'Relax, we'll both feel good.' I didn't feel good. I think I cried myself to sleep that time.

## Heroes to the rescue

"Next day, we arrived at the Hall of Fame. My baseball heroes were there. Ruth and Cobb and all the others. Brave men of character. Men of great strength. Men of great courage. Inspiring men. Men who would help me.

"And I swear to God," Mike said softly, looking at us for the first time since his story began, "I swear to God, they did."

"That night, as I held firm, he tugged harder. I said 'No.' Very, very firmly. And I wouldn't let my hand get free from holding on to the frame, so he couldn't roll me over. He was frustrated, but he got the point. He didn't touch me or have me touch him again. His playtime with me was over. Forever. We arose early, and he drove straight home, barely saying a word. He knew I would never be with him again.

## I never told anyone

"No one ever knew what he did to me. I made my peace with God and swore I would be a good boy, since God had taken away the evil. My ordeal was over. Or was it? It happened forty-five years ago, gentlemen, and I still remember every detail.

"My parents didn't ask why I lost interest in those teams or scouting. High school was on the horizon, and new teams beckoned. No more Little League, football, or Scouts for a high school man. Jesus, I thank God for that. Both my parents are dead now; they died without ever knowing of the evil. When my kids were reaching puberty, we spoke very intently of the evils of some adults. I wanted them not to be afraid to tell me, and so I told them about my nightmare. Only my wife and kids have ever known about it—until now.

"As for the men who did it, they eventually got caught and jailed. If you ask me, they should have been put to death."

# The Broker: Randy's Tale

After Mike stopped speaking, the breakfast room was very quiet. Silence seemed necessary to form a protective coating around the vulnerability Mike had had the guts to reveal. But pretty soon Randy began clearing his throat in a manner that could mean only one thing.

"Oh God," I said to myself. "It could be May before we get out of this room. True, the snow will be melted, but I'll have desiccated corpses propped in my chairs. Got to head him off …"

## A deal guy

Randy was at the Inn often and loved talking about his past. He was a "deal guy." Over the course of almost twenty years, Randy had visited over a thousand companies all over America who were qualified as "financially troubled." In his prior business life, Randy had been the president of a company going broke. He couldn't stop his company from going down the tubes, though he looked everywhere for an answer. In his next business life, Randy *became* that answer for hundreds of sinking companies. Getting to that position, however, was a longer and stranger trip than The Grateful Dead could have imagined. Fascinating, yes—but long.

To my surprise, Randy wanted to tell a very small tale. "This little story could be a metaphor for my work," he said. "Yeah, metaphor. I took about twenty minutes of a creative writing class at Towson State ten years ago. I'm going to tell you about bringing a dead man back to life, or at least trying like hell and getting some extra business cred because of it."

## Resurrection … and Rita

"Whenever an owner complained about the broad-based marketing campaign I used," Randy continued, "I always told this same story: If we are in a restaurant together and I have a heart attack, please scream as loud as you can for help. Don't just sit there, being polite, trying to catch a waiter's eye and then whisper that I am in trouble.

No. Let everyone know that I am dying. Let them know at the top of your lungs! Your company is dying. Let the world know it, so help, if there is any, will hear and come running.

"One night, my partner, Andy, and I were having dinner in a restaurant with a couple of men we were discussing a deal with. You guessed it. A man sitting right next to us had a heart attack. We didn't know if he was choking to death or succumbing to heart failure. Andy responded immediately, and the rest of us screamed for a doctor. Andy performed the Heimlich maneuver, but nothing happened. Next Andy cleared the man's throat and began mouth-to-mouth resuscitation. Within a few minutes, paramedics arrived and took over.

"The diners were moved to another section of the restaurant to give the medics room to spread the guy out on the floor and work on him. Unfortunately, the new location was only half a level down from the first room and had a window where we could see the poor guy all but pronounced dead right there on the floor.

"The man appeared to be over seventy. He had been dining with his son and several other family members. And he was, in fact, dead. His son came over to Andy to thank him for his quick response and his major efforts to save his dad. We found out during the conversation that the father had been rather frail, and this attack was not entirely unexpected. 'Nothing could have saved Dad,' his son acknowledged. 'But it was wonderful that somebody tried.'

"Now when we tell owners the story about screaming for help, it has a truer ring to it. If we had done nothing—if there'd been no screaming, no dramatic rescue attempts—the guy's family would have felt even worse. As it was, at least they saw someone try to save their dad. And owners should feel better that at least every effort is being made to try to save their company."

"Gee, Randy, you don't usually get into the human interest angle when you talk about your business!" observed Tony, who had shared breakfast time at the Abacrombie with Randy on several previous occasions.

"Oh hell, Tony. I'm definitely in touch with my feminine side," Randy chuckled. "Did I ever tell you about my company and Dolly Parton?"

"If that's the kind of knockers your feminine side has, you can tell the story twice."

"This story is not about knockers per se," Randy said. "Nor is it really about Dolly Parton. It's about Rita, a woman who worked at a truck stop in a small Southern city. She definitely had that Dolly Parton look. High hair and yeah, big boobs. The truckers liked stopping there for gas. One day, the owner wanted to sell. Rita wanted to buy. She did, and she worked eighteen hours a day to keep the place going. She even expanded it a bit. The truckers wanted someplace to sleep. So Rita went to the local banker and got a loan. On the lot next to the truck stop, she built a little motel with about forty rooms. Unfortunately, just down the road from the truck stop were all the major chains. So people passed the little truck-stop motel and kept going toward the bright lights of the places with more familiar names.

"Some truckers did stay at her little motel. Pretty soon, some of the local businessmen came to stay, but never for more than about an hour. In the middle of the day. With a close friend of a different gender. But even that traffic was not enough to survive.

"Rita had poured her life into the truck stop and the motel. Her friends were often the ones that came by to spend an hour with those business guys from in town. Even with a small bar and a restaurant, there wasn't enough money coming in to make it.

"The truck stop was foreclosed on by the former seller who had taken back a note. Oh well, Rita still had the motel. But the banker was getting nervous about her loan, which wasn't being paid. On the other hand, how hard could the local banker squeeze her? His friends in town were frequent guests at that place. Still, the loan committee wanted the money back. Rita would have to sell.

"Rita hired me. Maybe I could find an investor that would let her run the place. Rita loved it there. To try to make money, she had set up one room as a hair salon. Her friends got their tresses teased there. In the same part of the building, Rita kept one room full of her sparkly gowns and frilly dresses for heading out in the evening. She claimed she had once been to a party with Elvis Presley.

"Initially, the banker demanded all cash. Now, no one buys a motel going under for all cash. This place was the bank's problem, not Rita's. Buyers were proposing various amounts of cash down, but a loan in some amount had to stay in place. After a few weeks of resistance, I convinced the bank that getting some cash and exchanging Rita for a new debtor would be best for the bank. Rita would be out.

"At the court hearing to approve the sale, Rita protested mightily. If the bank could lend money to the new buyer, why couldn't they just keep going with her? Rita was adamant about staying. The court said it was the bank's prerogative to make the new loan. The sale was approved. Closing would take place in thirty days.

"Closing day on the deal was coming soon. Rita had moved from her house into the motel. And she wasn't leaving. When the buyer came by to do a final inspection, he was refused access to two rooms. Those rooms were where Rita was holed up. And she wasn't leaving. The buyer was getting nervous. Hell, I was getting nervous. Rita was standing between me and my fee. She had to go.

"At first we tried talking Rita into coming out of her room. It wasn't happening. She was crying a lot and talking about how unfair it was to take the place away from her after she had worked all those years. Admittedly, the banker and buyer and I felt very bad. The woman was having a nervous breakdown over losing the place. Lost in all the emotion, though, was the fact that Rita had run up a lot of debt. And that she had fed her friends for free at the restaurant and given away drinks at the bar so she could keep people around her. I figured it was time for her to pay the piper. I'd seen variations of this theme many times over. No one gets pleasure from watching someone lose what they had worked hard for, but that was something I could identify with. I'd had to come to terms with my own financial disasters, and now the owners I was working for had to face theirs.

"Some feminine side." Enzo looked appalled.

"Look, I believe very strongly that getting the owners away from the crisis is a good thing for their life. The failure occurred. Denying it doesn't make the owners better. Facing the consequences of their fate has to happen, and the sooner they do it, the faster they can start the next phase of life. Start to recover.

"Anyway, the local sheriff was called to the scene. 'C'mon out, Rita. You have to go.' Rita had cried all her tears out. She left the room in her finest ball gown, that Dolly Parton chest leading the way. Feisty as ever. Elvis would have been proud, for 'Rita had left the building.'"

Randy fell silent. Everybody did. But knowing Randy fairly well, I could see the motor in his mouth was idling—not off. I did a quick intervention.

"Hey, folks, if you want Randy's whole story, you can *read* it. Right here." I dipped into the armoire where linens were kept and fished out a manila folder. A big fat manila folder.

"This is Randy's story," I told the group. I could see and almost hear that Randy actually turned off his motor at the sight of the folder. Let the eighty typed pages tell my tale, I imagine he was thinking. One morning before the Inn had gone into breakfast mode, he had sat down with one of the university grad students who sometimes bussed my tables and talked. And talked. And talked. A month later, she handed Randy the manila folder. And quit her job at the Abacrombie.

## Randy's Really Big Tale

When he was a very young man, Randy developed a small business into a very big business that suddenly got too big. It was going under, and he could do little but watch, helpless, as it sank. The stockbrokers who'd sold stock in his company liked profits, and the venture capitalists would rather risk money in a new startup than one that was already heading south.

## "Going ... going ... gone": a beginning

So Randy was out of work. He answered an ad for a national auction company that had a great reputation. Over the years the two brothers running the auction house, left to them by their father, had built a firm that was recognized all over America for its expertise in disposing of machinery and equipment from major manufacturing companies that had failed. The large presses had to be sold to other manufacturers. Those expensive numerically controlled and computer-controlled pieces of equipment had to find new homes so the banks could recover their money from loans gone bad.

The auction firm had a rich, forty-year history, and the two brothers were sharp business guys. Up until that point, it had been a closely held family concern with few outside salespeople. But to expand, that would have to change. Outsider Randy was hired to go to Pennsylvania and bring in new contacts that would hire the firm to liquidate the assets of companies going under. Randy was to get ten percent of the fees he generated; the expectation was that Randy could make one hundred thousand dollars a year. But he was the first outside salesperson, so that ten percent might have been a wrong calculation.

Randy went to Philadelphia armed with nice business cards and a smile. He drove an old wreck. After going broke, he still had a few good suits, but there was no shiny car to drive. The nice brothers who hired him gave Randy an expense allowance and some company literature and said go forth and multiply—our fees, that is.

After calling on every bank in Philadelphia and seeing almost every bankruptcy law firm, Randy had booked absolutely no business. These people already had auctioneers they used, and there was no reason to go outside their circle to hire someone they didn't really know. Randy would have to go "upstream." His idea was to get to the owners before the banks took control. That could work, because the owners didn't have any auction contacts, and, in fact, didn't want their assets auctioned. They wanted to be left alone and allowed to turn the magical corner just ahead that would save the day. But how was Randy going to find owners who were going broke? They usually don't put out a sign announcing that fact.

## Clips and leads

Plant layoffs. People being let go. Why not get leads that way? Randy got the company to hire a clipping service to send newspaper clippings of stories about any business in a three-state area that was laying off workers. Plants with a reduced number of employees might have excess equipment. Maybe he could get the owners to hire him and sell the stuff for cash. That approach didn't work well either. The companies didn't want to be liquidated, so they didn't want to see Randy.

To help Randy out, one of the auction-company brothers let Randy have a few leads from some machinery dealers who had heard through the grapevine that so-and-so was going under. At that point, Randy signed a few small deals. Very small. In the first six months, six companies hired Randy's outfit to sell assets, bringing in about one hundred thousand dollars of fees. At ten percent, Randy was starving. He needed a new idea.

At the job interview, Randy had asked why the companies were always liquidated. Why didn't new owners just take over the ailing company, fix the financial problem, and keep going? No way, Randy was told. The bank didn't care about new owners. They just wanted their money back. By making loans at less than the auction value of the company's assets, the bank could just put the owner out of his misery, hire the auctioneer, and cash out. Whole. No losses.

A funny thing happened to banks in the mid-eighties. They became extremely competitive under America's heating-up economy and wanted to do nothing but make loans. Lots and lots of loans. Companies expanded. Capacity for manufacturing was growing beyond belief. Everyone put in new equipment to keep up with the exorbitant demand for stuff. And after a few years, there was an awful lot of equipment out there. Thus when companies went broke and wanted to auction the pieces off, the prices were not so high any more because there was so much equipment for sale. Soon the bank started getting ninety-five cents on the dollar. And then less than that. Eventually appraisal values were ridiculously low.

Randy's idea turned out to be the right answer at the right time.

## Using users

Users would pay more for equipment in place than dealers who had to find other buyers—after paying shipping and storage costs. So Randy started pitching something that no one else had thought of: sell the companies to users. When one company went down, the others scrambled for new equipment to expand their capacity and capture some of the new business out there caused by the other guy's failure. If you make widgets and he made widgets and he is gone, who would make the widgets his buyers had been buying? Your company couldn't, because you were at full capacity. So you bought the other guy's equipment and built an addition to your building and hoped that by the time you finished doing this, some of that business would still be out there for you.

Randy cut to the quick. The first large deal was a wire and cable company way under water. A strike had forced the closing of the plant, which, in the previous year, had produced over seventy million dollars' worth of wire and cable. Suddenly, if you wanted wire and cable, you ran into a backlog on orders, because a great deal of capacity left the market when this plant closed. Other major producers of wire and cable scrambled to add equipment. It would take months to build and install new stuff, but think of the excess added capacity!

It seemed too easy to Randy. He saw a clip from a lawyers' newspaper that said a lawyer acting as trustee for a wire and cable company wanted a proposal to sell the company's assets. So Randy called. It turned out to be a different company, and those assets were gone. But Randy asked if the lawyer had any other clients with equipment. Yes. In wire and cable! The company Randy worked for had just liquidated a large wire and cable plant in the Northeast. A plant this lawyer had heard of. So he would see Randy for a proposal. When Randy sat in the lawyer's office, the lawyer had another lawyer present who represented him. Huh? thought Randy. A lawyer who needed another lawyer?

Randy had nothing to lose. He pitched a deal they couldn't believe. Why not set an auction date? That is what everyone involved seemed to want. But wait, why not conduct a search for a user who could reopen the plant, put the people back to work, and get more money that way? Both lawyers perked up. Reopen the plant? Was this guy kidding? Over two hundred people were left without jobs when this plant closed. An auction would result in none of them being re-employed. But a plant reopening? The lawyers would be heroes! Had Randy ever done anything in wire and cable? The brothers' recent job gave Randy instant credibility, even though all he had done was help hand out auction numbers at that sale. Of course Randy had experience in wire and cable! He rattled off the names of every major wire and cable dealer in the country. Easy, they had just attended the previous auction. Randy had the names of every major wire and cable manufacturer as well. (Thank you, *Thomas Register of Manufactured Products*.) And every one of them was out buying equipment to expand capacity.

Though the lawyer was a little skeptical, the national presence of Randy's employer, coupled with a firm auction date for liquidation, gave him confidence he could get the most money for the sale this way. And if Randy could land a user, history would be made. Instead of closing a plant at auction, not only would more money be raised by selling to a user, but also people would go back to work. The lawyer had received fifty proposals, and only Randy's offered the hope of retaining jobs.

## Onto something

Randy went to work. His company planned its normal auction. Randy called dealers and outlined his plan. One dealer thought it was brilliant. This particular dealer had a contract in place for almost a million dollars' worth of equipment. Perhaps sale of the plant as an entirety would make the dealer more money. Randy was on his way. The sellers expected to make less than two million dollars. The final purchase price Randy got was over three million, fifty percent higher than expected. And the plant reopened. The fee was over two hundred thousand dollars, one of the five top fees earned by Randy's company in forty years. "Oh baby, now we got something," thought Randy.

A fortunate thing about the loan recovery business is that when you exceed the bank's expectation on a recovery, they say, "Can you do it again?" On the wire and cable deal, one bank was in Texas and one was in New England. They both gave Randy new deals to work. Referral business: the sweetest, easiest fee any salesman can make. He hoped they would never stop. But even two new deals didn't quench Randy's thirst. The brothers restructured Randy's commission; now he would get twenty-five percent. Let's get busy.

Randy was a bird dog. Find a deal, sign the deal, let the auction company sell the deal, and all would be happy. But the auction company liquidated stuff. They didn't sell to users. That one deal was just a quirk, the banks believed. So when Randy turned his new deals over to the office, they treated the deals as they always had. As auctions. They didn't contact potential users, and therefore none came to bid on the companies. Randy's plan was being undermined. Unintentionally so, but none the less undermined. Randy would have to sell his own deals.

Getting the clippings gave Randy access to owners. He was "fishing upstream," getting to owners even before the banks closed in, and he now had a pitch to make. Forget the auction crowd. Hire him to find a user for the company. The owner was dead in the water anyway and would have to make up any shortfall on the bank loan. Wouldn't the owner rather see the company stay alive, keep the workers off the streets, and get a bigger return from a sale? And didn't Randy understand the owner's position, since he had recently been the CEO of a company that went broke? Randy started telling the owners about throwing up three times a week. About not wanting to answer any phones, because creditors just bored into your soul looking for money. Why wouldn't the bank just leave the owner alone? Didn't the bank know that its tactics were driving the business into the ground? In fact, according to Randy, the bank did know. And the bank was pushing as hard as it could to get the company buried quicker. And then the owner wouldn't be driving the bus any more. The bank would take over and cut off the owner's balls. Sell the inventory, cut staff, and collect the accounts receivable. Just pay down the loan as far as they could and then sell what was left and hope it was enough for the bank to get whole.

Or.

Hire Randy to stave off the bank for sixty days, until new money could be found. Or new owners who would keep the company going. And pay the bank more than a liquidation would bring.

Owners liked Randy. He understood their position. He was on their side. So they hired Randy's company on a sixty-day contract to find a buyer who would keep the company a going concern. This approach greatly upset one of Randy's bosses, because nowhere in these new agreements of Randy's was it written that there would be an auction. And they were an auction company, one of the biggest in the country. Not to worry, Randy said. He would find users, and that would be that. Of course, that was just Randy being cocky. His bosses had every right to be concerned.

## Proving it

The first test came in Texas. One weekend, a friend of Randy's read a story about a large furniture manufacturer going into bankruptcy. Over one million square feet of manufacturing space. Randy had the friend call the company on Monday morning with an interesting offer. There was someone from the East Coast willing to fly to Texas that week to offer relief. Perhaps the guy would invest more money into the company if the deal was worthwhile. The CEO couldn't take the meeting fast enough. Randy was flying to Texas. To invest in the furniture business. As a representative of an auction firm. Some truth might have to be stretched at this meeting. Or at least creatively bent a little. Or Randy would be thrown out on his ass quickly.

Randy knew how to sell. First you listen. What was the guy's wish list? If he could have three choices, what would they be? Randy asked. Relief from the bank? Impossible. A turnaround in the sales volume of the company? Not likely. To sell out and cut his losses? Bingo. Randy said he was a Vulture Capitalist, not a Venture Capitalist. Randy cited as an example that he could have bought the wire and cable company for two million dollars, but was hired instead to sell it, and he realized three million dollars. Why not hire Randy's expertise, rather than sell at a discount what Randy could derive from a takeover? Man, one great sales story in your quiver of arrows is unbeatable. You have that first game-winning home run to talk about, and the manager with two outs in the ninth inning suddenly wants you up to do it again.

The CEO didn't want to hear about any auction. Randy had the answer. Randy was the guy who would put something together with other investors and keep the plant alive. The owner wouldn't suffer the indignity of seeing a seventy-five-year-old company go out of business, and gaining additional money would make his problem with the bank less stressful. Randy's company was hired. And approved by the United States Bankruptcy Court in Fort Worth, Texas.

A budget was agreed upon for marketing, and an international effort to find new buyers got underway. Randy had extreme confidence in his ability to convince other manufacturers to take over this business. He was wrong. It was too big and had too much too-old equipment. Also, like some of the other plants Randy had handled, this one produced a volume too high to be efficient. This plant manufactured tens of thousands of pieces of furniture a month, and there just weren't sales big enough to satisfy that capacity.

Gulp. Thirty days into a sixty-day program, and Randy was discovering that he might lay an egg. But wait a minute. The court order approving the engagement of Randy's firm stated that his company was the exclusive broker to sell the assets of this company. Flying back from Texas, Randy got an idea. Assets had always been disposed of by selling them to a machinery dealer. And the machinery dealers usually teamed up with a national auction company to buy them. Next, the dealers would cherry-pick the good stuff for their buyers at high profits; then an auction would be held to offload the rest of the stuff. Truth be told, if the price at auction wasn't as high as the dealers thought it should be, they would bid it back themselves and store the equipment for sale in the future when a buyer could be located at a better price. In this fashion, the banks would convert companies' assets into cash, and machinery dealers and auctioneers would make huge sums of money on the "upside." But when there was a glut of machinery, it limited the prices even dealers could realize from a sale, and banks began to lose money on the sale of assets. Companies would offer three choices to a bank of how to pay: one, all cash; two, a minimum guarantee at less than all cash and an upside split with the bank; or three, a commission sale.

Randy's company had been a major player in these deals. And Randy had been hired because the CEO, like Randy, expected a user to buy the stuff. But since that payday was not going to happen in this particular instance, Randy had to either get creative or strike out. Randy decided he would simply become the bank. He sent out a letter to all machinery dealers and auctioneers announcing that sealed bids would be accepted on the assets of the company, but only on a certain date.

## What the hell?

The two owners of Randy's company called for a little meeting and asked Randy what in the hell he was doing. Getting a payday, he hoped. But how could an auction company that worked with all these machinery dealers now be offering them a chance to buy a company they represented? It was unheard of. Randy suggested that they issue an affidavit stating that their company was not working with any other auction firm or machinery dealer, and that the high bid would be recommended to the seller as the one that should be presented at court to complete the sale of these assets. Randy admitted it was as odd as saying that General Motors was losing market share and should join hands with a foreign manufacturer to keep from slipping away. Oh yeah, that happened too.

Now the dealers and other auction companies reacted wildly as well. What's going on here? How can this happen? But Randy knew what would drive them to play in his newly invented game. Greed. Randy often described his job as being sort of like refereeing eight-year-olds fighting over a bean bag on the playground: You can't let Jimmy get the bag; you have to fight for it. When the initial shock wore off, all but one of the dealers and auctioneers responded the same way: when can we inspect the plant, and when are the bids due?

They just might be back in business, Randy thought. The sellers didn't attend the inspection visits, and when they did ask who was coming and heard it was a machinery dealer, Randy told them the dealer was there simply to appraise the goods for a potential buyer. He just didn't say that the dealer *was* the potential buyer. To make the bids legitimate, Randy set up bid procedures. You had to put up a ten percent deposit or your bid wouldn't be recognized. Hey, they were flying without a net anyway, so why not try anything?

On the day the bids were due, Randy had all the principals in the case assemble at an attorney's office to review them. About twenty people were sitting around a large conference table in an impressive room, including the CFO who hired Randy, the sellers' attorneys, the secured creditors, their lawyers, and representatives from the unsecured creditors.

Which user bought it, how much did they pay, and when would the plant reopen? Answers to these questions were what they had come to hear. Randy knew he had to make the presentation of a lifetime to pull this off.

Randy began his speech by talking about the quality brochure sent out to over ten thousand potential buyers. And he showed them all the *Wall Street Journal* ads that had been run nationally and internationally. Next he read from a list of over two hundred key companies he and his staff had called to inform them of this offer. And another list of companies who received a fax hyping the deal. Finally, he went over the fact that over one hundred prospects had been identified who signed confidentiality agreements before examining the assets in this case.

The lawyers and bankers were impressed. Those with experience in these matters had never seen such a thorough accounting of a marketing effort. Randy concluded, almost in Johnny Carson's Karnak style, "No one in his infinite wisdom could dispute that what was in these sealed envelopes had to be the true answers to the riddle."

Heads nodded agreement. "Let's get to the results!" But there was one last piece that really summed up the effect of the bid opening. Randy knew that each bank involved had called the dealers and auctioneers to get appraisals before making the loans. Liquidation appraisals. So these bankers had numbers that they knew they could get from reputable dealers and auctioneers if Randy coughed up a hairball with these bids. A floor of value had been set.

As Randy opened the envelopes, he announced the price bid and then the bidder. Such and such an amount by so-and-so dealer. Then another amount by another dealer. Then this many dollars from this auctioneer. Wait a minute, they cried. Where are the user bids? What in the hell is this? How did these guys come and bid when they were promised users at high values?

Randy was starting to lose the crowd. So he promptly went into Part Two of his speech.

Everyone sitting in the room had already gotten a liquidation value, and now some of the people who had approved all this stuff were themselves bidding higher. And Randy promised a greater return. Now, while they had expected the greater return to come from a user, it really didn't matter who bought the assets, just that the price was higher than a liquidation. Calm down, everyone, and let Randy finish the process.

Randy took another step to encourage them to give him their best offer: the top three bidders would be called and given one last chance to raise their offer. Only the top three would be called. Buyers had better be taking a good shot when they put their tickets in the box. Now the numbers were getting higher than liquidation value. How is that possible, when dealers had already been given a value in their earlier appraisal? Simple. They had time to go out and "pre-sell" some of the assets to customers who already knew this plant was gone, leaving inventory so big that these customers didn't want all of it but would gladly bid on a chunk of it.

## Punch-line logic

So in fact, Randy said, *users were buying the plant.* Huh? *Users were involved with every dealer who had bid.* Little pieces of the plant were going to various manufacturers around the world through the bids on the table. While no single user was buying it all, many users were in fact partnering with dealers to take a chunk of the plant they were reviewing. That is why the prices were higher than the liquidation appraisals.

The next thing that happened assured Randy's future in the business. His credibility for all time was born in that moment in that room. Randy picked up the telephone in front of all those lawyers, bankers, and owners and called the three high bidders. Number three said he was done. See? Randy had told them to bid their pocket limit, and they did. The number two bidder raised his bid but not high enough to be the top bidder. Their business was done.

"But wait—not so fast, little buddies," Randy admonished the possible readers of this stack of typescript. Randy called the high bidder on a speakerphone in front of twenty shocked people and told him he had an opportunity to raise his bid. Hey, he was already the highest, right? But the bidder didn't know that. So, Mr. Bidder, do you want to raise your bid? The man asked Randy what it would take for his bid to be the highest. Randy said truthfully that he might already be the highest, with his bid of 2.8 million dollars, but if the man would just make his bid start with a three-something, Randy was sure that bid would end up the highest. Okay, said the man, we bid 3.1 million. He had raised his already highest bid over two hundred thousand dollars. In front of all those witnesses.

## Behold, a miracle

Randy hung up the phone and turned to his stunned audience. They had seen a miracle. The buyer was paying over eight hundred thousand dollars higher than the liquidation appraisals. A thirty-three percent raise above what the bank could expect at an auction.

They took Randy's deal. And a new way of selling assets was born. The fee was over two hundred thousand dollars, and the brothers who owned Randy's company were shocked. Randy's reputation in the business was secured overnight. First the wire and cable deal, and now this. Dealers noticed, and bankers noticed, and lawyers noticed. All that remained was to get this deal approved by the bankruptcy court, and everybody could go home happy.

Again: not so fast.

At the court hearing, one person showed up protesting the sale, suggesting that he would raise the winning offer by two hundred thousand dollars. This would shatter the notion that Randy had gotten the highest and best offer and that all potential buyers had already participated in the process. The man sat in the witness chair and told the court he didn't get an opportunity to be a bidder. Randy was fuming. And Randy was ready with a rebuttal. He stood and addressed the court.

Bear in mind that attention to detail was everything to Randy. Pulling his marketing binder from his briefcase, Randy produced a dated Federal Express receipt from the marketing package sent to this man's office. He produced another list to prove that bidding procedures were issued to this man's company at the same time as all others. He provided an additional document showing that the man had visited the plant during the marketing time when Randy was involved. The man had simply chosen not to play. The judge would not allow the overbid. Randy's credibility skyrocketed. The sale as presented was approved. Randy's company got a huge fee. And it became a little different from the other auction companies. Randy sold to users, even when a dealer made the buy. No one else could tell that story to new prospects. Randy couldn't wait to get more clippings.

## Got milk?

Leads came from dealers, and dealers were great guys to know. Randy noticed a clipping about some dairies for sale. He flew to that city to meet the seller. It was a Tuesday afternoon. Said the seller: you must pay me one million dollars for two milk plants and an ice cream factory, or you are too late. And you must have the money by Friday, because that is when the other guy can close.

Randy had never been in a dairy before that day, unless you count the time his Cub Scout troop got a free ice cream on a trip to Henderson's. Three days to beat the other guy's deal. In cash.

No sweat.

The brothers Randy worked for had contacts all over the country, in every field of manufacturing. Randy called a milk machinery guy and then an ice cream machinery guy and laid out the deal for them. Both men got on airplanes from different cities the next morning and met Randy at the main plant. In the next twenty-four hours, people who could evaluate the equipment were dispatched to each location in three different cities. By Wednesday night, all the plants had been inspected and a value placed on all of the equipment. Thursday's round of conference calls concluded with the notion that they could pay the million dollars, get the deal, and make money. Each of the two dealers would take a third of the deal, and Randy's company would take a third. Randy would be paid from the profits on his company's third, assuming the company got the plants and made money at the future auction.

Randy knew the figure he could pay. A "cap" of what the backers would give the seller. But Randy had leeway. If he could buy it for less, the three guys putting up the money would love him and maybe give him more deals. Hence Randy wanted to buy, but at less than he was authorized. Instead of giving the seller his one million dollars, why not make the seller a partner in the deal? Why not give him nine hundred thousand dollars in cash, but then split whatever they got over 1.1 million on a 90/10 split in the seller's favor at the auction? Expenses and some profit came out of the two hundred thousand spread above the nine hundred thousand, and the guy could make more than his hundred thousand dollar discount by being a player and taking the lesser amount of cash up front. He took the deal.

The brothers who backed him loved him for this, and so did the two machinery dealers. Less risk and just as much upside. They hadn't figured the auction would bring in much more than 1.1 million, so any money over that was gravy. The sale actually hit above 1.2 million, and all were thrilled. Randy, they said, was a "shrewder magruder."

## "Swing me higher"

Remember that Randy had a clipping service to give him information on layoffs and other signs of a failing company? Now, when you get a clipping, you are reading a newspaper story. You are not getting a real lead, just the hope of a lead. You call the company and ask for the owner—and then what? Randy would say he wanted to meet with the owner to discuss a possible investment or buy of the company.

One clip talked of a gym set manufacturer in Pennsylvania, near where the great wire and cable deal had occurred. But when Randy called the company's listed phone number, he found service had been disconnected. Yup, that's what happens when you don't pay your bills. Randy crumpled the clipping and threw it in the waste can next to his desk. Not a lead.

But wait a minute, a man's name was mentioned in the article. So-and-so of Memphis, Tennessee: that was the owner. Randy plucked the crumpled paper out of the trash can, got the guy's number from Memphis Information, called, and spoke to a woman who said she was the owner's wife. Randy told her he wanted to buy her husband's company. Shortly thereafter, her husband's partner called Randy to tell him he could come to the plant for fifteen minutes the next day and state his case. The guy actually said, "If you aren't making sense in fifteen minutes, you'll be gone." Randy thought it was worth a shot.

Randy showed up on time and in fifteen minutes told his two best stories. Wire and cable first; then furniture in Texas. Okay, said the guy, you get another forty-five minutes tomorrow. With the banker who would be coming. At the next meeting, Randy walked in and saw three men in nice suits seated around the table while one guy slumped in the corner in jeans and a t-shirt. The suits talked and the guy in the corner said nothing. Blah, blah, blah, Randy told the two stories again, and the suits smiled and said they would get back to him. The plant was a long way from Randy's home. He had flown there for the meeting. The next morning at the airport, Randy met the same guys, in the same clothes. They smiled and said they were flying back to Tennessee. They would call him soon. They did. Randy had another shot at a big payday.

New ground had already been broken in Texas, and a few smaller deals had been completed since then. Randy was honing his skills and improving on his method of involving users with dealers.

The gym set manufacturer was one of five in the United States with a total capacity of about one million gym sets per year. Demand for gym sets was about eight hundred thousand per year, so margins were small and all of them suffered. Three of the five were in real financial trouble. At least one had to disappear. Randy pounded the phones. One user did want the hobbyhorse division. And the toy division with those little pegboard desks created interest.

The gym set scenario was the same story as Texas. Liquidation appraisals were in place. Those liquidators were now able to bid higher than their own appraisals because Randy had given them users who wanted chunks of the deal, though not the whole deal. And Randy remembered his most important piece from the Texas deal. The details of the marketing campaign.

Randy was ready. When it came time for the court to approve the sale, he got on the stand and told his tale. This many fliers were mailed. This many ads ran. This many calls were made. This many people were sent information packages after signing confidentiality forms, this many people visited the plant, and this many bids were received. But before the judge would approve the sale, he asked the buyer on the witness stand if he had paid his limit—or would he consider going higher? The man answered, under oath, pointing at Randy, "That man got the lint from our pocket, and we can't go a nickel higher."

The judge said it best when the union officials objected to the sale. "What else would you have me do here? The young man before us has turned the world sideways, and this is what we have as a result." The sale was approved. The thick document Randy had prepared convinced every one that the result was as good as it would ever get.

Two amazing things happened after the sale. The buyer asked Randy if he would mind conducting an auction of the machinery he didn't want in the deal, and the former CEO of the gym set company asked if he could work with Randy.

In round two of the sale, Randy used all his contacts from round one, and the auction was a huge success. Users trusted Randy to put them together with dealers who could pay more for large sections of the plant, knowing that if the auction didn't bring enough they would "store" the machinery for sale later at the right price. Suddenly the marketplace liked Randy's new method of selling companies. Randy made about two hundred thousand dollars for his company in round one of the sale and another hundred thousand in round two.

The process Randy had "invented" had merit. The CEO of the gym set company wanted to do what Randy was doing. Together they went to the brothers who owned the auction company Randy worked for and proposed a new division to sell exclusively "going concerns." Doing so would further distinguish them from other auction companies. One brother said Yes. One brother said Randy's process was a fluke. It wouldn't keep happening. A few good deals and a few big paydays didn't mean this method would take hold long term. He also said No, they wouldn't raise Randy's cut to forty percent, despite the fact that Randy, just in the last year, had brought in four of the biggest fee deals ever.

Over pizza and beer, Randy thanked the brothers for their support and left the company to form his own enterprise. But not until he went to Tennessee to see a banker. The banker from the gym set deal.

## Never forget "the guy in the corner"

Remember the guy in the corner at the first meeting in the jeans and t-shirt? He was the banker. His clothes had been lost in his luggage by the airlines, and he had only what he had worn on the plane. He didn't speak because he didn't have his power suit on. After watching Randy, he did speak in the end. He spoke about getting more money than they had hoped for. So when Randy asked the banker if he would hire him under a fledgling company name, and not the venerable auction company banner, the banker said, "I hired Randy, not the auction company. And if I have another deal, I want Randy wherever he is." After that meeting, Randy and the ex-CEO, along with the former plant manager of the gym set concern, began a new enterprise. One that would sell assets the Randy way.

Randy's new company was devoted to selling assets as going concerns or maximizing the values if the company had to be broken up and liquidated. For about a year, the three had enough deals going to stay busy, but not enough to be really comfortable financially. Soon a few good deals came along, and they made a little more money. But as in all three-way partnerships, the value of an individual contribution was skewed, with one or two partners' contributions being more, yet the money was split evenly.

During the second year, the new company decided to expand. The idea was to get more people putting money into the pot, thereby giving each owner a split of someone else's work. The company would be structured like a law firm. They ran ads in the *Wall Street Journal* for new partners and got a wave of applicants, professional men who were successful in other endeavors and willing to learn how the selling of troubled companies could make them rich.

It didn't.

Six men bought into the original company, which had grown to a total of nine partners located all over the country. Six new people searching for deals. Six new mouths to feed. Now a system was devised to have new partners earn by producing. Catch a fish, eat a fish. Don't catch a fish and starve. To get them started, Randy gave them each a deal he had signed up from leads the company gave them. Every new partner had at least one new deal to complete. So every one of the men who paid in got money back from at least one deal. Some completed two or three deals. None lasted long though.

Randy was swamped with referral business. The money was being split evenly. He was giving too much away. And one partner was taking advantage of the liberal use of his expense allowance. The three founding partners had, by the third year, off-loaded the six added-on partners. And after three years together, the original three went their separate ways.

## Alone in the sandbox

Randy knew he would do better by himself. The relationships he had with certain bankers and lawyers made his phone ring all the time. Randy never called a lead and never had time off. Banks were referring deals to him for one reason: Randy produced results. Consistently. Staying true to the method he had developed during the first wire and cable deal, Randy had been involved in over a hundred deals by then. The only worry was who would help him get all those deals completed. His nephew Tim provided the answer.

Tim was an excellent business man and a great guy. Tim had gone out on several deals with Randy and loved the action. Tim had two friends who were anxious to speak with Randy. A deal was struck. They would provide help in completing transactions for less than half of all money coming in, and Randy could keep sixty percent—instead of the third he was getting in the past three years, or the twenty-five percent from the brothers in that previous life. Much younger than Randy, the three new guys were raw and naïve, but very smart and hardworking. And even with the split being what it was, everyone was happy, because Randy had nonstop deal flow. Give a banker results, and he can't use you enough. Over time, more employees were added. None could match Randy, though.

When you get a court order to sell assets in bankruptcy, you are working for the entire "estate," not the owner. Owners confuse that issue. Although their fiduciary responsibility is to maximize the return to the creditors, many fight to hold on to a paycheck, or claim equity in a company that no longer has any. Owners don't always realize that when they borrow money from a bank, then buy goods from vendors, then can't pay it all back, there isn't anything for them. After all, they cry, didn't they build the company up from nothing? Didn't they pay the bank interest for years? Haven't the vendors made a profit on them from past sales of supplies? So what. In business, when you can't pay, you are no longer in the game. Adios. We all learned that lesson as kids playing Monopoly.

## "Never back down"

Take the first hands-on deal of Randy's young partner, Andy. The company made gun components and aerospace parts. Sales amounted to a few million dollars a year. The state-of-the-art CNC machinery and equipment (CNC is geek-ese for "computer numerically controlled") had real value to other manufacturers. Since this guy had lost several contracts, his sales were low, and his debt was high, he had to file for protection in bankruptcy court. An ex-Marine with a stocky build, the owner outweighed Andy by about a hundred pounds. When Andy tried to let the equipment dealer in to inspect the plant, the owner said it wasn't going to happen. Andy knew that would mean no payday. He emphatically demanded that the inspector be allowed in. They stood in front of the owner's desk and got nose to nose. The words got louder. (Andy says he remembers the spit from the guy's yelling hitting his face.) But Andy wasn't backing down, even though he looked down on the man's desk just then and realized that the components of a gun were lying right there. He hoped there were no bullets in the drawer, because the screaming was getting louder.

Eventually the owner listened. Okay. Let the inspector in. When Andy returned to the office and recounted the trouble he had on his first visit, his first deal, the other guys asked him what gave him the courage to stand his ground. How could he stare and shout down a larger man twice his age who was fighting to keep his company alive? Andy replied, "Because the whole time I was thinking, hey, if I let this guy win, I will have to face Randy. And Randy'll tell me I don't have what it takes to be in this business."

Andy was right. Randy always taught his new partners never to let an owner stand in the way of getting a deal done, because that person was blocking you from getting paid. Randy felt owners like that were taking money out of his or his partners' children's pockets. Any "deal guy" willing to let that happen had to go.

## "The right thing"

Besides being a badger about never letting go, Randy has another trait that has contributed to his success: he believes one hundred percent that what he does in making a deal is the right thing to do. If the current ownership is unable to pay his debts, then the ads, letters sent and faxed, and hundreds of telephone calls Randy makes to find solutions for the debt recovery will result in the highest and best return to creditors. In many instances, that belief has been proven correct—when a banker or lawyer insists on turning down the money Randy puts on the table, and another person's method ends up bringing much less than what Randy's approach would have.

## Banks, owners, and mutual misunderstanding

There are different philosophies in banking. Some say the best loss is the first loss. See a problem, face it immediately, get out, and take your medicine. It isn't always that simple, however. Banks that Randy made deals with have gone broke and out of business just like the companies Randy sells. These were major banks with large losses exceeding hundreds of millions of dollars. When an aggressive lender hits the streets, it puts lots of deals out there. The old-fashioned system, whereby the bank lends money only when you don't need it, doesn't always apply.

One bank Randy worked with extensively grew in a very short period of time from handling loans worth about eight hundred thousand dollars to holding over ten billion dollars' worth. Where did those new loan officers come from? One loan officer Randy made deals with had recently been a Xerox salesman. Now Xerox is a great company, with some of the best sales training in the world, but it does not teach banking. Or how to read a business plan. Or the pitfalls of various industries that real bankers are trained to look for.

Next, the banks sometimes add to their chances for failure by pushing loans. The idea is to get more money into the streets quickly. This practice is referred to as getting more "footings" in the street. Or, "getting a bigger footprint." Take the loans away from the competition. Charge less up front and be a little loose and risky, but load higher fees into the documents, so if the borrower gets a little behind, or his inventory is out of balance, the interest and fees go up. The borrower might start out at a great rate, with almost no equity down, but when the business doesn't quite materialize as planned, then sock the guy with a penalty rate. And charge monthly override fees. And monthly review fees as the loan disintegrates into the "workout" department.

Think about this. The bank participates in a deal where an owner puts up a few hundred thousand dollars and they put up a few million. He gets fifty percent of his inventory on a credit line. And eighty-five percent of his accounts receivable also go on his credit line. And his cash flow is starting to come up short. Real short. His inventory is walking out the door and getting smaller, because he can't buy enough to replace it; and that's because he doesn't have enough cash. His receivables are getting bigger for a while, but then they start to shrink when sales decline. He can't borrow as much any more. But he needs cash. He always needs cash—he really doesn't have the margins he expected, hence he isn't making the ten percent profit he told the bank was inevitable. He is making only about five percent gross profit. True, though it's a small margin, it is a profit.

Not enough, though. You see, the bank wants six percent on their three million. That adds up to about fifteen thousand dollars a month in interest only. With sales falling, there isn't fifteen thousand a month in profit.

The borrower has to cover the payroll and payroll taxes. He has to keep his company car payments up. Someone has to suffer before he does. First, the unsecured creditors. The owner used to pay within thirty days of receiving a bill. But cash flow gets tight, so he drags payment out to forty-five days, and then longer, sometimes much longer. The vendor selling him supplies crosses his fingers and keeps shipping supplies. After all, he can't afford to stop selling supplies, or his own sales will decline.

And the customers buying this company's products are also having cash flow problems. That means that this owner's receivables are coming in late, so late that the bank disqualifies them from the credit line. Now he can't borrow against them. The company is now entering the death spiral.

Randy's intimacy with the financial situations of his clients comes from experience. He has visited over one thousand owners in the last twenty years. In every kind of industry. Plastics, furniture, aerospace parts, auto parts, steel yards, playground equipment, Mickey Mouse gumball machines, the hockey games where the men slide back and forth on the rink via rods you spin, even electric football. Once Randy owned the company that makes the plastic trigger sprayers we all have at the kitchen sink. That company held the patent for years and provided eighty-five percent of all sprayers to the U.S. through sales to companies like Moen, Price-Pfister, Kohler, and Delta. There was a metal stamping operation in Kentucky that made parts for Lexmark and Grindmaster. In many cases, Randy wasn't just the broker, but also the owner for some period of time.

Sadly we must return to the death spiral. As it swirls out of control, every owner has a moment where he blames everyone but himself. He says my customers went belly up, and that is killing me. The equipment can't make the product as fast as it should, and as a result my costs are too high. The union is killing me with wage demands.

That fucking banker is charging me too much, or not allowing me enough slack on my loans. Shipping costs are ruining me. How can the competition sell for that low? We can't make it that cheap. In a thousand interviews with owners, none has ever said, "We miscalculated costs and need to get out." Or, "We underestimated expenses and can't continue." Or, "We paid too much for this business, and, while it makes a modest profit, it's not enough to pay back the high load of debt we put on the company." Randy would fall over if he heard an owner just straightforwardly fess up and face the music. We are not built to take blame in this country. It is always someone else's fault.

Usually there is more than one reason for the failure, but no one takes any of the blame. When loans are put into the street on bad deals, the shareholders of the bank will lose, but the guy who made the loan isn't always blamed. When Randy asked one lender why a particularly bad deal was made, he said, "The month we made that loan we were trying to make the Chairman's Cruise. That was the prize if you got ten million dollars in the street in one month." It would have been cheaper to forego the loan and just send the banker to Aruba anyway.

Bad loans raise the issue of which owner gets squeezed. Say you are a recovery officer in the workout department of a bank—the department where bad loans go. And in your portfolio there are a dozen bad deals. Five of you work in that department. If you get down to seven or eight bad deals, then the boss might say, Hey, we can cut Jones and give the other guys each one extra deal and save some payroll. At a certain point, the banker stops squeezing his bad loan clients. Randy has witnessed this many times. So, Mr. Owner with a bad loan, pray that your workout guy needs you as much as you need him and drags your case out a lot longer. Or that the workout guy's lawyer sees a long term bill-out by milking you along. No, these things are not always as simple as you think.

After educating rooms full of breakfast eaters with his knowledge of lending practices, Randy's Abacrombie audience who had met him over the table at other times often asked him to tell "the one about the guy who ..." or "the one where so-and-so gets his ..."

Here are some of the tales he told when there was time for him to take requests. One reason he got them typed up is that even the tale-teller sometimes gets sick of the telling.

## "Locked in the closet"

Two stories involved getting locked in somewhere. At times a banker or the bank's attorney would call Randy and say, Hey, just pay a visit to this owner and see if he is receptive to selling. No harm in that. On one deal, Randy called the owner saying he wanted to discuss an investment in that guy's company. No problem, come on down. Once in conference, things got hectic. The owner was paranoid about how Randy knew he was in trouble. How did he know the walls were closing in on him? How did Randy know he had been meeting with a bankruptcy attorney and contemplating a filing to head off a possible bank foreclosure? The owner started rambling and becoming very agitated.

Randy tried to tell him that he did know the banker, but that he knew of no bank plans at that point. The owner didn't trust anyone anymore. He stomped out of the conference room and said he would be back after a quick call to his attorney. What if Randy was foreclosing right then? he must have been asking himself. What if Randy was ousting the owner with the bank's support right on the spot? The owner couldn't take a chance. He locked the conference room door. And Randy was inside looking out the glass wall.

"What are you doing?" Randy called.

"Sit tight until we sort this out," said the owner. So Randy sat—while the owner called his attorney, who advised his client to keep Randy there without talking any further until the lawyer could run down to the courthouse and file the Chapter Eleven documents. That way he'd have the time stamp on the papers before Randy served foreclosure documents to the owner and kicked him out. What? In reality, Randy's company never had any such authority in any deal. But this incident showed the level of impact of any meeting Randy scheduled with an owner. Randy never knew the back story of what was going on just before his arrival. But he could always tell from past experience when an owner was coming unraveled.

The second lock-in situation was more comical. Randy's company was meeting the owner to sign the agreement to sell the company. Randy took another guy with him to start reviewing the inventory and the equipment for the marketing materials. The meeting took place in the front of the building, where the offices were housed. The plant was connected with the offices by a narrow hallway. The secretaries all saw Randy and the owner meet, but they had no idea what was going on. Randy had to leave to fly to another meeting in another city, but the man reviewing the inventory stayed behind in the distant rear section of the plant. The secretaries never saw him. When Randy left, so did the owner.

An hour later, the IRS showed up. They were there to seize the assets. The office people would have to leave; the company was being closed immediately for nonpayment of taxes. The famous yellow tape was stuck across the door and the chain and padlock put in place. All were gone now—except Randy's guy in the back of the plant. No one told him to leave, because no one knew he was there. When he finished his list and returned to the front of the building, it was dark and everybody was gone. When he tried to leave, he found the door chained shut from the outside. He was locked in. He phoned Randy, who couldn't stop laughing. The trapped man finally got out through an office window, but he didn't find it as funny as Randy did.

## Flying above the herd

Picture this. A young man left pilot training and returned to his Air National Guard unit in the Midwest with a pair of wings and a pocketful of dreams. He answered an ad about a job that seemed perfect for his station in life. Seemed the country needed countless hotels and motels built; this was the booming seventies when America really took to the highway. Where did we put these motels? The first builders of the "chains" were men who picked spots in small towns near the expanding interstate system: whammo, a hundred-room box sprang up with the help of investor money that poured in to the founder or a major franchisee of that chain. After all, everyone knew we needed more boxes with a hundred rooms closer together as we drove the highway, because we couldn't stand to drive another fifty miles before we slept.

The ad he answered said the company needed a man to examine locations for new motels. A pilot's license would be helpful; a small plane could cover many new spots in a short period of time. Why drive, when the boxes with rooms were so far apart? Once the young man accomplished the goal of locating more spots, driving between spots would be easier, see?

The young man got hired by the investor team and started going from small town to small town along the highway, securing spots for the next box of rooms. Soon the group owned ten, then twenty of the boxes with the familiar name out front. The young man got farther and farther away from home base, because now there were lots of boxes where he started. As said in the movie *Field of Dreams,* "If you build it, they will come."

In this way, the young pilot learned the business literally from the ground up.

Now, if he could find the great spots and oversee the building of the property and hire the local management team and watch the investor group make all the dough while he got a salary, well whoa, why not get his own investor group and be the head honcho? Who had a better résumé than he did, having just seen two dozen properties open?

The young man found his first site for his own "Investor Group." Property number one was born. Then two, three, and four. And then lots of investors saw the young man still in his twenties expanding rapidly, and they wanted their star hitched to this guy. So he grew and grew. After all, the tax code let the investors take multiple times their losses—money invested that had not yet been repaid by profits—and soon the properties would be full and profits rolling in. Every day, the investment history of this country proves P.T. Barnum right in saying "There's a sucker born every minute."

Now the young man was building his tenth, fifteenth, twentieth buildings, and soon number twenty-five was going into the ground. But the boxes were being built in places with minimal local population to support a motel, and reliance on the highway traveler was essential.

Owning so many boxes with rooms required a management company to run the operation. Of course, different investors owned different properties, so the young man started a management company with built-in business, running the boxes owned by the people who really put up the money. The management company took a percentage of each one every month. Here's another way to look at it: other people's money "bakes the pie," and the management company "eats the first piece" every month.

The house he built to live in was not far from the airport, making it easy for him to fly out and locate sites for new boxes. But the house was far enough away from the airport that driving there seemed inefficient. Hey, the "Little People" drove. The poor little souls who spent time commuting when he was flying his cute new helicopter from home to the plane at the airport. He was becoming a tycoon, and tycoons were "above" the common man.

Buying properties meant becoming familiar with the movers and shakers in each new town where a box would be built. Press releases trumpeting the next opening gave him exposure. He was a somebody. A season-ticket-for-all-the-ballgames somebody. Those management fees were great. And of course the young tycoon had to wine and dine the local important people to get the best spots and most favorable zoning, and he had to show the investors he was on the yellow brick road to the pot of gold.

There was a catch to all this. Several, as a matter of fact. Funny thing about that great site on the highway he found. Across the street, two or three competing chains found the same damn spot. So, while the numbers showed a need for a hundred rooms to satisfy the travelers at this exact spot, once all three chains each built a box with sixty to eighty rooms, there were now around two hundred. Not one of them was ever full or could raise prices, since the chain across the street would blast a lower price ten miles up the highway and snatch that traveler away from the other chain's box of rooms.

Next, the tax laws changed, wiping away the shelter advantage investors had come to expect. Finally, the problem of wear and tear: when the properties did have a high occupancy rate, it seemed the guests wore out the carpets and drapes and furniture, so the ones that made a profit had to be refurbished with the excess money. What's a tycoon to do? The banks were now wanting their money back, the outside investors were heading for greener tax shelter hills, and the management fees were getting lower because those other, better-known chains were choking his ability to raise room rates. It was getting tough to justify taking the helicopter to the airport to get in the jet to go look for more spots for boxes when the investors disappeared and the banks said "no more" to any new loans.

This one story highlights in almost every feature how in America we seem to get little pockets of opportunity to explode from nothing to something, yet in reality we just ride one big wave into the shore and then can't believe the ride is over. When Randy spoke to this young tycoon about all the money he owed, he pointed out that the helicopter was pretty expensive, to say nothing of the jet at the airport, and—when a contractor arrived with the new, imported marble for the walk-in shower—asked the guy if he didn't think he had gone a bit overboard. The guy mocked Randy. Great men in America who built great things were above the herd, he said. Men with vision needed to comfort themselves to be free to think clearly and work on the job of growing America.

For all his "vision," the tycoon couldn't see reality. Tens of millions of dollars of other people's money had built his empire, as well as millions more from the banks who couldn't wait to get on board. After all, didn't every monthly publication tout his genius? And the jet was impressive. And important people found it exciting to go into the clubhouse with him and touch the ballplayers up close.

Profits? Return on investment? Mr. Tycoon said that the absence of these was really Congress's fault. Changing the tax laws was holding back progress. How was America to grow if the government wouldn't let him take money from investors who would then take money back in losses from other taxpayers, so he could build more boxes of rooms so his management company could get at those lovely monthly fees to keep him flying above the herd?

There wasn't much point in trying to re-educate this guy. So Randy just sold the box of rooms the bank had its lien on and got the investors back as much as he could. The bank didn't get a hundred percent of what they invested, which meant the outsiders got bupkus. That damn Congress.

## Two guys and their motorcycles

Randy knew of two deals where, at the settlement table when they sold their businesses, the two "partners" left the table with millions. In both cases, they had started in a garage and built large companies with annual sales in the millions to Americans hungry for more of everything. Funny thing about American business, as exemplified by these partners. They hadn't really made very much in profits, although they made several hundred thousand dollars a year each in salary. The real money in their business—in American business— rolls in when the company is sold to someone else for millions more than it might be worth. Here are the stories of two sets of owners who each rode off into the sunset on their new Harleys, while the buyers and their investors and banks found out that paying too much leads to disaster.

The first example of this principle was a company that produced a mostly handmade product that many people could produce in their garages at about the same cost. So it wasn't the genius of making the product better or faster than others that made the boys rich or their company desirable. It was the way they sold the product that made them special. They built a sales empire across the country to sell their particular brand of a common, easily made product. Fifty million a year in sales big. A million dollars a week big. Obviously if you were a man looking to make a big salary, you would want a company that had a lot of sales. How can you take out five hundred thousand a year if the sales were just ten million? No, the fifty million a year made this company one of the biggest in the country in its particular industry.

And the two young men in their twenties who started in the garage had really only expanded into a bigger garage. Three hundred workers in a factory building hand-making the product that couldn't be mass-produced by machines. In fact, almost no sophisticated equipment or unusual knowledge was required to make the items. What made this manufacturer unique was its sales method. "Shelf space" is one way to look at it. When you went to buy their type of product, the display item was theirs, and orders poured in.

Forget margins (small) or profits (less than one million a year). Somebody believed he could take sales of fifty million and jack them up to five hundred million. So instead of paying about five million dollars (the safe figure, five times earnings), the buyer paid over forty million dollars to acquire the company. It happens every day. What is Google's market value versus its actual profits? As of the day Randy asked this question, the answer was "over fifty times earnings."

So the bank ponied up about forty million, and the buyer put in two million, and the sale was consummated. Now think for just a minute. Let's say debt service, that is, the interest payment on the loan, is only five percent annually (in reality it was much higher). Spending two million a year to service its debt and taking in only one million a year in profits, this company was insolvent and destined to fail on the day it was purchased. Does this really happen? Ask the two guys who left the settlement table, bought a Harley apiece, and toured the country to celebrate America. Hosanna for the greatness of being able to find a guy willing to pay eight times what the company was worth, and Hallelujah for a buyer's banker who couldn't see that. Hell, the guy who made this loan probably got a bonus! Forty million in loans on one deal!

How does anybody find a banker who would make such a deal? The answer is, "It's easy." Westinghouse Credit Corporation lost over a billion dollars in business loans before closing. Finova Capital Corporation, more billions lost. Many commercial banks avalanched by mountains of losses. Why? For the same reasons people lose money every day in the stock market on companies that fail: a banker is betting that the one he is putting his money on won't. For that is truly the American Dream. "I can pick winners while others pick the losers. And if it's other people's money I am betting, it's even easier." The cyclical nature of banks is to lend money to make the interest. One cycle may involve commercial real estate or residential houses, until they lend too much. Credit cards are good for a while, but then the banks give too much credit, and that cycle comes up a loser. Why not business loans, when all the other banks are doing it?

And who makes these loans? Is it the guy who finished first in his class at Harvard or Wharton who now works as a loan officer? No. The Wharton guy is the one who wrote the great business plan to show the bank how he couldn't lose, and, since he is very smart and beat the loan officer in every class the two shared in college, the loan officer lends him the money. "Hey, the boss at the bank will see that I'm smart and making the bank a boatload of money."

When a bank closes a loan, a funny thing happens. They make a profit that day. That's right, they give you ten million dollars, but they make one hundred thousand dollars of profit that day. It's an origination fee. It's profit, because the lender gave the borrower only 9.9 million and kept one hundred thousand. Neat. Let's make more loans and rake in millions of dollars of profit. Now, as long as the borrower pays back all the money the bank lent, the system works fine. But the banks don't always get their money back. Even the Harvard guy and the Wharton guy don't always hit it right. The fact is that in America over half the companies are losing money every day. Check the tax returns. It's true. So if you lend money to the half that loses, you can't get paid back the ten million. You might only get back nine million. Or less. Which means the other guys, who put up the equity money (which doesn't get paid back until the bank is paid back) get ... zero.

Now the bank can win even if the new owner loses. If the bank lends less than the assets are worth, they can just close down the company and sell the assets. Bye-bye company and bye-bye employees and bye-bye equity investors, but hello full return on the bank's loan. They hope. And if they miss on half the loans, they charge enough on the other half in interest and fees to make a profit anyway. They hope.

It happens every day. Ask the guys at Quaker Oats if they made a good deal on Snapple, which they bought for a billion because they wanted to get into the soft drink business, and then sold for a few hundred million. Good thing we still like oatmeal after that debacle.

## Two more Harley riders

This story shows the faults of the banking system and the lack of integrity shared by many. Randy calls it "selective ethics." We don't set out to do something wrong, but we sometimes elect to lower our ethics in situations where we can't see any harm in it.

Two guys were making auto parts in Detroit. Their company wasn't big, but it provided them with a nice living and employed about sixty people. But they were getting to the magic age of fifty. Wouldn't it be nice to enjoy life without working? So they put the company up for sale. A man from Toronto made an offer, and the deal was headed to close. The man buying the company arranged a loan from a bank in New York, and the closing date was set. The banker headed to the airport on closing day, ready to fly to Detroit where the papers would be examined and signed, following which the money would be wired to the seller's account.

But it was snowing in New York, and the plane couldn't leave. Damn. All that paperwork was sitting in Detroit with people waiting at the settlement table. So the banker made a selective-ethics decision. Call the buyer and tell him to have the papers signed and sent overnight to the bank's office. In the meantime, the banker had the money wired to the seller's account. Now, the selective ethics of the others involved also came into play. The sellers did sign the papers, and they did get the money, and they did buy two Harleys for their "ride across America" start to retirement. But somehow the papers never got to New York. And so the bank had no proof of who owed them money. None.

Just a wire transfer to two nice guys who went riding into the sunset without knowing that they got the money without the buyer sending any proof of closing. More selective ethics come into play. The banker didn't run into the boss's office and lay out the scenario. Didn't say, "It was wrong to wire the money without going to the closing." Instead, she said to herself, "Let's just see if we can't get the buyer to send the papers with some prompting." One month of trying produced a lot of "He's not in" or "He just left for the day" or "He's on a trip to see a customer." One month dragged into two. And by the way, since there was no proof of the loan, the buyer didn't make any payments, either. None. Nada. Zip. Now people in the legal department were saying, "Where are the loan papers for this deal? Why hasn't any money been paid yet?"

There didn't seem to be much the banker could do. Fess up? Nah. The banker called Randy and said, "What can you do about this? The bank is out about two million dollars, and we can't legally chase the guy because we have no documents." Well, if the guy who made this loan had balls that big, then what did Randy have to lose if he tried to outclass him in the cojones category? Randy's fee was five percent, so he was looking at a hundred-thousand-dollar reward for getting the money back.

Randy flew to Detroit on his own nickel and showed up at the plant unannounced. The workers knew something was up because the banker had been calling in a panic for weeks. And these employees had worked for thirty years for the sellers, whereas they had no loyalty to the new buyer. At ten o'clock in the morning, when Randy met the operations manager and the office manager, he didn't say who he was. He said only that he had to see the buyer immediately. The two men said they didn't know if they could get hold of the new owner. Randy told them he would be back at three o'clock to lock the doors and confiscate the property and building. They didn't know if he could do that. And neither did the buyer who made the loan. So the guy who pulled this no-papers and nonpayment stunt arrived at three o'clock. At that point, Randy knew his balls were bigger. The first words out of the guy's mouth were, "I knew somebody would show up here sometime."

In his two months of operating the business, the buyer had realized two things. One was that he had paid too much for the business and wouldn't be able to make the bank payments on the loan. And the second thing was that, since he showed a lack of integrity by not sending the closing papers, the banker probably didn't trust him anymore. Duh.

The buyer signed papers to allow Randy to sell the company, feeling he might be avoiding a case for fraud. Forty-five days later, the bank got back most of its money. And of course Randy got his fee and expenses.

Selective ethics. Many of these stories reflect that common characteristic. Only you, the typist, Randy, and that banker know what really happened.

> *Dear Mr. Randy,*
>
> *I am very sorry, but I can't continue working on this. It's very interesting, and I really, really need the money, but your story seems like it's going to go on forever and I have to get back to my studies.*
>
> *Yours truly,*
> *Mary Ann*

[The typist's note was the last item in Randy's Big Story folder. Weird! Randy himself had told me he expected the typed-up tale to be over a hundred pages long. Well, apparently the rest of the story was nowhere but in Randy's head.]

## Randy's Big Tale Gets Bigger

"What the fuck …?" Rick muttered. During the last couple of guys' stories, Rick had stood by the Abacrombie's bay window flipping through the fat manila folder containing Randy's "big story." Some parts he barely skimmed, but others he had appeared to read with near-Buddhist concentration.

"Would you look at this?" he demanded, flapping the typist's "I-quit" note for all to see.

"Who can blame her?" asked Tuck with an exaggerated sigh. "There's only so much a person can take."

Randy appeared dumbfounded. He had had no idea that Mary Ann never finished typing his story. He'd paid her by the hour and figured she was a fast worker.

"Christ. I don't believe it. A detail man like me never went back to see if the job was completed." Randy sat silent and glum for a long moment. Then he brightened. "Well, hell. I didn't take up too much time today with Rita and the dead guy, and you seemed to like 'em, so how about I just tell you the rest of my tale right now?"

The snow by now had frozen to an impenetrable crust. The outdoors around the Abacrombie looked like a moonscape. We sat back. We knew re-energized Randy would just keep going, and going, and going.

## Not on my watch

"Here we are in a city that was built by brewers and tin can makers," Randy began. "You know, some families in America have owned large industrial companies for over a hundred years. Plants wear out and need to be refurbished. Renovation is costly. Often a plant can get away with not being renovated for about twenty-five years." He continued, "That timing works very well, because, in about twenty-five years, the older generation turns the business over to the next generation. They, in turn, generally die about twenty years later and leave enough money for 'Junior' to refurbish the plant for another run of twenty-five years."

These remarks set the scene for Randy's picking up where his typed story left off: at a large Midwestern complex that made metal parts for the world. Every worker connected to the plant unknowingly relied on one thing: that the old folks would die and leave the money for the plant to be retooled.

"If they don't die and the next generation can't have the money to retool the plant, then the plant itself might die. Machines breaking down. Tools wearing out. The roof needing to be repaired. When Dad left the plant to Junior, who left the plant to his son, who left it to the founder's great-grandson, he also kept up the tradition of dying on schedule, allowing his money to be put back into the plant."

Damn science and medicine! After one hundred twenty-five years of running on schedule, medicine advances, and people live longer. But the plant was wearing out at the same schedule. So the owner called Randy and cried "Help." The owner was sixty-two and running the plant on schedule; he knew he needed to put millions into refurbishing. He was eager to do it, partly to keep his hundreds of employees working and the parts shipping, but mostly because "This place ain't going under on my watch!" The owner couldn't stand the thought that his legacy would be putting the family business out of business.

The bank would only go so far with loans. The owner needed Mom's money by way of his inheritance, and Mom wasn't ready to leave Earth. Within forty-five minutes of meeting Randy, this guy looked him in the eye and said, "She is ninety-three, blind, and in a wheelchair, and every day I ask myself … is this the day I push her down the steps?"

Actually, this guy was a wonderful person who was just expressing his exasperation. And Randy was able to do two things for him. Sell one piece of the business to raise capital and get a little money from Mom to see the owner through the crisis.

As of this writing, Randy doesn't know when Mom finally died, but he does know that the company is still alive.

## When a banker calls

"I was at a point in my deal-making career when I was flying four days a week to somewhere or other, which meant I was also flying home. After a long day of three flights, two out and one halfway home, I got a message while waiting in the Pittsburgh airport for that final leg of the trip. I was almost home. But not quite. The banker said, 'If you can be in La Crosse, Wisconsin, at nine o'clock tomorrow morning, there is a deal for you. If you can't make it, we'll call someone else.'"

Randy told us he looked at his watch. It was almost nine at night. Heading to the ticket counter, he called home and alerted his family he would not be coming. This was an all-too-frequent scenario.

With a new ticket in hand for the last flight going anywhere near La Crosse, Randy set forth. After landing, he drove for several hours to his intended location in just enough time to wrinkle the sheets with two hours of sleep.

"I spent a lot of nights like that. Short nights. In hotels. Most rooms are the same. Bed or two beds, nightstand, table to eat or work at, and dresser that you never put your clothes in because you weren't there long enough to unpack. And of course the ever-present armoire with the TV that traded stares with you. The major difference was which side the bathroom was on. This is critical for weary travelers who need to know which side of the bed to crawl out of for that 4:00 AM pee."

Randy made the morning meeting. The banker was pleased. Bankers are not about the money they make but the power they have over others. "One guy used to tell lawyers he could call me anytime, tell me to put on my kneepads and go blow so-an-so, and I'd comply," Randy laughed.

Of course he saw it differently. He was averaging about a hundred thousand dollars in fees for his company each time he answered those calls. While the banker viewed it from the power position, Randy just counted the money. You had to be wherever they wanted you, whenever, and that was that. Why say no and let the banker call someone else? Randy's company's commodity was service, and if making drastic changes to his personal life was part of the deal, so what? That was the price you paid to succeed in that business.

As an example of the inconvenience of doing deals all over the country, Randy cited the case of a new "deal guy" about twenty years his junior. Randy was in one of those identical-feeling airports at 9:00 PM waiting for yet another flight. His meeting the next day required certain information, which his staff back at the office was gathering for him. Randy called the young guy at about 9:15 PM. The young partner said, "This is my family time. Please call me tomorrow." Randy stared at the receiver in his hand. What? Family time? Randy had put this guy onto enough deals over the last year to earn the guy and his family two hundred thousand dollars. And the young guy would get a healthy cut from the deal Randy needed this information for. Family time? What the hell is that? Randy called back. The guy's wife answered this time. Randy told her that the guy should start looking in the paper for a new job. Randy was a founding partner and still out traveling during "family time," so perhaps her husband was in the wrong field.

Meanwhile, back to La Crosse. Randy got the deal, but the completion of the transaction was very unusual. The court order allowing the engagement of Randy's firm had been agreed to by all three of the banks that were secured creditors. The buyer was a publicly trading company that proposed no cash at closing. They would sell inventory and collect receivables and pay off the bank over a six-month period. They also offered stock in lieu of the payout method. Two banks agreed to take cash out over six months; the third bank opted for stock, because they had already written the loan down as a loss. The banker who took stock won, because, in the time frame when he had to hold the stock, it went up almost fifty percent in value.

"But in the courtroom where we went for approval of the sale, the judge noticed something nobody caught but His Honor and yours truly," Randy said. "I was due cash at settlement." Randy stroked the thick silver hair at the back of his head.

The judge asked each banker in open court if they were accepting the terms of the deal. Each said yes. The judge announced that the deal was approved. As Randy raised his hand to speak, the judge said, "Hold on, young man [actually, Randy was about forty-five by this time], I know what you want." The judge stated that, according to the terms of the sale, Randy was to be paid cash at closing. But since the banks were not getting any cash, each banker would have to bring a check for almost a hundred thousand dollars to pay Randy's company their fee at closing—as per the terms. No, no, protested the bankers' attorneys; Randy has to wait until the banks collect their money. But, as the very honorable and smart judge pointed out, they had all just agreed to the deal terms and Randy had specifically stipulated in the terms that his company got paid in cash at closing. Apparently this merry band had never before done a deal in which they sold assets without getting any cash at closing.

"When I split the three hundred thousand dollars with my partners, I remembered that banker's kneepads comment. Being ordered around wasn't so bad. In fact, that banker could call me anytime!"

## Randy's statue in Arkansas

Manufacturing plants are located all over America. Not just in big cities but sometimes in very remote areas of the country. In such locations, a particular plant may be the entire economy for that area. Close a plant and crush a community. Such was the fate of a small city in Arkansas.

Two hours south of Little Rock, there was a small dimension stock plant. "Dimension stock" is the term used to describe parts of furniture. Maybe a plant made rails, or seats, or drawers, or table legs, or parts of sofas and chairs. But somewhere else the piece of furniture was assembled in its final form. So this plant made something that depended on others to make into the final product. And the biggest customer for their dimension stock went out of business. These workers had no more customers to sell to. They had made a great product and never missed a deadline and sold at a low margin, yet still a bad thing had happened to them. Was this the end of the town?

Randy arrived and found the mayor of the small city at the plant. The mayor told Randy that, up until then, the worst thing that had ever happened during his term of office was a dog biting someone.

And now this crisis! What could the mayor do to help Randy sell this plant? And get the people back to work? The mayor offered to drive to Little Rock and pick up prospective buyers at the airport. He offered whatever he could to help. Randy ran the ads. And made hundreds of calls. And sent faxes. And FedExed information packages to everyone who might need a beautiful woodworking plant with a great workforce. In the middle of nowhere. In Arkansas. Remember, Randy totally believed in his process.

Of perhaps one hundred fifty prospects, only one guy wanted to visit. But he liked what he saw. He bought the plant to make hardwood floors for high school gyms. The workers had jobs again. The mayor thanked Randy publicly, via the local papers, saying the town should erect a statue of Randy in the town square. Randy thought the statue should be of this mayor who cared so much for his town and his people.

## "Fore!"

Two of the funniest moments in Randy's deal-making experience came from one man. He was a cantankerous seventy-something who had run his plant like a kingdom for decades. But he ran out of cash. "Selective ethics" then came into play: he took out the scales that weighed the rolls of steel his plant processed. He began taking chunks off the ends of the rolls and selling the steel while leaving the full rolls on his inventory so the bank would lend him more money. The bank sent out an audit team to check occasionally, but the man always said the scale was broken and being repaired. Just count the rolls, and you'll see it matches our inventory. It always did. But how can you look at a ten-foot-high roll of steel and know how much steel is really there without weighing it? You can't. This guy was in real trouble.

After being the "Little King" all those years, he wasn't about to listen to Randy, who had been sent by the bank to get him to sell his company so they could get their money back. No way would he sign. A plan was devised. A court hearing was scheduled to allow Randy's company to be hired to sell the guy's company. But the owner kept saying he wouldn't sign the agreement. The bankers' lawyers had arranged for the sheriff to show up at the guy's house in Florida where his wife was living at the time. As if on cue, she frantically called her husband to say there were men in their home tagging the furniture and telling her she had to leave. The bank was executing the foreclosure on his property. The owner put the telephone down, leaped across the conference table, and began choking the banker. It was hysterical. A little old man flying across the room to grab the throat of his nemesis, the banker. "Make them stop, make them leave!" the old guy screamed at the banker.

The old man sat down again and was informed that the bank would stop the Florida procedure as soon as Randy's agreement was signed and approved by the court. Randy knew how nice it felt to have leverage in a deal, and this was some awesome leverage. The guy signed, his wife was left alone, and Randy began to market the company.

But the old guy wouldn't give up. He would sell it to a user but never a dealer. He wouldn't live to see his plant broken into pieces. Forget the fact that millions in inventory were missing, and money owed was far more than would ever come in, NO DEALERS ALLOWED! Here Randy had a guy standing between him and his fee.

Randy sent letters and brought in the dealers. The old man was furious. Seated in his office on the day Randy told him a dealer was coming, he flew into a rage. Red-faced and screaming, he gave Randy a piece of his mind. And then he looked over Randy's shoulder and out the office window. Suddenly, he took off down the hallway. On his way out of the office, he grabbed something. Randy didn't know what it was. By now the guy was out the front door of the office and screaming at a man up by the steelyard, about a hundred yards away.

Randy trotted behind the little running maniac and finally saw what the man had grabbed. The guy threw a few golf balls on the ground and swung back the club in his hands. BAM. BAM. BAM. The balls were flying over the visitor's head and bouncing off the metal building where all the equipment was. The visitor was spinning around screaming, "What are you doing? What are you doing?" Randy started laughing so hard he almost fell down. Finally the old man ran out of golf balls. Calm returned. Of course, eventually the company was sold, and Randy got his fee. But that owner could never be used as a reference. He hated Randy. Like many other owners, he blamed Randy, not his own mismanagement.

## "Hey, keep the deal"

One of the reasons bankers called Randy so often was that his company would go and take a look at any deal—at no cost and with no obligation. Randy would fly anywhere in the country and agree to tour a plant and meet with an owner, paying for air travel, car rental, and hotel accommodations out of his own pocket. After the trip, Randy would get back to the banker and give an opinion.

Often bankers would merely tell Randy about a certain deal, making no promise about his being engaged. Sometimes, to distance themselves, the bankers would give an owner who owed them money the names of three firms, not just Randy's, so the owner could make the final choice of the firm to hire. Sure, the bank would apply pressure, but let the guy choose his own firm. That way, if the deal turned out badly, the owner had to take the blame for the choice. Banks are risk-averse, and their lawyers even more so.

In this particular deal, Randy met two lawyers at the Birmingham airport—great bankruptcy lawyers he had never met before. The banker was present as well. They all went to the factory to meet the owner and tour the facility. Randy checked the inventory. He reviewed the accounts receivable ledger. Looked at the purchase documents. Studied the payroll and the backlog of orders. As usual, the owner was declaring that if he were given more time, his company would pull through, and the banks would be paid in full. Did that mean that the guy was standing between Randy and his fee? No, not at all. You see, this time the owner was right. If Randy sold the plant at that time it would bring almost half of what was owed to the banks. The strategy put forth by the owner made sense to Randy. The guy should be given more time. They shouldn't sell the plant at that time.

No fee. Not even his expenses covered. Why not push for the sale? Because in Randy's understanding, business credibility and integrity are the cornerstone characteristics in being hired again and again. Brokers who put a sale for a fee ahead of good business decisions don't last long. In this case, turning down a chance to sell, thus helping an owner buy more time, was absolutely the right thing for all. Over time the owner made it and paid back the bank. And Randy made new friends who were impressed with his integrity. Two years later, when one of those lawyers represented a three-hundred-million-dollar-a-year trucking company, he called Randy to do that deal.

## "Happy birthday, honey"

Men who are successful in business fail in relationships just like other men, and maybe even more so. When that successful businessman marries for the second or third time, he may choose a woman quite a bit younger than he is. Money and power are great calling cards. Dancing at the country club, or flying away to Vail, or buying that three-carat diamond ring can make an old geezer look pretty good sometimes to a pretty young lady. So if his business fails after that marriage, he may not tell the new wife. She might leave.

Since the new wife has her name on the new house you bought her, she also has her name on the new bank loan you took out to expand the plant (and pay for some of the work on the new house). The old wife, the "ex," was saved from bankruptcy because she got the house, car, and stocks in the divorce. The new young wife got the geezer and the future, and the future wasn't all that bright.

This particular geezer made backpacks. Hundreds of thousands of backpacks. And backpacks are very popular. All the kids have them. Many kids over the years have had them. And his new wife loved him and her new house and the country club where she loved to dance. He was a great husband who deserved a great birthday gift. She bought him that antique car he had always admired. For about fifteen thousand dollars. Now she didn't have that kind of money in her checking account. So she just sent the bill to his company. Weren't they rolling in it? He was in tears when the car was delivered to the plant. Not tears of joy. He knew the jig was up. He would have to tell her everything. And she might take off at that point.

Randy worked with the guy and got as much as he could for the backpack plant. By then, foreign imports were undercutting his sales because of his high sewing costs. But the brand name had some appeal, so a buyer came forward. The sewing went offshore, and some workers kept their jobs. Randy feels pretty sure the antique car never went to the guy's house, and he doesn't know if that wife is still around.

## "I gotta keep the house"

When a loan is made, there are always personal guarantees to be signed. You pledge your house, the stocks, and all the assets of the plant against the loan; otherwise, the bank won't give you the money. When signing these papers, no owner believes he will be out on the street one day. Of course he isn't going to fail. People who believe they will fail do not buy companies to begin with. Naturally, the wife also signs. Her name is on the deed to the house. That's fine. The loan is for less than the company assets are worth, right? So the bank would never need the house.

Right.

Months later, the owner fudges a little on the inventory, and maybe he creates an invoice for something going out next week on this week's eligibility list. This way his borrowing base gets higher, and he can get more cash. But then the damn customer he pre-billed cancels half his order. Wait—he already told the bank the full order shipped. He is fucked. Unintentionally, he has now committed bank fraud. And his loan is out of covenant. And more sales have fallen short, so he needs even more cash.

Even very ethical men and women have fallen into this trap. They felt certain the new sales would be higher, offsetting the early billing or the inventory over-counting, and all would return to normal. But sometimes that doesn't happen. The banker might catch you. Your loan might have been changed at the bank because the guy you took to lunch and the country club to play golf, the guy that gave you the loan, is gone. Your loan is in the workout department. The new guy looks a little different. He doesn't seem to care about you or your wife or kids or the other stuff the first guy talked about when he was trying to get you to use his bank. "Where is my money?" is all the new officer talks about.

When a loan goes bad, it takes a while for the consequences to appear. Sometimes it's a few months before the rumbling starts. Once in a while things are better by then, but mostly they get worse. Phone calls for more information start the downward spiral. Please give the new banker some up-to-date inventory numbers. A new accounts receivable spreadsheet please. Why don't the current sales numbers match the projections you sent in three months ago? Nagging questions. The owner has excuses but no good answers. Then a meeting is scheduled at the guy's office. And please bring in your wife.

This is known as the "come to Jesus meeting." It is where the new workout banker points out that his employer had been generous enough to take a huge risk and allow his shareholders' money to be partially managed by this owner, who borrowed the money in good faith but seems to have fucked up somehow and submitted bad information. On purpose or otherwise. Whew, does this guy ever take a breath?

And then the banker turns to the wife. "What kind of car do you drive?" Or "What school do your kids attend?" The banker doesn't want the money he isn't being paid back supporting private-school tuitions or Mercedes payments. At one such meeting, the wife started to cry early, and soon the husband joined her. Randy saw this heartbreak as completely unnecessary. He asked out loud if the crying made the banker happy. "Happy? I'm happier than a two-dick dog," said the banker. His point was made. The screwed couple had a good life and nice cars and private schools, but the shareholders were paying for it. All of that would have to go if the bank wasn't paid back. Ah, those personal guarantees.

Another example came Randy's way in California, where houses can be extremely expensive and can therefore contribute greatly to repayment of a loan shortfall. So when one owner was refusing to sign over to Randy's company, the bank applied real pressure. The banker's lawyer, Randy, and the owner sat in the owner's office where the owner refused to leave and let Randy take over. The lawyer reminded him that the Porsche outside was company property and therefore really the bank's. The owner didn't budge on his position. "Take the car with you," he said; he wouldn't sell his company. "Could you give me that phone, please?" asked the lawyer. He called the guy's wife and put her on speakerphone. The lawyer told her that her husband would need a ride home—and that she should start looking for a new house, because he was going to start foreclosure immediately and she couldn't stay in the one where they now lived. Was there anything she could do? she pleaded. "Yes, dear, have your husband sign these agreements, and you can keep the house." The lawyer watched the owner sign the papers and even let him keep the Porsche. "Just leave immediately and do not come back," the lawyer said; and just like that, Randy had another deal to sell.

Personal guarantees are not really meant to have the bank end up with more houses. Personal guarantees are signed to make sure the bank gets your full cooperation when you fail.

## Boats, cars, and ...

Little Mr. X's business had been good to him over the years. He had made millions and liked his toys. The first Hatteras yacht had been replaced by a bigger one, but he couldn't part with the smaller one, so he had two. He hung pictures of them on his office wall. Randy admired them.

And those little model cars on the desk—the Bugatti, and the Bentley, and the Rolls Royce—were just like the real ones at home in the owner's garage. Out the window you could see the plant, with hundreds of workers whose fate was in the balance of his daily decisions.

When Randy pressed the case that the bank would like its money back, the little man began to cry. Sob, actually. Randy said he commiserated. Understandably, the man was upset at coming so far in life and now facing the loss of his company. He tried to console the guy. "No, no, it's not that," wept the guy.

"Look at me … I'm just over five feet tall, and I weigh too much. There are three things I love in life: boats, cars, and fucking young women. If you take away my boats and cars, I'll never fuck a young woman again."

Randy suppressed his laughter. It would have been comical if the guy hadn't been so serious. Hundreds of workers could lose their jobs, and this man's main concern was whether or not he would ever bed a young woman again. People always amazed Randy when that stress point hit home.

## Be the first one on the beach

Sometimes family members, often two brothers, own a company together. Dad has left them the company on a 50/50 basis. But one guy gets tired of the business before the other, and he wants out.

Consultants are brought in, accountants check the books, emotions heat up. A price is set for the one to buy out the other. Randy's advice is strong and simple. Be the first one out and head for the beach!

Randy had seen many failing companies in which the financial trouble started when the buyout forced the remaining partner to make payments to the guy who left, or to the bank when he borrowed money to give to the exiting partner. It happens often. After thirty years, one brother leaves—and, less than a year later, a major customer dries up. Or a catastrophe occurs in the plant, badly damaging costly equipment. Or a competitor comes up with a better mousetrap. While both men may have worked and taken a paycheck during those thirty years, only one is punished for the downfall, which sometimes occurs within months of a partner's leaving. Timing in life is everything. To every person who says, "Yes, but the remaining guy may grow and get bigger because a competitor fails," Randy says, "Show me those cases."

## I hired a muffler salesman?

A large manufacturer in Mississippi had two banks as secured creditors. One bank wanted Randy to be its "deal guy," and the other bank wanted someone else. The owner of the company picked Randy. A hearing was scheduled to give the company permission to engage Randy's firm. Of course, the other bank objected.

On the day of the hearing, the banker who backed Randy was there with his lawyer. The owner of the company was there with his. The other bank was represented by one of the sharpest attorneys Randy had ever seen: a man with a strong stare and straight face and a brow serious enough to make you tense up a little. This damn guy knew what he was doing.

When Randy took the stand, he was first questioned by the owner's lawyer to establish his credentials and then turned over to the friendly bank's lawyer. He asked a few puffball questions and that went well. Next it was the unfriendly bank's turn.

Starting with his current employer, the stern-browed attorney went backwards through each layer of Randy's career. What do you mean you once ran a troubled company? Tell us more about your sales career. What about those muffler shops you sold? By then they were going back almost ten years.

The lawyer kept going. Tell me about your service record. How many companies have you ever run? Where did you get your college degree? Did you graduate from college? What kind of high school did you attend? This guy was a pit bull. The hearing was running late. And the lawyer wasn't finished asking questions. They would have to adjourn for the evening and come back in the morning. The lawyer gloated, "I hope you packed some boxer shorts because we aren't finished yet!"

In point of fact, Randy didn't have any clothes for the overnight stay. He didn't want the lawyer to know that, though. When the judge adjourned the hearing to the next day, Randy made his way to a department store and bought a fresh set of clothes in order to be ready.

On the way out the door the friendly banker couldn't resist making a comment. "I hired a fucking muffler salesman? Is that what you are, a fucking muffler hustler?" Randy knew the banker was kidding, but many a truth is said in jest.

When the hearing resumed the next morning, the unfriendly lawyer started up again. He covered so much of the same ground that the judge finally stopped him, saying he had now heard more about Randy's life than anyone needed to know. And also that he had not heard any reason why the owner couldn't have Randy as his consultant. Maybe there was a better qualified guy out there, but the owner had a right to his choice unless that choice was completely unqualified. Randy seemed okay to the judge.

Walking out the door with the court order approving the hiring of Randy's company, the lawyer who had been grilling Randy smiled, shook his hand, and said, "Hey, it's nothing personal—I was just doing my job." That attorney became better acquainted with Randy throughout the case, and the two men ended up friends. Over the next seventeen years, they worked together on several matters. Recently that attorney was appointed to the bench in the United States Bankruptcy Court. Randy knows that the District is lucky to have such a qualified judge.

Once Randy was hired on that case, the real task, of course, was to come up with a good result. The company manufactured kitchen cabinets. It was a huge facility, almost four hundred thousand square feet. The place was in such a remote area that the nearest motel was over twenty-five miles away. So the owners of the plant built a mini-motel consisting of three rooms and a small pool to house suppliers and customers when they came to the site. During the former ownership by a company in the United Kingdom, the current owner had been the operations manager for many years. In fact, he was one of the originators of the concept of RTA, which stands for Ready to Assemble. Instead of shipping big cabinets full of air, the cabinets were "knocked down" into pieces that could be shipped in flat boxes and assembled on the buyer's site. The man who ran the plant was probably the smartest Randy had ever met. He had worked diligently to run an efficient company with a hardworking employee base, and he had also set up the most beautiful showrooms Randy had ever seen.

The product was being sold all over the country in large chains, not just in the Mom-and-Pop type of stores. The fax machines were humming with orders all day long. You would walk into a location, pick out the cabinets you wanted, and within a few days that order was manufactured and shipped to you. Installers would show up and lo, you had a beautiful kitchen. Or a beautiful bathroom: this company began marketing fancy cabinets as "bathroom furniture" long before others did. They made only mid-priced goods and high-end goods, staying away from the lower end, cheaper products. And they sold over twenty-five million dollars' worth of cabinets a year.

An outfit called Service Merchandise had been the cabinet manufacturer's biggest customer. A change in company philosophy sank this ship. Service Merchandise called one day and said that they were no longer going to sell cabinets, and their three hundred plus locations would have the displays removed. Over eight million dollars a year in business lost on one phone call. Certainly no amount of management skills or quick adjustments could overcome losing one third of your customer base through no fault of your own.

This turnabout occurred less than six months after the owner had purchased the plant from the parent company in England. The purchase price had been based on the full twenty-five million in sales. The bank had supported the very high purchase price because that man running the plant had delivered profits for thirty consecutive years. Losing that much in sales dug a huge hole to fill. But the owner was committed to trying. He scrambled his troops. Cut costs where he could and went out to find more sales from another national chain.

This owner's downfall furnishes a simple outline of many nightmares Randy had to visit. New owners pay what seems like a fair price.

The bank lends money on the history of the company. Some outside force changes everything in an instant. But no one can adjust to the new world economy that fast. Think of any business losing one third of its revenue overnight. Hell, think of your family income cut by one third starting next month. Could you pay your bills? Certainly not in the same manner you do now. Things would have to change. Would your creditors mind waiting while you make adjustments? Remember Randy's earlier comments about the banks. They wouldn't normally wait, and, in most cases, they shouldn't. The cabinet manufacturer might bleed the company's inventory or run down all accounts receivable, depleting their assets, trying to stay alive. But banks act quickly to take the assets over and get their money back before they take a loss.

Randy, the ex-muffler salesman, went to work. Beautiful brochures were sent to over ten thousand possible buyers and beyond. The owner called Randy and blew his top. One of their smallest customers had called, demanding to know how a cabinet installer making less than one hundred thousand dollars a year could buy a company that owed almost ten million dollars in debt. Why did Randy mail that guy a brochure? The banker got wind and challenged Randy on the notion that the expenses approved were to sell the company and not to advertise Randy's firm by having a mass mailing like that! Holy shit, he *had* hired a muffler salesman.

As always, a lot was riding on the outcome of this deal. Randy already knew his reputation was based on results, and people were getting testy early. But there was an answer for sending the mailers to people who were small in the industry. It started chatter at the bottom of the food chain and spread quickly. Within a week, every cabinet guy in the country knew this deal was in play. Little installers were talking to distributors who were talking to other manufacturing reps who were running into their bosses' offices to say that this company was for sale. If you sent it to just the top ten big boys who might have enough clout, how much talk would you cause?

There was also another reason Randy reached out to all within earshot of a deal. A longer shot reason, but worth the try. Suppose one of those little Mom-and-Pop shops knew someone with money. Lots of money. For instance, suppose your son had left the family's tiny shop where he grew up watching Mom and Dad sell new kitchens to his neighbors, and he went off to the Texas oil fields and became rich. And he wanted to get out of Texas and come home. And maybe buy a kitchen cabinet manufacturing company at a deep discount. That, in fact, is exactly what happened. So maybe mailing the brochure to the little guys works. Maybe the former muffler salesman knew this because he had been a good muffler salesman.

The big guys all had their shot at the deal. Every major manufacturer got involved. The owner was a legend in the industry. Everyone respected his products. All knew they couldn't survive if they lost a third of their sales instantly, so no one questioned how well the company had been run. This was a bankruptcy via an outsider decision and had nothing to do with bad management. But the place was just too big to take over. And far too remote. Unless you used the small airstrip one mile from the plant, you were looking at several hours of driving from Memphis. Very remote. If only they had more sales.

One major company in the plumbing fixture business sent a few company officers in a private jet to see this place. They were considering expansion into "bathroom furniture" by selling high-end cabinets to go with the beautiful fixtures they already marketed. One other visitor was there that day: the son of the Mom-and-Pop shop owners who had gotten the brochure and wondered loudly why. Randy kept the two groups apart, but he always let visitors know other people were there inspecting the place too. Competition, you know. Or, at least the façade of competition.

The boys with the jet walked the plant and ate the fancy box lunch some chef had stashed on the plane that morning. They thanked Randy and the owner for the tour. As they left on the drive to the tiny airport to depart one said, "Hell, if we stuck a guy down here to manage this site, he'd either get divorced or commit suicide within six months." Randy agreed that the site was remote, but Randy was the only one to hear that thought.

Many people looked. During this deal, Randy had developed another method in his selling technique: weekly reports. Getting approved over one bank's objections and knowing this case was high-profile, Randy spent a chunk of every Sunday night writing a report on the previous week's activity. Who got mail, which ads ran in what publications, who Randy called about the deal, who signed confidentiality agreements, who was planning a visit. He sat at his desk at home every Sunday night and faxed that report to all the "Parties in Interest." That meant each lawyer and banker, the owner, and the unsecured creditors' committee members (and their attorneys) received a full accounting of what was going on.

They didn't have to wonder, as the first few weeks went by, if Randy was getting to the right people. The weekly report also listed the "who's who" in the industry. Randy had mailed, called, and faxed every key player in the country. He had run ads in the international *Wall Street Journal* as well. Not bad for a muffler salesman! The players were all looking. Sure, some Mom-and-Pops were mailed stuff, but the big names made those early fears disappear. The big guys were all there, coming to visit, as the weekly report pointed out.

And they dropped out one by one. Oh shit. Another liquidation in the making …

Was it my "hostly" imagination, or were the guys in the breakfast room visibly bracing themselves for an hour of liquidation lore? It was definitely not my imagination that Burt—patient Burt—pushed his plateful of crumbs aside, folded his arms on the table, and dropped his head onto his arms.

That's when I made an announcement: everybody needs to take a pee break.

(As both author and host, I now invite readers to do the same.)

# Respite

*Also usable for changing shoes,*
*making a phone call,*
*stepping outside for some air,*
*or just escaping Randy's Rampage*
*for a couple of minutes.*

OK, guys. Back to Randy and the incipient liquidation.

The banks were owed over ten million dollars. Manufacturing had stopped. No orders were being filled. It cost too much to run the plant without a full sales capacity. Efficiency at twenty-five million was different than efficiency at seventeen million. And the banks didn't want that inventory depleted. They wanted the accounts collected. They wanted a new buyer to restart the plant right away, because everything was there waiting for them.

"Not going to happen. Too big. Too costly. And now when you walked the plant, there was no more humming sound of production. Shut-down plants are as quiet as a walk to the death chamber. Trust me, they're eerie."

By the eighth week of the marketing program, the only thing Randy heard as he walked the plant was the fax machine ringing. He walked into the vacant sales office and saw tiny, rolled-up papers on the floor. Long ago, the fax machines had run out of paper. The floor was full of orders. It dawned on stunned Randy that the last major presentation the company had made was a pitch to Sears. They wanted to be in Sears on a national level, with displays in every store. That would make up for the lost sales from Service Merchandise. Sears loved the idea. In fact, Sears had put the company's products into the Sears catalog that had just been sent out. People all over the country were picking out their new kitchen cabinets and going to their Sears store to place an order. Orders which were lying on the floor in the sales office where no one worked any more. It was too late.

"When I told the story in each week's report, all the bankers and lawyers realized they were in trouble," Randy said. "Everyone who needed to had received information. Everyone had rejected the notion of buying the plant. The bank was crunching those liquidation numbers. It didn't look good."

About three and a half million dollars on a good day was all the bank could expect from a liquidation. Gulp. Under water for sure.

The bid deadline was only a few days away, and they expected nothing. Literally nothing.

On the morning of the bid deadline, Randy had breakfast at the only place in town to eat. The friendly bank's lawyer joined him. And the son of the Mom-and-Pop shop stopped at Randy's table to say his bid of five million dollars would be walked over to the attorney's office within the hour, thus meeting the deadline. Randy's negative expectations swiftly departed. But his response was, "Whoa there, son, five million is not what we discussed."

"You see," Randy explained, "I had crunched numbers with this guy for days, and I knew that there was close to six million dollars of purchase price in his bid range. And then I lowered the ultimate salesman's boom. I told the guy, that is, Mr. Mom-and-Pop Junior, 'Remember those guys at the plant the same day you were there? They may play at 5.5 million, so you'd better get closer to six million if you want this deal.' (Of course, those guys were the plumbing guys who had no intention of bidding and had dropped out weeks before, but Mom-and-Pop's son didn't know that.) He walked away saying he would see what he could do."

The banker's lawyer was stunned. He said, "Randy, if you blow a five-million-dollar offer when they couldn't get more than 3.5 from an auction, you'll be shot."

"Yes," I answered him, "and if I leave five hundred thousand dollars on the table, that ain't good either."

Randy and the lawyer walked over to where the bids were due and opened the one envelope there. Five million six hundred thousand dollars. The bank's lawyer almost lost his pancakes. In one moment, he had witnessed Randy finesse six hundred thousand dollars from the only bidder on Earth.

The plant reopened. People went back to work. Three years later, however, Randy was called again. Seemed the place was in financial trouble once more. The lawyers involved called Randy's new involvement the reunion tour. Same players all around. Same court, same broker, same marketing campaign worldwide. But this time, there were no rich guys from Texas. Randy knew no one could operate this behemoth again, and this time he brought in the dealers.

"Now the bids were coming from machinery dealers and auctioneers. And one real estate bid that would make you blink," declared Randy. "This place measured over four hundred thousand square feet under roof. It took a lot of heat to keep the pipes from freezing, a ton of insurance in case of fire, and security to keep some local kid from hurting himself in there."

Randy recommended the sale this time at around three million dollars. Thus it plunged from twelve million when the English company sold it to about six million in the last sale, and now about half of that—if the banks took the deal.

"What if we keep it?" asked the banker. "What if we cleaned out the equipment and just kept the building? What could we do with the building?"

On a conference call, Randy told them all that if the banker kept the building, he could make it the world's largest bowling alley—but that was about it. And the banker took the deal.

"You have to have a sense of humor," Randy said. "As we parted at the courthouse and I said goodbye to my lawyer buddies, I mentioned that I was glad there would not be a round three on this deal. You see, I was a commission guy, and the lawyers were paid hourly. The lawyers got the same fee each time it sold. I, on the other hand, had gotten only half as much this time around, for the same work. But hey," Randy acknowledged, "half as much was more than enough."

## The day Randy walked on water

Over time, Randy grew more and more confident that his method was the best ever for dealing with financially troubled companies. "Touch every possible prospect, create a level playing field on which all could bid, and allow access to information: that was the way to get the best possible offers for any company I represented. And make sure every player knows what he or she needs to know to put in a winning bid. Make sure the buyer understands what I firmly believe: the owner signs Randy's Agreement, but the buyer makes the deal. The way I figure it, the buyer bakes the pie we all eat. Make the buyer happy, and he will make everyone happy."

In the three hundred plus companies where Randy has been the consultant, the one absolute principle he has lived by is always to secure the confidence of the buyer. "Lie to a buyer and you won't last long. You must also understand semantics. When I told the guy who bought the cabinet company to remember who visited on the same day the buyer did, I didn't say they were bidding. The bidder inferred that from my comment."

Randy elaborated: "If someone asks if they are the high bidder, and you say, 'I can't say that your current bid will win, but I can say that X bid will win,' you haven't said whether anyone else is really higher than he is already, or that if he keeps his bid where it is that he won't win. The other side of the same coin is this: when I tell you that you are not bidding enough, it is never a bluff. Listen closely and you'll know what to do."

I noticed that Burt had abandoned his snooze-posture some time ago and was listening as closely as the rest of us.

"I built an outstanding reputation for getting the highest and best prices, and the bidders will attest that they were always treated equally. If you lost a bid, it is because you wouldn't do what I told you was required to win."

Buyers make their own choices, Randy reminded us. "If they bid their pocket limit and lose, then they didn't really lose. Someone else just valued the deal more. You, not the other bidder, take yourself out of the game. The client is the estate, meaning the equity holders and all creditors. Maximizing value is always the goal." Randy said it was his firm belief that finding users who might also save jobs always maximizes value.

According to Randy, you seldom see a shut-down plant that is being sold at a straight auction go to a user. He explained the rather simple reason for this: "The auctioneers aren't even looking for a user. They don't believe in Randy's way," lapsing into royal third person, "despite Randy's almost twenty years of consistent success."

But some bankers and lawyers and owners have "believed"—almost in the religious sense—and these stories reinforce how well-placed their belief is. For a case in point, Randy invited us to Illinois.

A large machine tool manufacturer was going under. The seventy-five-year-old company had been making lathes, grinders, and machine tools for other manufacturers to use. This particular company placed machines all over the world. But the new expensive machines they made were being underpriced by foreign imports with cheaper labor. There were thirty-plus shareholders in the family, some of whom still worked in the business. Many had simply inherited their stake in the company. Its future looked bleak. The bank and the unsecured creditors were owed a lot of money. Time to close and go to auction.

The president of the company heard Randy's presentation and knew his method would give all concerned the best shot at recovery. No one expected the shareholders to get a dividend; they just hoped not too many creditors who had long supported this enterprise would lose.

With the president's support of Randy granted, the Board of Directors, family men who were respected in the community, was next. The directors agreed that Randy would give their company the proper send-off. And then came the meeting with the bankers, lawyers, and largest unsecured creditors. It took three great pitches, but at the end of the meeting Randy was sure all involved were in his corner.

And then one lawyer piped up, "We have to get 4.2 million dollars to make us happy here, Randy. Can you do that?" Randy ran his hand up the back of his neck, seeming as nervous and excited as he must have been when the question was put to him.

Belief in what you do is a great thing. Randy immediately responded by making an impassioned plea: "No one in this room can ever mention the needed figure again. To anyone." Saying the figure aloud put a ceiling on the deal, Randy explained. Why would anyone pay more if they knew the sellers would be happy with 4.2 million? The people in the room were shocked to hear such brazenness. They had all seen the liquidation appraisals. "Hell," said one lawyer, "if you get more than 4.2 million, then you must walk on water."

Common sense plays a role in every transaction, Randy pointed out. There were twenty-five thousand pieces of equipment all over the world that had been made in this factory. And although the parts business for repairs did not amount to a large sales number, only about 3.5 million dollars annually, it was still hugely profitable. No one else had every drawing for every machine ever sold. No one else knew how to tool every part for every machine. And no one else had the parts inventory already in place. That is the premise from which Randy started.

Randy called every repair facility that had worked extensively on those twenty-five thousand machines out there. Getting the list of them was easy. The only place they could buy parts was from the seller. Of course every competitor was called, along with every company in a similar business. Ads ran nationwide and worldwide. The telephone rang off the hook.

By then, private investment companies had seen Randy's ads. People started to know that when Randy's company worked a deal selling a company, it would be sold and on time. If you wanted a company Randy represented, you needed to act quickly and listen to what he had to say.

"Within three weeks of starting to work the deal, I had written offers exceeding 5.1 million dollars," Randy gloated. "I sent out the weekly report with a reminder that I had already walked on water. Hey, if you can't toot your own horn, who will?"

By the deadline, three companies were willing to pay 7.1 million dollars. According to the established bidding procedures, only the three bidders who were highest by the deadline would be able to continue bidding in an open auction in court. On the hearing date, the judge took one look at the crowded courtroom and asked the attorney for an update. It so happened that this particular attorney was one of Randy's favorites. They had worked together many times. Randy knew no one did a better job for debtors, and the lawyer knew his clients would get the best result with Randy's firm. After stating that there were three bidders present and that all wanted to consider going higher, the judge turned the courtroom over to Randy and went to his chambers, where he would wait to be called when the maximum was reached.

Meetings took place right on the spot. Then each group went into a separate room to negotiate a final bid. Of course, each one begged to know what the other guy was doing. "And each time I said, 'Forget him—just bid your absolute pocket limit. If that is enough, then you win. If someone outbids you, then they valued winning higher. You didn't lose. You just didn't want to go any higher.'"

Bidders wanted a "last look," a chance to give a bid and wait to see if it was topped. Then, on their "last look," they could determine if they wanted to go higher. Randy retorted that if they were willing to go higher if they had to, then they must not be at their pocket limit now. And round and round they went. Up to 7.6 million dollars. Which was seventy percent above the "walk-on-water number," the original 4.2 million the banks said they wanted.

Everyone got money from this deal. The banks were paid in full, and so were the unsecured creditors. It was one of the few bankruptcy sales where there was even a dividend for shareholders.

"Bottom line," Randy summed up, "never say the price you expect out loud."

## "You could see the horns on his head"

"Some owners feel a sense of entitlement," Randy recounted. "They started a company many years ago and worked long days to build a great enterprise. It is theirs. Theirs. How can it be taken away?

"Sometimes family members are involved—wives, sons, daughters— and they make it even harder when Dad has to let go. Many cling to the threads of an unraveling business as if grim death were waiting at their door, not just the end of their business."

A call came from Randy's banker buddy in Illinois. Could he go to Mississippi and work on a case the bank needed help with? And could Randy recommend a lawyer down there who knew his way around the court system? Yes and yes. Randy gave them the name of the attorney who had badgered him for so long on the witness stand in a prior matter. By now Randy and that guy were friends, professionals who respected each other's contribution to a case. A meeting was arranged down at that lawyer's office in Mississippi.

The banker, an attorney from Chicago, the banker's boss from New York, and Randy all met to discuss strategy. It seemed that the owner of the company didn't trust the banker. Why, then, would he trust someone who was being recommended by the bank? With the background now explained in such a way that it seemed the owner had almost no chance of hiring Randy, off to the plant Randy went.

Randy met the owner and his wife the next day. Nice people. Well-mannered, well-groomed, polite. How did Randy come to know their troubles, they asked. Randy didn't lie. He answered that he had done previous work for the bank.

"Oh, so then you might have noticed the banker's horns," interjected the owner.

"What?"

"Yes," the owner said. "I believe the banker is the devil. If you look close enough under his hair, you can see the horns."

The guy was dead serious. Randy couldn't laugh.

The man's wife sat there and let her husband go on and on about how the banker would do and say anything to take over his company. That the banker was evil and could never be trusted. When Randy pointed out all their unpaid debt, the husband and wife shrugged. "They make too much money anyway. And we aren't stealing any, just going through a rough time. And if they'll let up a little, all will be well."

By probing with deeper questions, Randy soon became aware of why the money drain had occurred. The Mississippi operation was well run and did indeed make a profit, so much so, in fact, that the guy wanted to expand. If he could add capacity and bring out his new sports drink—similar to Gatorade—the banker would get his money. With that plan in mind, the man bought a plant in Phoenix, Arizona, and moved into a townhouse there to get the new plant going. Unable to meet the purchase price, he took money from operating revenue and skipped a few vendor payments to get the cash to buy the Phoenix plant. And now his creditors wanted their money back. Just hold on everybody, the owner begged. Just hold on. Sixty days was all he needed.

"Remember," said Randy with the humility Abacrombie patrons had come to know and love, "I was a good salesman. And good salesmen listen. Okay, I told the owner, if he really believed the story he was telling about almost turning the corner, then he'd better hire me immediately."

Not because the owner should trust the bank. But because the bank trusted Randy. Therefore, if the owner was right, and sixty days would prove him right, then Randy would get him the sixty days just by being hired. Hell, just sign Randy's agreement and the owner would be home free. If the owner wouldn't sign, then he must not believe his own story.

"Even the wife couldn't fault my logic. So the guy signed, and I went back to the lawyers and the bankers, who, after they witnessed this turn of events, thought I just might be able to bring Lazarus back to life."

Randy did the same thing he always did. Calls, letters, and ads up the wazoo. This case illustrated another feature of Randy's work ethic. Always go when the buyer wants to go. Not everyone celebrates

Christmas, so if people wanted to inspect the plant two days before Christmas, halfway across the country, so be it. Many of Randy's deals spoke to this same "get up and go" philosophy.

Randy gave us an example. He had found three individuals who appeared to be good prospects: they insisted they were about to buy another facility for bottling and intended to strike the deal within the next week. If they were to change their mind and invest in the Phoenix site, they had to see it on December 23. Randy flew out to Phoenix without hesitation. After landing around noon, he met up with the three buyers who had just flown in for the inspection. They got a rental car and headed to the plant. By now it was about one in the afternoon: no one was around. The plant was locked tight. No one had cell phones back then; no one could be reached.

The three buyers became skeptical. Was Randy the court-authorized broker or not? Why couldn't he get them into the plant? What was going on here? "I didn't flinch. I said the man who was supposed to let us in went home sick, so I was calling someone else to let us in. I knew I'd better be quick, or all of us would miss the turnaround flight back to the East Coast. And maybe miss Christmas."

Randy called a locksmith. Told him he had left his keys back in Mississippi. "Who are you?" demanded the locksmith, "and why should I open the plant for you?"

"BECAUSE I HAVE A FUCKING COURT ORDER IN MY POCKET HERE," Randy bellowed. "NOW OPEN THE DAMN DOOR."

"Pay me cash and sign this authorization slip," was the locksmith's reply. Thirty minutes later the visitors group was heading back to the airport.

On Christmas Eve, Randy was home. The owner of the company called and went nuts. "How dare you break into the Phoenix plant? You had no right to go in there without my guys present." Later Randy found out the owner had ordered "his guys" not to be there when the visitors arrived. "Remember, the owner didn't want to sell.

But that locked door was standing in the way of me and my fee. It had to be opened."

Trust was evaporating between Randy and the owner. Randy had contacted many new lenders for the owner and presented the owner's business plan, hoping to replace the current lender and allow the owner to keep his company. Unfortunately, no new lender wanted to do that. "Of course that was my fault, the owner insisted. It couldn't be that a lender didn't want to make a loan to a guy who would skip paying bills and the bank and use the money as a down payment on a new plant. Talk about a trust issue! Somehow the owner never saw it that way," Randy added.

And about that new sports drink. Seems it was actually being bottled in a third site owned by the guy's two sons—whose equipment was eerily similar to what Dad used in the other two plants. Where did that new equipment come from? And if the sons' plant was in the business plan as having been started by the owner's company, why weren't those assets also the "liened" property held by the bank?

The owner was running out of time. A hearing was scheduled to present the results from the marketing program. Randy had indeed found a user who wanted the plant, someone willing to pay considerably more than the liquidation value. Almost enough, in fact, to make the bank whole. Naturally, the banker wanted the deal. The owner was told he could show up and outbid the highest offer or face the fact that his reign was over. Had the owner not bought the Phoenix plant, he might not have been in this situation.

Every lender they tried to secure turned the owner down. There were no new loans to be had. And yet the owner stood up in court on the morning of the hearing and said he was outbidding the other buyer Randy brought. Where was the money coming from? Randy had no knowledge of any lender backing this guy. The owner said Randy didn't know because he couldn't trust Randy, who had turned out to be the evil representative of the evil banker. The owner had been hoodwinked, and he was now hoodwinking Randy back. He waved a Letter of Confirmation of a loan large enough to make his bid real.

The judge involved was, in Randy's estimation, perhaps the best bankruptcy judge he had ever appeared before. "To this day, I admire this judge's courage and leadership on the bench. Everybody who comes before him receives every possible opportunity to save their companies."

The judge announced a recess before ruling on the sale and called Randy into chambers. He told Randy to verify the loan letter being waved about in court and report back in thirty minutes with an answer as to its authenticity.

The letter in question turned out to have been signed by the owner's brother. It stated that money would be loaned after a secured creditor had been obtained. But none had been obtained. When Randy testified after the break, the man proclaimed loudly that Randy must be evil to turn his back on him like that.

"Some owners never get it," Randy ruminated. "They never see the simple realities of their situation. No one was evil. No one was the devil. A man had simply spent more money than he had and couldn't pay it back. Nothing more complicated than that."

The judge thanked Randy for his hard work and confirmed the sale to Randy's buyer. And Randy's credibility in the state of Mississippi was cemented in place.

## "Even numbers stay ... odds go home"

"Over 175 million cassettes sold annually: that's what the cassette manufacturing company I was called to next could claim." When Randy went there, he found an immaculate plant with thirteen "lines" in place. "I heard the constant hum of plastic moving about, going from little pellets to the cassette cases we all still have dozens of. Guys, if you are over fifty, and I know some of you are, you probably have owned at least a hundred cassettes in your lifetime. Cassettes were what made vinyl records obsolete."

Randy went on. "This particular factory made more cassettes a year than any other factory on Earth at the time. The equipment was incredible. Efficiency like you wouldn't believe. At no time was the product being touched by human hands until it was being packaged. But almost three hundred workers monitored the machines.

And then came CDs. So long, cassettes. Oh well, it was a great run.

"When your plant makes a product people want badly at a particular moment in time, you never know how long that run will last. Technology keeps moving. Leather machine straps in 1880 became rubber belts a few years later. If you once made transistor radios, you are long gone now. History proves again and again that progress kills a fair number of businesses—without the owners or workers ever doing anything wrong. Time just passes them by."

So, Randy told us, the owner who operated the cassette plant saw his sales plummet. Computer chips could do what the cassettes had done. Those talking stuffed animals and dolls with those sewn-in cassettes suddenly wore little computer chips in their stuffing instead. And this guy didn't make computer chips. He made cassettes. Music people didn't want his product either. The customer base was dwindling to the vanishing point.

A huge plant required to produce a huge number of products has to run full tilt on straight shifts all day and all night. The cost of operations is spread out over a large number of parts. Cut production, and the cost per part zooms. When the owner got into trouble, he called for a turnaround consultant to help. "You couldn't fire any of the machines," said Randy, "so to cut costs, you had to let workers go. At full-out production, three hundred workers were needed. With decreased demand, some of them had to go home."

When a large layoff is required, what is the fair way to decide whose job gets taken away? Seniority isn't always a fair basis for the decision, because people are hired for their skill set; in this plant, a guy with three years' experience could do the same thing as a guy with ten years, even though at that time he might be making less money. So do you fire the last people employed and retain the high-cost guy, or do you cut the high-cost guy who has been a faithful employee much longer? "Hey, somebody has to leave," Randy said. "Often, a lot of somebodies have to leave."

Randy continued, "People in my business have to separate their feelings from the individual faces. Turnaround managers who step in to revise a plant's operation will tell you it's gut-wrenching to demand layoffs. In truth, the owner wants yours truly, or the other consultant the bank recommended, to make the cuts. That way he can blame the loss of workers on the bank. But how do you cut a workforce in half? The choices are to lose half your workers or lose all of your workers. What is it going to be?"

Although identifying who stays and who goes has never been done this way to Randy's knowledge, one possibility was the "even and odd" method. "You line up all the workers and say, 'Go outside and check your license plate. If it ends in an even number, come to work tomorrow. If it ends in an odd number, don't come back.'"

Randy said that people in his shoes joke about this mythical method. It would blindly make a decision that no human wants to make. Random fate would make the call. "I never forget that those workers are someone's mother, father, wife, sister, brother, or husband—with hopes, dreams, and several mouths to feed on the check he or she just lost. Do not think for one minute that people like me ever forget that."

Burt turned to Randy with a new light in his eyes. "So," he said. "That's what you worked for day and night."

"Right," agreed Randy. "It wasn't all about Randy. It was to keep as many workers as possible on the failing company's payroll."

Randy went quiet, stretched, continued: another year and, tomorrow, another Christmas Eve. Why was Randy flying halfway across the country again, going away from home, not towards it? Because one man of a different faith didn't know from Christmas, that's why. His personal calendar just noted a free day for him to go out West and inspect a particular plant for a possible purchase. Randy, who *did* know from Christmas, told his kids goodbye, promising to get back as soon as possible.

The weather forecast for the entire country was cold, with snow falling in every part of the U.S. where it snowed. Delays going west made Randy late getting to Nebraska. No matter. The prospective buyer was coming from another city in the East, and he was late too.

Randy and the prospect toured the plant with the temperature outside at five degrees and snow blowing down sideways. Randy, of course, was cordial to the man, hoping he didn't make this trip and risk missing his kids' Christmas for nothing. The prospective buyer was actually a wonderful person who realized too late what traveling those particular days might mean to Randy, and he apologized for his scheduling of the tour when he did: unfortunately it was then or never.

With the plant tour completed, both men hustled back to the airport to head east. Quickly they realized they were not going to be leaving anytime soon. Snow was piling up everywhere. Planes couldn't take off or land, not there, not in Chicago, not in St. Louis, not in any other place where planes took off to fly east. Christmas was about thirty hours away, and Randy was over two thousand miles from home. This was the first time in all his years of traveling that he started to fear he might not be home in time. Soon, however, a voice squawked that his plane was leaving. Whew. He would be at least halfway closer to home when that plane landed.

Someone up there must love Randy. His next plane also took off, pretty much as scheduled; he made it home on Christmas Eve. Barely. "Here's my message to families of those who travel for business: hug your road-warrior husband or Mom or Dad when one of them comes through the door, and be thankful that they try so hard for you.

"Roadies know: constantly making your way around the country is tough. Maybe I never battled daily rush-hour traffic en route to and from the office like people who don't travel, but all business travelers can tell you Christmas Eve stories that have turned their hair gray."

What keeps the road warriors fighting is that sometimes their hard work is rewarded. That prospective buyer bought that plant. And sold cassettes for the "books on tape" crowd. The world may never again need as many tapes as it did in that factory's heyday, but many workers remained employed because the buyer and the broker made that trip.

## Speaking of tapes

Randy said that his previous story reminded him of another deal involving tapes. The men in the room made groan-suppressing noises, but I could tell they were intended mainly for effect. Randy had his listeners' ears.

"Despite technical innovations, it used to be that nothing beat a particular kind of recording tape, used in the music industry, which was manufactured in only one plant in the world." The factory that Randy spoke of made many kinds of tapes and had a remarkably large sales volume. Debt was high compared to the huge sales volume. Again, fast-moving technology passed the company on certain products. Sales went down and margins disappeared. Another plant closing loomed on the horizon.

Some of the world's greatest classical musicians, rock stars, movie soundtracks, and world-class orchestras used only this one kind of tape to make a master recording. And suddenly—because its other products, such as cassette tapes, were failing in sales—the whole company might close down.

A national magazine ran a story about the demise of this company, and panic hit the streets. Musicians actually checked to see how many extra feet of tape they had left open on reels previously recorded, hoping the extra footage could be used in the future. This tape was gold. Randy and his partner Andy loved to hear such stories. If the tape was that good, someone had to buy the company just to get this one product! Someone did, and the "solid gold" tape is still being made today.

212 TﾠHE IﾠNNKEEPER TﾠALES

## The most expensive dinner he never ate

Was it my guests' need for me to bring in more provisions that made Randy launch into his next segment? Randy didn't waste a minute on downtime.

"The bank was in New York, but the deal was in Chicago. An auto parts chain owed millions to the bank. The landscape was changing in auto parts. Traditional stores were losing sales to big box stores. Now you could buy a lot of auto stuff cheap at Wal-Mart that you used to have to go to the little guy for. Some of the products with the best profit margins were no longer selling. Here was another innovation that killed a business."

As Randy explained, the banker involved with this auto parts chain was owed millions. Over twenty million dollars to be more accurate. Over sixty locations were operating in the Midwest, along with a huge warehouse distribution center to service those stores. Could this be written as a real estate play? Maybe some of the locations could be sold to those movie rental guys looking for space in strip malls. People seemed to want movies more than auto parts. When they went to the strip mall, anyway.

With sales waning, management was cutting locations. But these efforts still weren't enough. Randy was called into the deal to see if someone would buy the chain. It was the biggest at the time in its large geographic area.

Randy toured the main facility where literally millions of auto parts were stored. The parts arrived in trainloads and were distributed several times a week to waiting store managers, who pushed truck floor mats and air fresheners, license plate holders, and tire black spray "to make your ride look (and smell) more beautiful. Oh yeah, they also sold brake parts, plug wires, the distributor cap for that old Chevy, and even whole engines that had been remanufactured."

Sales annually exceeded one hundred million dollars. "But the big box stores stocked more at each location than the little guys could. And you were already in the big box store buying groceries, a lawn mower, flowers for the garden, dog food, and toys for the kids, so why not grab those auto parts while you were there? The only time you went near that little old auto parts store in the strip mall was when you wanted a slice of pizza from the shop next to it."

Randy and Andy went to work. "Ads, mailings, calls, faxes: same things you've heard me talk about many times. The program gets repeated because it works."

Randy pointed out that when the biggest guy in the marketplace falls, it doesn't mean that the next biggest guys just move up. Sometimes they are sleeping. Or too slow to respond to the changing market. Or thinking about selling pizza because the guy next to their store seems to be busier than they are with their auto parts. "On the other hand," he said, "if you are one of the smallest in the marketplace, you are also sometimes the hungriest."

And Randy knew this banker well. He was a "land mine planter." This is a term that Randy coined when he found a banker willing to back a new owner and roll over the debt rather than take his loss now. Some bankers simply rewrite the loans with an owner in place, often giving him even more money at closing, and starting at a higher level of debt.

"Believe me," Randy said, "it happens. If the banker liquidates today and gets hosed on a loss of, say, ten million dollars, he looks terrible. If he can simply rearrange the deck chairs, maybe no one will notice the boat is sinking."

Of course the new guy the banker lends money to has to have some credibility, or no one above the banker's level will buy the deal. "Remember, however," Randy pointed out, "that the banker's bosses don't want losses in this quarter either. Not if they can be put off to the future. It's like planting a loan like a land mine. It may blow up later. But not now."

While legitimate buyers were willing to pay eighty to ninety cents on the dollar for "good inventory" with a substantial down payment, the "little guys" in the marketplace saw a chance to grab a huge market share by paying one hundred cents on the dollar—with no cash down. This amounted to millions more than the buyers with real money would pay. Also, going with the real cash money guys meant taking losses now, whereas rewriting the loan to the new "little" guys meant it could be dealt with in the future. Hey, Randy didn't control the bank's philosophy.

"Once I tried to change things," Randy recalled. "I hopped a plane to see the top man at the bank handling a particular loan. I just couldn't understand how a bank with over ten billion in loans could keep planting land mines."

The bank had dozens of lenders making hundreds of loans. The way this bank was structured, the head man had two divisions: East Coast and West Coast. Each featured an underling who answered directly to him. Randy wanted to keep working for the bank. He didn't want the "land mine" philosophy to be tagged as his company's idea. Randy knew that, in time, these land mines would go off, since people couldn't possibly pay back the loans in full. When Randy bluntly told the top guy he had major problems with the bank's method, the banker said, "Well, I don't. Because my East Coast head and my West Coast head tell me I don't." In other words: Randy, thanks for your time, but don't worry yourself about the bank's policies or their future.

"With this guy in charge, the bank soon failed completely," Randy grinned.

"Now, back to the auto parts deal," said Randy. With so many locations and so many parts inventoried and so many millions, the paperwork was very complicated. And there were lots of pieces to be fit into the puzzle. One lawyer involved had his offices in the Sears Tower building. That would be where the closing was to be held. The seller, his top managers, his lawyers, the bankers, the buyers, and their lawyers all assembled at the Sears Tower office.

Day One of the closing began with everyone in stiff shirts and ties. Suits of course. Lots to discuss. But progress was being made. After a grueling day of paperwork-related stuff, the banker making the new loan said, "Let's go to dinner." They agreed on a multi-star restaurant. About a dozen hungry people went off for a wonderful time. Wines, steaks, dessert: the banker spent over twelve hundred dollars. Hey, no problem: the deal was worth millions.

Day Two was more of a grind. The buyers were becoming aware of their leverage here. Why not squeeze a little here and there to make the terms even more favorable? The banker had already showed everyone his hole cards and there was nothing he could do about it. Yes, the buyers got picky on Day Two, hence closing went on forever. Again, late that day, it was time to eat. This time the lawyer hosting the closing would have his firm buy dinner. Another twelve-hundred-dollar meal. At another great Chicago restaurant. People were getting fat on the deal, and the closing wasn't even over.

By Day Three, Randy recollected, nerves were so frayed they were just about shot. The banker was irritable, because no one was giving him the respect he felt he deserved—but that was partially because he had already played his hand. The buyers were making everyone mad, because they were now asking for the moon and sun and stars and weren't putting up a dime. Even the lawyers were getting tired, despite the fact that they were billing out many hours on this closing. Day Three was coming to an end. Everyone needed a break. People had spent three days in close quarters, sweating in hot suits and tight shirts and ties, then sleeping on sofas in conference rooms during the many mini-meetings that took place in those three days.

The lawyer hosting the show called timeout late in the day. "Come back in one hour," he said, "and be ready to finish this mother."

When the closing resumed in the big fancy conference room, everyone was shocked to see the lawyer in charge wearing flip-flops, shorts, a loud Hawaiian shirt, and dark sunglasses. He announced that the battles were over. He was going to change the demeanor and get the closing over with so everyone could head for the beach. Impressive style. Not the first time Randy had seen this man's personality in a deal. It was just what the participants needed to change the mood. A few hours later, everyone agreed that all points had been negotiated, and they were done. Let's go eat.

As ten of the twelve guys crowded into the elevator to head for yet another of Chicago's finest restaurants, everybody but Randy joined in on the chant: now that the deal was done, Randy was going to pay. After all, he was the one getting the big commission. "They were right," Randy laughed. "I was going to make a bundle on this one. But before I could jump on the elevator, the lawyer said, 'Hold on, Randy, you can't go! You have to stay here and review the documents to make sure they're right.'"

By now the doors were being held open by ten hungry guys begging to get at their steaks and crying, "If Randy can't go, just give us his credit card, because he is definitely paying, whether he eats with us or not." Slipping the card out of his wallet, Randy wondered how hard this unintentional party-on-him would bite him.

Bottom line: "They spent the usual twelve hundred dollars, and I never ate a bite."

## "Fifty cents on the dollar"

The Abacrombie guests had heard Randy's war stories about the relationship between owners and creditors, failure and rescue. They came to recognize that, while owners are often much to blame for the failures, so, often, are others in the deals. Like bankers. Banks have historically grown themselves into failure time and again. Mark Singer's recently reissued 1985 book *Funny Money* outlines how banks parceled out loans, clipped "origination fees," and made serious bucks while the loans they sold "upstream" to the bigger institutions eventually failed and crippled some other banks, including large ones.

"If you're expanding your bank rapidly, you aren't always able to hire top people, the ones with a rich banking history," Randy pointed out. "You sometimes get cowboys willing to play Monopoly with other people's money. Pay them well, give them a fancy office, and let them make loans. It'll all work out, right?"

One office Randy visited on the West Coast was fancy and then some. Gorgeous. In fact, its loan department occupied the entire floor of a high-rise. Heading that department was a man nicknamed "Fifty Cent" long before the emergence of the rap singer by that name. "Just how did this 'Fifty Cent' get his moniker?" Randy had wanted to know.

There were offices for twelve loan officers on that beautiful marble floor. Great mahogany desks. A beautiful kitchen where some flunky would prepare lunch when the honchos were too busy making loans to go out to eat. But ... where was everybody? Only Fifty Cent and his secretary were left. The other eleven had been let go long ago, when this loan office closed. Only the head of the office remained, and his job was to clean up the losses from over seven hundred million dollars that had been loaned since they opened a few years earlier.

"It was supposed to be a money-making machine on the West Coast; instead, it turned into a drain that helped send the big bank back East down the tubes," Randy said.

The workout guys back East had taken over all of the loans. Fifty Cent had been in charge out West. He remained employed because he knew all the details of all the loans, the ones his troops had made before they were let go. Randy got to know Fifty Cent well during the time they worked out several deals together. Randy found him to be one of the nicest guys he ever met: full of integrity and willingness to work hard.

"So, tell me, Fifty Cent, how did you get that nickname?" Randy had asked one day.

"Well, the East Coast guys called me that because, when the deals were worked out, the bank only recovered fifty cents of every dollar the West Coast office had made. Only about three hundred fifty million dollars was recovered from seven hundred million dollars in loans. I've been 'Fifty Cent' ever since."

Over dinner one night, near the end of the workouts, Randy couldn't resist asking how Fifty Cent had gotten the job of heading the West Coast loan office of the big bank back East. Was he an ex-banker from somewhere else? Did he run a financial institution or a workout department before that gig? Did he hold a degree in economics or business?

"Well, it's simple," said Fifty Cent. "I played basketball in college with the guy at the bank setting up the West Coast office, and he knew I needed a job."

## Finally slowing down a little

With his youngest daughter in college, Randy said he felt it was time to slow down. He cut a deal with Andy, his young partner, selling him the stock in the company that had taken care of his family for years in the past. The sale permitted enough investments for Randy to work less and travel less.

In his twenty years on the road, Randy had gone from being the youngest guy in the room where a deal was being made to being one of the oldest. Amazingly, his wealth of successful experience didn't seem to matter much to some young bankers. At meetings where Randy would present his ideas, some young bankers dismissed his admittedly unorthodox notions without a thought.

"And just how many deals have you completed?" Randy would ask a new workout guy sitting in the room.

"What does it matter?" the banker would say. "This is how we want the deal done."

Randy shook his head. "A guy with experience in talking with over a thousand owners, who had completed over three hundred fifty transactions in forty-one different states, almost half of which were in Chapter Eleven in a District Court somewhere, didn't seem to merit much consideration by the new blood among the deal-makers. Banking hasn't changed much. The new guys want to exert their power more than they want to listen."

Randy still works a deal when his old friends call him. Andy has ably taken over the leadership and carried the flag of their company. Take a break, guests and readers. Go to **TheInnkeeperTales.com** and drop Randy an email.

# Alpha Males: Herman Digresses

"Jeez, it's still daylight," Jim said, nodding toward the nearby window. "I expected it to be dark by the time you wound down, Randy!"

Everybody in the breakfast room looked exhausted. It wasn't just the length of Randy's tale. It wasn't just his breakneck story-telling style. It was mostly the gut-busting work itself. Heart-attack-inducing work. Type A–personality work to the $n$th degree.

I couldn't help thinking about other "alpha" business guys who had talked and bragged here in the breakfast room. In the back of my head was a question about whether Randy's passion for winning deals carried over into his personal life, especially his sex life. My guess was that it had to. I've often noticed that men who are aggressive with each other in the business arena are often over-the-top sexual aggressors as well. As Herman the Host, I was definitely not about to put the question to Randy. He'd told us about *what* he had come out on top of, and *who* was another matter altogether. But I couldn't resist telling the guys some of the wilder tales other top-dog business guests had spun here in the breakfast room.

## Dangerous waters

Sean's tale sprang to my mind first. Sean was a New Yorker all the way. He worked hard all day making money and went home at six to take a nap. That's right. He slept until ten, then got up and dressed to hit the streets. He made well over two hundred thousand dollars a year back when that was the equivalent of a lot more. He lived in a low-rent apartment but had the clothes of a millionaire. So he would hail a cab and hit the clubs to go "fishing." Now, he was engaged to a wonderful woman out on Long Island where his family lived. But when he called her at eleven to say goodnight, she was off to bed. So was he, but that bed was usually someone else's.

Things got sticky, though. He fell hard for a beautiful Italian girl who wanted more than a good dance partner and lover. She had her eye on a little Mercedes convertible, actually. One that cost about ninety thousand dollars. With a car phone.

Making this car her birthday present was a huge mistake. Now, she had to park a car in New York (about six hundred dollars a month), and she could check up on Sean using her new car phone. When he finally realized he was pretty much engaged to both women, he knew he had crossed the line. But he didn't act quick enough. Both found out. Both dumped him. He couldn't find the Mercedes right away, but the payment book still had coupons.

The big bad businessman, ruthless by day, sat outside his Italian lover's apartment that night whimpering like a child, only to realize she had a man inside with her: a scared man, in fact, who could see through the peephole that Sean was upset about his girl's new friend.

Sean waited there all night Friday night. Then all day Saturday, sitting in the hallway, hoping for the door to open. The new couple had food inside, heat, and a bed. Sean had the cold hallway and a hard floor. Sunday morning he gave up. The alpha male tycoon decided that there were other fish in the sea.

Sean was one among many acquaintances and business associates who proudly or shamefacedly told me their tales. Garth was another. Garth was an exceptionally good-looking man, and extremely self-possessed. He was a killer negotiator and a low talker, the kind you had to lean in to hear better. It made women get closer so they could smell his aroma. And he could look them closer in the eye while he set the hook.

## The metrosexual

Of all the men I met in business, Garth was the most successful. Successful at scoring new lovers, that is. I'm told that all he had to do was walk through a plant, and in about an hour, some female would be mesmerized by his look. Most men had their initials monogrammed on their cuff. Garth wore his initials below his left nipple, where no one could see them under his double-breasted jacket. But he knew that monogram was there. Once a top manager in a personal grooming products company, he always had his "man purse" full of stuff. Like eyeliner, just a hint. And hair color, in case the gray crept in overnight. And an array of smells. His fragrances must have come with a guarantee. They worked.

Garth had a wife. He always had a wife. And he was always looking for a new one. When I met him, he was on number four or five.

As the tale goes, Garth once went on a business trip with a guy who wanted to spend some time with his mistress on a short cruise. Garth agreed to go along on the cruise to cover for the man by making his wife believe the trip was all about business. While his friend spent four days in a cabin with his sleepover buddy, Garth played blackjack in the casino on board. He played with the same dealer for four days. Days and nights. I don't know if he won any money on the cruise, but he did ask the dealer to marry him. She said yes. When the cruise ship docked, Garth called his then-current wife to say he wouldn't be coming home. He had been dealt a new hand.

## Love or money

Type A men need conquest, need to conquer in order to feel good. But the feeling fades, so they have to conquer again to get the same high. Rob was a case in point. He was insatiable. He went through several women a week, old, young, and in between. He was one of the most successful business people I met, but his life was a wreck. He was utterly consumed by the drive to make money and make love. I don't know which was more important to him. I do know his obsessions won and lost him a fortune.

If Rob couldn't pick up a date, he'd find willing partners in topless bars or enlist call-girl services. Some weeks he spent five thousand dollars on hookers alone. To Rob, sex felt like conquering even if he paid for it. But he didn't often have to pay for it. He was incredibly good at picking up women. Unfortunately, sex got in the way of doing business, because he would often try harder to make a deal with a secretary than to complete a deal with an owner.

## Therapy

Guests love to tell tales on their friends. One guest, who made me promise not to use his name if and when I retold his story, had the following story to regale us with.

"We were business buddies. Not friends. I needed to have contact with him for business reasons, so I told him his other stuff was starting to interfere. He said I was right. He needed help, and he went to get it.

"At about 5:00 PM, right after his first therapy session, he called me to say he was on the way to recovery. Even in that first session, he realized that he saw women only as sex objects. He didn't respect them as people. He was relieved to know he could change.

"At 10:00 PM that same night, he called again. He told me he had gone to a clothing store in the strip mall to get a new shirt, and, well, he started to flirt with the salesgirl. He admitted to her that he had a sexual problem, always wanting more and more women. He told her it might seem depraved of him to come right out and say that he wanted to fuck her, but he didn't care; he just couldn't help himself. Apparently she couldn't help herself, either. It seemed that all the sex talk had made her horny, and the depraved part gave her an idea. Why not show the world just how much they both loved sex? She fucked him right there on the sofa in the store window."

"Defies logic, doesn't it, how brilliant, successful guys can totally lose their perspective in their drive for sex," Enzo observed.

## Rotten tuna

Reclaiming the breakfast podium, I told the guests about one guy who loved to take a "friend" on the road with him. It gets so lonely at night after a hard day of making money, right? On this particular trip, his traveling lady got to the hotel before he did. He had called the hotel to say she would arrive before him, so they gave her a key and she went to the room. But while waiting she got hungry. A tuna sandwich would be nice, she thought, so she dialed room service. But when the kitchen called the front desk to okay the order, the front desk realized that no one had authorized the woman to order food; she was only approved to enter the room. So the front desk clerk called the guy's house to see if it was permissible for his "wife" to order room service. The guy's real wife answered the phone. When the clerk said, "Is it okay for Mrs. So-and-so to order room service?" the real wife got a little crazy. I mean, she knew she wasn't in the room. Or maybe she just didn't like tuna.

When he arrived and heard about the mishap, the business traveler gave the clerk two hundred dollars to call his real wife and say it was a mistake: the front desk had gotten the wrong room number, and no one was staying in her husband's room but her husband.

## Sales and sleaze

A tale told by a company owner who stayed at the Abacrombie a while back amply illustrated one business principle: sex sells. I decided to pass it along to this crop of guests.

A company that sold automotive products to dealerships, very good products with a great reputation, suddenly found that its sales in one region had stopped. Not just dwindled: stopped. The owner sent the sales manager out to investigate why they were losing account after account. Was someone else simply giving their products away? Did someone invent a better mousetrap? Maybe another company's ad campaign was better than their marketing?

Nah. The truth was that the competition had hired a new sales force of particularly friendly women. So friendly that with each order the used car manager received some very personal services which he alone could enjoy. A manager who had been so "served" didn't care what your company did with price or delivery time, didn't even care if the products worked; your company wasn't offering what he was getting from the competition's sales force.

Tony looked disgusted. "Listen," he growled. "Everybody knows that any woman can 'cold call' a location and get into the manager's office faster than a man. But I guarantee you not many of them provide sex to close the deal."

"But when they do, the sales go through the roof," I laughed. "Or at least that's what I've heard here at the breakfast table. Here's another example."

I recounted my friend Larry's story about how sex had built sales volumes into the tens of millions of dollars range very quickly. Back when "big box" stores were first developed, they moved enormous amounts of home goods and could take an upstart company into huge sales rather quickly, due to high volumes. So how do they get the edge?

Larry had the answer. When the buyers came in for the pitch, Larry's female assistants all had on trench coats and large black-rimmed glasses. All wore their hair pinned up in a tight bun. Each product line and sample had a different assistant to show it. After the presentation was over and prices had been projected on the overhead screen, Larry asked for orders. To help the prospective buyers make up their minds, he had the assistants take off their trench coats, revealing that underneath they had on nothing but skimpy teddies. While the buyers admired the teddies, the assistants let down their hair from the bun and lost the glasses. As the company CEO again asked for the buyers' orders, he added that, for each product shown, the assistant would accompany the buyer to his hotel at no additional cost. This approach resulted in ninety million dollars in sales in one year.

"Talk about sleazy," muttered Rick.

"Sleazy, yes. But how proud of this sales technique was the owner? He hung a shadow box with a teddy in it on his office wall to remind buyers on future visits what might come with next year's order."

However, while the "teddy technique" resulted in ninety million dollars in sales, it also helped bankrupt the company. Seems the sales to big box stores came with a returns feature that wasn't expected to materialize. Let's call it "inventory on wheels." The buyers weren't afraid to place large orders because they knew that if the merchandise didn't sell, it would be shipped back to the company. How much, you say? About twenty million dollars' worth.

A warehouse had to be rented to hold all the stuff coming back. And the bank had already loaned money on the shipped orders accounts receivable. But now instead of money, all Larry had was merchandise. Too bad for him the bank wanted money instead of a visit from the girls.

## A pox on both his houses

By now I was rolling full-steam ahead and launched into another story. "Lots of guys who get rich buy a new house before selling the old one." I had a tale to tell about one guy who was sorry he did that.

Seems that while away on a particular deal, this guy spent a lot of time alone in a very remote town. "Had only one titty bar," in his words. Nevertheless, he fell into heavy lust with a lady who had also ended up in that remote town. He used her in many ways, and she used him too. Why shouldn't he enjoy her and her many ways back home where he lived? He owned a big empty extra house. And she wanted to escape the remote town. So she packed her bag when the deal was done and headed to the big city to live in her rich friend's big old empty house. He was delighted with the plan. He could just pop over from his new house and spend some quality time with his new friend from the bar.

Of course, the plan didn't work. Although his wife had moved all the furniture from the old house to the new house, she had left many trunks full of her seasonal clothes in the attic of the old house. And the seasons were now changing.

His wife went over to the old house to fetch some cashmere sweaters stored in the attic. Inside the old house was a very sexy lady lounging about without a care.

"Who are you?" said the wife, "and what are you doing here?"

The sexy lounging lady replied that she was the girlfriend of the guy who owned the house. She was staying here with him.

226 THE INNKEEPER TALES

Within hours, all the locks had been changed in both the old house and the new house. When the guy came home, he couldn't get into either one. He lost both houses in the divorce, and he lost his new play-friend when she had to stay in a motel that reminded her of the motel in the remote town. She decided she might as well just head back up there, where she could make a thousand dollars a week showing her body to a whole lot of men, not just him.

# Fantasy Baseball: Jeff's Tale

Jeff had come down to the breakfast room wearing his team shirt and his team hat. Though the hat changed its angle and direction from time to time, it never left Jeff's head. The logo was for a type of car that is sold today, but since it was Jeff who had given that name to the team, the logo really stood for Jeff's team, not the car. How did Jeff come to own a team?

I don't know how many of the guests marooned at Abacrombie's had ever wondered about team ownership and team owners, but, as a rabid fan of baseball myself, I've thought about them for years.

I tend to think we ("we" meaning fans, of course) all love to hate the owners—fat cats whose grandparents founded breweries and car dealerships, or lawyers who seem to get rich from someone else's ills. These people didn't start a little business and grow it to become a major league team; they simply forked over a check and became the boss. You can buy a piece of baseball memorabilia and feel closer to your heroes than these kinds of owners are; they just happened to have enough money to buy the whole team and call the shots. Surely (in my own thinking), anybody who has followed baseball for years must know a hell of a lot more than the asshole in charge. What does winning a lawsuit, for example, have to do with running a baseball team? I often questioned how it was that none of the individual victims of asbestosis ever got enough money to own a team, but the guy who filed the lawsuit got hundreds of the victims' court-awarded millions.

But I digress. Again. Sorry. Let Jeff tell his tale.

## Sacred ground

Watching baseball is like a religion to Jeff. When he was a kid, his mother took him to church every Sunday to instill in him a love of God and all that is holy. Jeff's father, on the other hand, took him to Memorial Stadium where he worshiped living gods.

In a late inning of a game he attended when he was quite young, the Yankees, passionately hated by Jeff's father, were coming to bat. When Number Seven stepped up to the plate, Jeff's father rose to his feet, and so did everybody else in the stands. He pulled little Jeff to an erect position and announced, "This will be the last time you'll ever see Mickey Mantle bat in person. This is his last year." Jeff was puzzled. All these fans were cheering for the other team? No, Jeff's father explained, they were showing respect and regard for the many accomplishments of a superstar, no matter that he was in the enemy camp.

A young boy can learn an immense amount about life at a baseball game. (Jeff and I saw eye-to-eye on that.) Rules are the sacrosanct center of baseball's universe. Dimensions of the bases are set in stone. Foul poles dictate the boundaries. Umpires control the game, calling balls and strikes. You have a team—this is not golf—and you back up your teammates. The manager decides who will play and bat in what order, and who will pitch. Baseball teaches you that there is order to the universe.

There is a winner and a loser in every game, but there are many games in a season. As in everyday life, you can't win them all. And even if you lose a few in a row, there are more games to come. If the season ends and you are not world champions, there's always next year.

Jeff would have given anything to own a team or be the manager. The manager is the boss. The manager rules the players, even though he probably can't pitch, hit, or run the bases. To be the manager, Jeff felt, would be Heaven on Earth. Jeff was Catholic, but he knew he would never be the Pope. He was a religious fanatic about baseball, but he could never own a team. Or could he?

## A field of dreams

With Fantasy Baseball, all things are possible. For the sake of the other breakfasters, Jeff explained what "Fantasy Baseball" is. The term describes a game whereby fans get a number of people together to form a "league." The league conducts a draft at the beginning of the season and holds an auction in which each member organizes a team of real major league players.

Eager to get my two cents' worth in, I added that the original term was "Rotisserie League Baseball," after a book from the early eighties about a game invented by a group of men over dinner at New York's Rotisserie Restaurant.

## Not about cooking chicken

In the winter months in early 1985, a friend of Jeff's called to invite him to a meeting of several others who wanted to discuss Rotisserie Baseball. They were all too old to play real baseball any more, but they loved the game and wanted to be more involved than mere spectators. At the friend's apartment, a hockey game was showing on the TV screen in the background, but the talk was of a new book Jeff's friend had brought along for all to read.

"Get this book," he urged. "Follow these rules. And we can all own our own baseball team. I'm talking about a team made up of real major league players and managed by you and me, the smartest guys in baseball. We'll compete with other teams, using the daily statistics of real players. Forget where the Indians, Royals, or Dodgers finish. We'll each have our own team to control. And no matter who wins the 'other baseball'—known to most people as the Major Leagues— 'real baseball' will be our own teams in the Rotisserie world."

Jeff was speaking a mile a minute at this point. Even the non-baseball fans were amazed by Jeff's enthusiasm for a game that seemed so very real to Jeff. And it *was* real: as real as going to work, or buying a car, or watching a movie. You really did own a team— with real players who went out onto real fields in real ballparks and played real games, which then translated into your team's individual statistics and gave your team a real place in the Rotisserie standings. This arrangement not only made you root for your home team; it also made you a genuine fan of every team in the major leagues. Your guys played in Toronto, and Detroit, and Oakland. They went on the disabled list, and you lost them. They got sent to the minors, and you had to replace them. You'd better know who some dumbfuck shortstop from Triple A was, because the big team just moved your guy to the pine and inserted that dumbfuck.

"Where did you get the statistics?" somebody in the breakfast room wanted to know.

"In the old days, the local Sunday papers published the stats of all pitchers and batters," Jeff replied. "But the real bible was *USA Today*."

Tuesday of each week brought *USA Today's* American League Statistics page. Crunch some numbers—home runs, RBIs, pitching, catching, and so on—and you have eight lists of rankings for each person's team in your league. Collate those stats into one number, and you had the standings for your league. Accumulate the stats weekly, and you had a season going for you, all based on what real players did in real games.

"Your league is real just like the one the Orioles play in. And you can cut that stinking pitcher with the high ERA, even though the major league manager still trots him out there each week killing the Birds," Jeff said.

Nowadays, Jeff told us, there are dozens of Fantasy Baseball books out there, but Jeff's league never ventures away from the original set of rules or the original eight categories.

"Tradition. Like that other baseball."

## The Word according to Jeff

Jeff said he didn't want to bore his listeners with too many details, but he thought he should explain a bit about how his league worked. Each owner put up $260 to start, which bought him 260 units to buy players. "You had to field a complete team with players and pitchers at each position and stay within the budget. Misspend and you would suffer the consequences. Spend wisely and you might succeed. You had to scout those players. Dig up data, and beat the other guys."

Suddenly couch potatoes were on the move, Jeff told us gleefully, doing actual research in books and magazines to find out all the details, even the most seemingly insignificant, on a player they might draft.

## First draft

A few weeks after the opening meeting of Jeff's league, the first draft took place at someone's office. The room had no windows, and everybody smoked. (It was 1985, remember?) Within minutes, the place was in a fog. A smoke fog and an information fog. You had to know who just went, and for how many units; you had to know who was left, because you still needed a second baseman who might hit a few homers.

This first draft was a momentous occasion, although those first-time people who each "owned" a team didn't know it. To make each member's team feel more like his own, one guy brought in baseball cards from Topps, the most popular brand. As an owner landed a player, the guy would toss him that player's current card from the freshly opened box. The next day, one owner had a wall laid out like a baseball diamond with each card mounted at the appropriate position.

Enzo wanted to know what was so momentous.

"Well, for one thing, one owner was a woman," Jeff answered. "See, these guys were liberal enough in 1985 to know women were as smart as men. Sherrie finished second in the first year and proved to them she wasn't just 'as smart,' but probably smarter."

## Baseball was changed forever

More momentous was the way the participants watched baseball: from that day on, it was never the same. You no longer cared if the home team won or lost on the grass-and-dirt playing field. It was only important that your Rotisserie League pitcher threw a shutout. Or that your player hit a grand slam. Your joy and despair didn't depend on the outcome of the home team's efforts on the physical field.

In the early days, Jeff said, you waited two weeks to know where you stood. Two weeks equaled a "period." At the end of a period, each owner compiled his (or her!) team's numbers and sent them in to a secretary of the league, who then published the standings. There was a league commissioner as well. You could trade players, release players, and pick up players, just as in the major leagues. Those Tuesday *USA Today* stats were solid gold.

Pretty soon, *USA Today* caught on to Fantasy Baseball and began giving daily boxes, far more detailed than the regular box scores that appeared in the local papers. And information on each team in the Big Leagues. Perhaps a comment about a pitcher going south with a sore arm. Or a hitter with the flu. Stuff you didn't see anywhere else. Jeff wondered how many papers were sold just because of Fantasy Baseball. While sports commentators started to remark about the geeks who were doing "Rotisserie," and players made crude remarks to fans who taunted them for bad outings affecting an owner's fantasy team, the plain truth was that Fantasy Baseball was having an enormous impact on the baseball world.

Judging from the multitude of magazines, tout sheets, and books on strategy that were emerging, more and more people were becoming Fantasy disciples. And then came the Internet. Instant access to stats. Sweet mother of all orgasms! You could know instantly who did what. You could find out where you stood every day, not every two weeks.

"Today," Jeff said, "you can find out your team's standing after every at-bat. There are software programs in place to see pitch by pitch what's happening, and the stats are instantly recalculated to show you where you stand, even during the games."

As a kid, Jeff reminisced, he knew batting averages and homer totals. He knew who had the best ERA. He could tell you who was hot and who was cold.

"On my home team, that is. But today I can spout off the most inane material on almost six hundred ball players. I have to be able to do that if I want a chance to win my league. And so can thousands of other team owners in thousands of other Rotisserie leagues."

"All hail to the originators there at the Rotisserie Restaurant. May they find their rightful place one day in the Hall of Fame in Cooperstown," Tuck intoned.

Jeff shot Tuck a quick look to see if he was being sarcastic, but Tuck was definitely not one of the breakfasters who, as non-fans, were beginning to get a glazed look in their eyes.

## What to do about winter?

Heartened, Jeff went on. When winter seemed cold and dull, and baseball was a distant wish, the league invented a way to make winter warmer. Owners could take a trip somewhere together and hold a winter draft for fun. Just the practice of saying the names, knowing they owned a team, would help participants get through those bleak, gameless winter months.

"You could have your winter team, and it would never change during the year. You would put that sheet of paper away and see how that group did at the end of the season," continued Jeff. "You couldn't make changes. This was not to be confused with the team you drafted in April; this was just a practice team."

Everybody thought the plan sounded great. Where should they go? To the Baseball Hall of Fame, obviously.

For that first winter venture, Jeff rented an unimaginably long RV in which eight guys set out for Cooperstown on a Friday afternoon. The RV was huge. And plush. And drove like a dream. Jeff brought the portable TV he had just given his daughter for Christmas, and one of the other owners brought a stash of porno. Crank it up! Someone plugged in the set as soon as they were on the highway, and the men gathered around the screen to see someone else's daughters do things to men they hoped their daughters wouldn't.

I noticed that the breakfasters who didn't give a damn about baseball, fantasy or otherwise, seemed to be perking up.

"But the screen was black," Jeff told them, "and smoke started coming out of the top of the television. Holy cow, the porno was cooking the TV!"

Actually the current had been set up wrong, hence the TV didn't work; the guys could only imagine what those women were doing on the darkened screen. However, they were philosophical about it. Let's talk some baseball, man.

Just past Scranton on the interstate, the RV began losing power. Soon it was clear that the thing couldn't go any farther. The vehicle had just crept past a ramp where cars were coming onto the highway. It seemed a good time and place to try reverse. Hey, in reverse, the RV could actually move! They began backing up onto the long, steep on-ramp.

At the top of the ramp was a service station that surely could help them out. No chance. But the station guy knew where a man lived that did work on RVs. He was two miles away, up the side of the mountain. Up that little two-lane road there. Two fucking miles up the side of the mountain. "Back 'er up, let's go!" was the battle cry.

One guy in the league was named Pope. His team was called "The Vaticans." The other league owners referred to him as "the hub," since all things center around the Pope. Pope climbed out and put himself in charge of the three guys clearing traffic behind the RV as it inched its way backwards up the mountain. There were lookouts at the back window of this forty-some-foot rig, and the driver cleared a path through the occupants so he could see all the way out the back window, spotting Pope as he was walking away from the RV facing oncoming traffic. Pope walked slowly, and the driver backed the big bus up the hill slowly. Two very slow miles.

When the driveway they searched for was in sight, they pulled in backwards as if all was normal. A man came out of his garage, put a mechanic's creeper on the ground, and disappeared under the RV. The baseball geeks stood around wondering if, between them, they had the several thousand dollars this guy would surely charge to fix it. After a few minutes, the man slid back out into daylight. Said he would send his wife to town for a part. It would take about half an hour.

The Fantasy Leaguers paced around. Man, they were in trouble now. But very shortly the guy's wife returned. Back on the creeper: the mechanic disappeared under the vehicle again. When he emerged, he said, "Start it up. Try going forward."

It worked. Jeff said the guys were now guessing a price tag in the hundreds. Between them, they could do that. They hadn't gotten to Cooperstown yet, so they still had some cash.

"That will be thirty-two dollars," the guy said.

"We could have kissed him. Stop looking, Diogenes—we had found an honest man!"

## The league must have a guardian angel

Onward Christian Soldiers. When they got to the place on the interstate where you had to leave the highway and take a two-lane winding road, they noticed they had left something else behind besides the interstate. Light. They had no lights. Zip. Nada. No headlights at all. And it was getting dark. Real dark. Oh, they got out of the RV and pulled on wires and tapped on connections and checked fuses and twisted the bulbs, but no lights came on. Start creeping up the road, boys, and keep your eyes peeled for oncoming traffic. Wonder how far it is to civilization.

After a few miles in the dark, they spotted a gas station. Help at last. But here was another station with no help. Whatever happened to "service stations"? They did get a flashlight though. And what the heck, why not peek under the hood again to see if they could find the problem? Unfortunately, no one really knew what they were looking at. Slam went the hood. Bang went the driver's door as they climbed back inside.

And let there be light! The headlights came back on!

"Do not question why God makes these things happen; just go with the flow," said Jeff. And that's what the RV did.

At Cooperstown they found a peaceful cathedral honoring their religion. The town was winter-quiet; echoes of their heroes, all the greats, resounded everywhere. And the next day, with snow falling gently on the RV, they huddled around the small kitchen area and held the "Hall of Fame Draft."

"And no matter where we are, every winter since then we've gotten together to draft a winter team. And that team is always called our Hall of Fame Team!"

"How important to you guys is winning?" I asked. "Is it about the money?"

"Nah, half the money is used for parties during the season, and the other half is split among the top four teams. No one cares about the money."

## Ta-dah!

After the first year there was a party, the money was split, and everybody went home. The winner got the glory, but after he spent the money, he had nothing else to show for it. The winner in the second year fixed that. He took the winnings and had a trophy made.

"Not the six-inch trophy you won in Little League. No sir. He had a trophy made that would make your dining room table look small, Herman. It's over a foot square at the base, then it rises up in a tower of wood with a great figure on top telling the world that you are the fucking winner, man. This is a monument to the fact that you kicked everyone else's ass."

He added that since the guy who paid for that baby was named Culler, it became known as the CULLER CUP. The guy even had side plaques made for the wood towers which were engraved with the name of the winner from the first year and Culler's name as the year-two winner. Wives came to the first two awards ceremonies, but after they saw how wacky their husbands were over this monument to wasted prize winnings, they never came again. And most wives begged their husbands not to win, thus sparing them from having that monstrous trophy come into their homes.

Jeff's name is on the cup once. Commemorating just one magical season when he won. There are nineteen other names marking the years Jeff has lost. But in Fantasy Baseball, there's hope every spring.

# The Homebuilder: Jim's Tale

The next guest to tell his story was Jim. Jim wasn't a tall man, but he was built like Popeye—he had lifted weights all his life, and, born a hundred years too late, he liked to hunt and fish for his dinner.

This predilection would have given Jim stories to entertain us till spring, like the time he shot a deer with a bow and arrow, and it ran out of the woods across from his house and ended up keeling over at the McDonald's drive-in window—right in front of the cop car that had just been served. Dressed in his camouflage, Jim just nodded at the officers inside their car and dragged his kill back into the woods. But outdoor adventure was not to be the dominant theme of Jimmy's tale.

## Jim gets hooked

Although he had a shirt-and-tie job, Jim loved to work with his hands. He thought he might like fixing up some real estate. His wife's best friend, Jane, was in the real estate business, so he asked her to show him some fixer-uppers.

Jane showed him a house that caught Jim's interest. The asking price was forty-five thousand dollars. Jim instantly said he would take it. It was a dump. It had been over thirty years since anyone had put a paint brush to the place. The kitchen could have been in a museum for ancient appliances, except that the filth would have turned museum visitors away.

"I loved it," Jim grinned. "I figured I'd renovate that puppy and make a fortune."

There was so much to do he didn't know where to start. The attic, he decided. Work his way down from the top. But hurry, because the roof was leaking badly. Probably the best thing about this mess was the furniture Jim found in the attic. An old parlor set from the late 1800s, a mirror and a chair. The attic itself, as well as the rest of the house, was a disaster.

Windows were leaky, and the furnace was shot; there was no hot water, and the electricity sometimes made a sizzling sound when somebody hit a light switch. Fifteen thousand dollars later, the house had heat, new cabinets in the kitchen, a usable bathroom, and replacement windows. The house sold for a ten-thousand-dollar profit and an education in what not to buy. Along the way, Jim spent some of the profit on the start of his new tool collection. Who knew what a Sawzall was until then?

## "Welcome to your new home"

Though Jim's first semi-disastrous adventure in real estate didn't scare him, the next project should have. Jim wanted to buy ground to build a new house, and he wanted to buy it in a high-roller area where homes went for over half a million, easy. He found two acres that would cost about one hundred fifty thousand. He considered taking the deal. Then Jane called.

"Hold on, Jim, we can buy over two acres with a four-bedroom house and barn for less than one hundred seventy-five."

Amazingly, the property was right in the middle of Desireville. He told Jane to secure the house quickly. When Jim and his wife pulled up in the driveway, Jane was waiting for him.

"Sorry, guys, this place is not fit to live in."

The property had been the center part of a plant nursery which had been in operation for half a century. The owners had sold off land over the years to make ends meet, and the little farmhouse sat on the last two-and-a-quarter acres left. For five years after his wife's death, the owner had lain dying in one small room. No one tended to the nursery. Shrubs and trees and bushes left in planter pots had rooted through the bottoms of the containers and grown so tall the two acres were more like a jungle than a nursery. Disturbing as this tangled forest was, nothing prepared Jim and his wife for what they would find at the house.

Wandering outside was a three-year-old wearing a t-shirt and no pants. The old woman caring for the child was lying in the kitchen.

Yes, as in the words of that famous commercial for electronic "Help" necklaces, she had fallen and couldn't get up. The dogs running around hadn't always bothered going outside to take care of business. Stench, trash, and the creepy aura of the owner's recent death greeted Jim when he went inside.

"Whew, we gotta knock this sucker down and start over," Jim told himself.

"Remember now," Jim pointed out, "the ground was on the 'Ridge,' the area I most desired. And over two acres for just a little more than I'd be paying for a smaller lot not far away. This place had a house and several outbuildings, too."

Jim's wife was a gamer. She said "Go for it." Jim's girls took one look and said they would never set foot in such a place. "Oh ye of little faith!" Jim told Jane to write the contract. She was flabbergasted.

"How bad was it?" I wanted to know details. A building as old as the Abacrombie had probably gone through some pretty bad days itself.

"Well, to give you an idea," Jim said, "before anyone could live there, my wife and I endured two gut-busting years tearing out walls, rearranging well equipment, pouring concrete patios, and putting in a new kitchen, floors, and bathrooms. During that time, we took thirteen commercial-size dumpsters full of trash and debris off the property."

In addition, Jim threw away six refrigerators that used to house products for the nursery; these appliances had turned to blocks of ice with ancient product frozen inside, like glaciers hiding prehistoric bones. And it took months to dismantle a fourteen-foot-wide, sixty-foot-long house trailer, overgrown by trees, which had formerly been used by the nursery caretaker.

One brand-new John Deere lawn tractor gradually gave up its life over the twenty-four-month period when Jim hit every rock, tree stump, and hidden treasure with the blades swirling as fast as they could go. His wife always knew where he was on the property, because she could hear the loud "clang" as the blade tried to cut into another stone.

In time, a revitalized house emerged from the jungle and junk, now containing three bedrooms where there had been four tiny ones. Outbuildings demanded attention: a small edifice called the "milk barn," where milk used to be stored to keep it cold, and a rather large barn on the back of the property. The barn roof was bad, one wall was caving in on the side, and there were several rooms full of old nursery business records and chemicals from the busier days. One freezer remained plugged in there, and in it was a frozen block with God knows what inside. One day the smell from the barn grew too much to bear. Someone had turned off the freezer, allowing the glacier to thaw. Jim ventured in to turn the freezer back on. A few days later, the smell was once again buried in a block of ice.

After two years of hard labor, Jim and his wife moved into the house. And why not? There were now hand-painted sinks and a Jacuzzi tub in the bathroom. Beautiful brass fixtures at the sinks. Custom cabinets in the newly expanded kitchen. Jim proved to his daughters that old was not always bad. But "old" took a lot of work to look this good.

"My daughters eventually became believers," Jim said.

The barn became Jim's long-term project.

"How long?" I wanted to know.

"Ten years."

Groans could be heard around the table. "You going to tell us about each one of those years, Jim?" somebody murmured.

Jim obligingly summarized instead. A new roof, rebuilt outer walls, new wood siding all over, a workshop with hanging chandeliers, and a beautiful stained-glass window bought at auction from a Vanderbilt mansion. Jim's wife calls the added-on library and playroom area "the treehouse that every boy wants." The kids, by the way, the ones who vowed never to set foot on the property, bring their friends over all the time.

## One of the original Reister houses

Next, Jim and his wife bought a property in a small town just north and west of Baltimore. The town had been founded in the late 1700s. John Reister had built a hotel/tavern/restaurant as a rest stop for people traveling from Maryland to Pennsylvania. This particular house had belonged to one of John Reister's sons, suggesting that it was among the first built in the area.

When the house was first erected, over 230 years ago, it was just a small log cabin, little more than a huge kitchen hearth and a room to sleep in. The hearth survived to the present day, and so did the crane that held the food bucket. Its brick walls house built-in ovens.

"That hearth probably baked bread and rolls like you serve here at Abacrombie," Jim observed. (My inn is only a few decades "younger" than the one Jim was speaking of.)

Over time, the house was expanded so that by the 1850s it held three rooms downstairs and three on a second floor. Records indicate that one Reister family member, born in the house, lived there her entire life until her death at age ninety.

"Some people say she still walks the upper floor, but I have yet to see her," Jim said.

Houses of such antiquity have special problems resulting from their original construction. When a house was built back then, Jim explained, a stone foundation left a space underneath the dwelling to allow air to flow under wood floors. That way, the floors stayed drier than if they were just lying on the dirt. After the stone foundation was set in place, trees would be cut down and placed across the foundation. They would over-hang the stone foundation by a foot or so. Then floors and walls were constructed on top of them.

As the decades went by, the ends of the trees would rot off from being exposed outside the foundation. As a result, the outside walls would droop slowly, bending the floors inside lower around the edges. Naturally, the ceilings droop when the walls droop, and the second floor bows down. Windows and doors shift as well.

"Inside a house this old, nothing is ever level," said Jim.

"Bummer!" Tuck had apparently never had much experience with old buildings.

"Nah," Jim replied. "It takes a long time to occur. You never notice it while you're living there. But the cumulative effects of over two hundred years of drooping is fascinating. A house like that seems almost like an A-frame when you look at it from the outside."

In 1970, a new thirty-by-fifty-foot barn-style addition had been affixed to the back of the original structure. It had a fourteen-foot ceiling and a small loft area where some former owners had slept on two "Murphy" style beds that folded down from the walls. Not totally forsaking all modern conveniences, Jim and his wife added a bathroom with a Jacuzzi tub—even though, for some reason, they disconnected the modern furnace and heated the place with wood stoves.

"Well," I put in, "remember somebody once said that consistency is the hobgoblin of little minds. Maybe Ralph Waldo Emerson ..." I love to astonish my guests.

Jim ended his tale: "Today, my wife runs a business from that building."

## Jane finds another dream home

At the outset of Jim's next real estate venture, Jim didn't get first crack at Jane's new listing. She was considering the place for herself. It had three bedrooms and stood on one acre left by a dying uncle to his niece, who lived out of town.

The heir asked the attorney for the estate about its condition, knowing the place had been occupied only by an invalid relative for many years. She was right to worry. It was a mini-disaster. The roof had leaked for so long that the ceilings on the second floor had collapsed, which apparently made little difference to her uncle, who had slept downstairs. The niece wanted to know the value of the land. "About one hundred thousand dollars an acre," the attorney estimated.

"Fine," she said, "get me the hundred thousand."

Jane decided not to buy the house for herself and instead gave Jim first crack at it. Without hesitation, Jim said yes.

Jim cleaned up the mess and repaired the roof and ceilings. Put in a new kitchen and new wiring. Renovated the bathroom. Installed a new well and septic system. Some sweaty work, a few thousand extra dollars, and the mess became a property he could rent for over a thousand bucks a month or sell for twice what he had put into in the place.

"Of course, my wife and I didn't sell."

## The old mill town property

By now, Jim had built up a significant workshop of tools, "for a white-collar guy, anyway," he laughed. He went to auctions frequently and bought not just saws and hammers and drills, but professional-grade power tools at a fraction of what home improvement or big box stores get for new ones.

When Jim wasn't working his professional job, working alone on the houses was better than paying a therapist. Time to think about life and get a workout too.

Jim's next project partnered him with "Em," short for Emily, one of his daughters-by-marriage. Em was creative and, in Jim's words, "kind of funky" in her style. Eclectic. Not a female version of the white shirt, stiff tie, pocket-protector guy Jim had grown up as. Jim adored her from the get-go. And she had game, like her mother, so when Jim suggested they buy a property together, Em was right there with him.

Em needed a house, something she could get equity started in, rather than continuing to pay rent. She liked the small town of Ellicott City, a mill town over a hundred fifty years old, with quaint shops on the hilly main street running through the village. Em and Jim bought half a duplex on a corner near the top of the hill.

The renovation plan was for Em to rent the first floor out to a business tenant, while she would live in a second-floor apartment, which she and Jim would fix up. Upstairs were four rooms: a kitchen in the back, then a bathroom, next the bedroom, and then a large living room at the front of the building. Above that was an attic, nice but nothing special.

"A guerilla carpenter, that's me," Jim told us. "I attack something full force. I never pay any attention to what damage it may do me!"

Why not lose a ceiling in the living room and take advantage of the pitched roof design to make the new ceiling cathedral-style, rising to a level of fifteen feet in the center? Cool. The wide-plank oak, over one hundred fifty years old, which had been the floor of the attic over the living room, became side walls downstairs: beautiful.

The attic above the rest of the rooms was converted into a storage loft, approached by a small staircase hidden in a closet. Jim and Em ripped plaster walls to expose the wooden frame walls within. They left the old wood exposed. A tin ceiling went into the kitchen, along with new tile floors. Amateur-tile-mason Jim loved playing with his new power tile cutter. He and Em would try anything. How wrong could they go?

The bathroom got the full treatment. New fixtures and a bathtub from one hundred years ago, "with those cool old feet." A circular rod overhead held the antique shower system. Some orange paint here and there, and the place was "all Em. Years later, she still lives there," Jim said.

"I once had an old place," Tim put in. "Upkeep cost a fortune. And it was impossible to heat till I put in vinyl replacement windows."

"Ah, the windows."

We settled back, knowing Jim was off and running again.

"Sixteen rotting frames. I put vinyl-clad windows in every one of them."

But the old mill town had one of those historical-architecture committees that insist on everything being or looking completely authentic. No, no, no, those replacement windows will never do! Jim and Em got a citation from the committee. The windows had to go. In their place had to be wooden replacements.

About one hundred feet from the property, clearly visible from one of Em's windows, stood a house in the middle of the block with the exact same windows that Jim had just installed. No, no, no, said the committee: the corner building was more prominent and could be seen more readily, and therefore it needed to be more historically correct. Almost seven thousand dollars later, custom-made, wood-framed windows were installed after the brand-new vinyl covered windows were removed.

"Em and I made sure we didn't rattle the committee any more after that," Jim chuckled.

## "This is the last one"

Along the "Ridge" where Jim lived, many of the old frame houses were being replaced by larger brick homes as time passed. One old house had been falling down little by little over the years. Weather had caved in what had served as an old garage, too, and it stayed that way until the owner died.

This property included one and three-quarters acres of beautiful ground backing up to a golf course. It was amazing that the place had not already been demolished by somebody whose imagination was limited.

"But me, I'm a visionary!" Jim said. "I saw the wonderful lot where everybody else just saw the crumbling house. You can always renovate a house."

Jim drove by a thousand times and wondered if he should write the owner a letter: why not sell the house to Jim and live there as long as he liked; later, Jim could renovate. The guy died before the letter was written. The day the real estate agent listed the property, Jim rode by and pulled into the driveway.

"Jane," Jim shouted into his cell phone, "the house we want is for sale. Get over here quick and write a contract!"

Although the sign had been up for only three hours, another prospective buyer had already made an offer of a figure close to the asking price. Before the ink was dry on contract number one, Jane delivered number two, which read "full price, all cash, no contingencies, and close in a week." Number two won, and Jim had another house to fix. This was to be his swan song.

Again the place started out a disaster.

"Picture this," Jim regaled us with horror-story gusto. "There was an ancient fuse box with six fuses in the basement of the two-story house. That meant two circuits for each level. Apparently, at some point in history, the two fuse circuits for the second story quit working. So the owner plugged in one of those bright orange extensive cords on the first floor and threw it out a window. Then he put the bright orange cord through an upstairs window. And then he plugged in one of those plug extensions that hold several wires at once. Not a modern power bar, mind you, with a circuit breaker, oh no, just a plug-in with about four openings. And extension cords went from room to room including the bathroom. All the power on that level was fed through his bright orange extension cord from below."

Jim didn't know how many years the old guy had lived with that system, but he had been there over sixty years total.

"So you rewired the place."

"No. *I* didn't. Had to admit that was a job for a real electrician. As for the plumbing, let's just say it all had to go. And I hauled in a real plumber."

By now Jim was becoming better at his carpentry skills and ever more willing to try new things, like taking out the back wall of the house because the kitchen was too small and building a thirty-by-fourteen-foot room for a family area. With a working gas fireplace.

"Think maybe you were reading too many *House Beautiful* magazines?" I needled.

"My wife sure thought so," Jim laughed. Then he got that house-beautiful, wishful-thinking look in his eye again. "I put sixteen windows in the new addition. Sure wish I could've used those windows I took out of the other house and threw away." He brightened. "You should see the porch I added onto the front—the old-fashioned kind with a low wall and a big porch swing!"

But upstairs was where Jim pulled out all the stops.

Since this was to be his "last masterpiece," he showed no shortage of creativity, or as his wife said, he showed a total absence of brains, putting far more into the renovation than the place was worth. The attic was gutted and a new floor put down. Lights were installed, and two new small windows went under each eave for light and air. A window bench was built under one of them. Wood planks covered the entire ceiling so that it looked like a floor. Bright red paint was the finishing coat on the side walls—five layers to give the color a rich depth. New carpeting finished off the neat hideaway bedroom Jim had built.

At that point, there were no stairs for getting up to that hideaway. But not to worry. The house originally had four small bedrooms on the second floor with a bathroom at the top of the stairs from the first floor. Two rooms were on each side, none very big. Knowing that he was "movin' on up" by creating a room in the attic, Jim split one of the original four bedrooms and put a bathroom in half of it, then installed closets and a staircase up to the attic in the other half.

Now there was one larger bedroom and two smaller ones on that level. And two bathrooms instead of one. And now it was possible to get up to the attic.

New heating and air conditioning were added and the basement cleared of the old plumbing, water heaters, and furnace. At last the masterpiece was ready to rent. Jim found a tenant who treated the house with the love it deserved; however, within a year, her circumstances changed, and she couldn't afford to stay. The house went on the rental market again. This time the prospective tenants made Jim leery.

"How many people can sleep in here at the same time?" That seemed to be the primary question asked over and over.

Jim envisioned his lovingly renovated house being wrecked by a horde of tenants all moving in at once. Rather than see that happen, he sold the place. Jim is now out of the house-buying and remodeling mode.

"So much risk. So much hard labor," Ben sighed, nodding his head slowly, "for places you don't even live in. Some you never did."

"Well, you're a rebuilder too, so you know how good hard work feels. And how doing things you thought were beyond your grasp makes you proud. Look. I could've showed you guys snapshots of a couple of the places. But the important part is what a picture could never show."

# Hachigame: Eric's (and Shane's) Tale

"I think you guys might like to hear the story of Hachigame," Eric abruptly piped up from where he had sat quietly through the last several tales, changing position only to silence his cellphone's occasional rendition of Beethoven's Fifth. (There'd been enough digitized "duh duh duh DUH, duh duh duh DUH" to drive the snow-marooned men crazy.) "One of these days you're going to see or read about Hachigame or see it up in bright lights in your hometown."

Hatchy-what? Japanese food, car, or graphic novel? New computer game? Whatever. We'd soon find out.

## Shane and stardom

"This story isn't so much about yours truly as it is about a guy named Shane. Shane is the guy who made yours truly a star!" chuckled Eric, enjoying his own story in advance.

Eric met Shane through his son's business. Shane, one of the workers there, had written a movie script. Shane craved a career as a filmmaker, but he was barely on the ground floor, plying his craft as an occasional actor and director in theater productions. Like many people in the creative arts, Shane had to keep his day job, as the saying goes, in order to eat and pay the rent. Hence, the "straight job" where Eric met Shane.

Shane was a thoughtful and interesting young man who seemed to move to a different hum.

"That's 'hum,' not drummer." Eric made sure we noted the distinction.

"What I mean is, when the pace around Shane accelerates or slows down, Shane stays on an even keel. No need to rush. No need to worry. What will get done will get done." At times, the customers made the job atmosphere chaotic. Other workers sweated as their stress levels elevated, yet Shane kept the same calm control he showed on much slower days.

Further defying the stereotype of "artistic temperament," Shane was a highly responsible person. He was always on time for work, never asked to leave early, and was always willing to cover another worker's shift when necessary. Eric liked Shane's demeanor. They chatted frequently about Shane's ambition. It was a kind of ambition Eric recognized. It was that "blind faith" ambition which had driven Eric himself thirty years ago. The kind of ambition which still drives him to new adventures today.

Shane had spent the last two years writing his script. Its title was *Hachigame,* pronounced something like "Hatchy-gammy," meaning "horseshoe crab" in Japanese. The movie was a documentary-style whodunit to take place on Smith Island, a speck of dry land off the southern tip of Maryland. Shane had assembled a small but enthusiastic crew, including several actors to play the three main roles. He planned to conduct interviews with island residents who would suffice for other characters. On tape, these characters would answer questions, and their answers would then be spliced into scenes where their answers fit the script's needs. The island itself would become a character. As the script unfolds, a young man returns to the island after a fourteen-year absence to find out how his father was murdered, along with two other men: a real-life triple murder that had never been solved.

Mr. Watkins, a retired detective who had been the lead investigator on the case, had been the best friend of the murdered man. The dead man's son was now returning to explore the past. Shane had given Mr. Watkins' character a small part, just one or two small scenes to introduce the former policeman in the film; then the main focus would turn to the other characters.

Shane studied Eric and said, "You could do that role for me. You'd have just a few lines." Now the closest Eric had ever come to the movie business was attending the same high school as filmmaker John Waters. That was forty years ago—and in fact Eric never even met him. In short, Eric was nowhere near being an actor.

"But hey," Eric said, "this film thing could be a hoot. And then I remembered something that really made me want to do the part."

As a child, Eric's older sister had told him that back in 1920, when their father was a baby living with his parents in Los Angeles, he had played the infant child of Mary Pickford in a movie. "I could hear the silver screen calling me," Eric admitted.

## How to make a movie without any money

Shane's film could not even be classified as low budget. It was pretty much "no budget," depending on borrowed equipment and low rates paid to the professionals involved. Heavy-duty marketing would be needed to make a splash even locally when the film was completed. Eric knew the film was Shane's dream. Both Eric and Shane had the alluring spectre of *The Blair Witch Project* lurking in their imagination; of course Shane, like hundreds of other aspiring filmmakers, wanted to make the next indie smash-hit. Eric saw in Shane the same spark Eric had had in his early twenties, the spark that makes people feel they can do anything. So why couldn't Shane make a movie? He could. He would. With whatever meager bucks he could muster, Shane was off to Smith Island to make a blockbuster. And Eric was going to play Detective Watkins.

Shane called Eric about a week after shooting began and said he was ready for Detective Watkins to show up to make movie magic. A script was emailed to Eric just a day before he was scheduled to head for the island and perform his one scene. The dialogue was a mere paragraph. No more than thirty seconds at most. It would be a snap. And oh, by the way, could Eric please bring his antique truck? It would be the perfect vehicle for the detective to drive in the movie.

In fact, Eric had been to movie sets before. When the movie *Diner* was filmed, the director needed antique cars, and Eric took one of his to audition for the shoot. While his car never made the movies, it was fun to see the clutter of a movie set with its many bright lights, multiple cameras in various positions, and seemingly endless miles of wire and cable stretched across the area. Eric had also been on one of those Universal Movie Studio tours where huge sets were established as background for feature films. He had been to costume and wardrobe areas holding the actors' many changes of costumes. He remembered the vast amount of catering equipment set up on location to feed the grips, cameramen, sound people, and dolly drivers, as well as the actors, on a real movie set.

As the small ferry boat arrived at the dock on Smith Island, Eric wondered what the set of *Hachigame* would look like. Walking down the dock towards the road, Eric saw a car pull up. Out stepped Shane, who introduced Eric to the two men with him. Following a ten-minute ride around the island to see everything (there are less than 150 houses on the island), they arrived at the "location headquarters," a small, recently built two-bedroom house with a tiny kitchen and a screened porch. Luckily with air conditioning, as summer heat was beginning to blast the area.

"As writer, director, producer, and sometimes cameraman, Shane was the bomb-diggity on this movie," Eric said.

Shane's dream and his passion were what had persuaded three young professional actors to shoot the full-length documentary of his imagined version of the triple murder from years gone by.

The lead character was the mid-twenty-something man returning to the island where he lived as a child before leaving abruptly with his mother at the age of nine. Three years after he left, his father had been killed. No one had ever explained to him the circumstances of his father's death. The young man decided to return to the island with his girlfriend and another man to unlock the secret to his father's demise. One of the three "real actors" played him.

Shane had developed a creative way of avoiding the need to hire actors to play Smith Island locals. By doing the film in a documentary fashion, he could interview island people about things from the past and incorporate their answers into the film later where the script called for them. The residents were not told about the "triple murder" portrayed in Shane's movie. He felt they might be less cooperative if he did, since they'd be apt to see portraying their island as the scene of a horrendous crime as being detrimental to their image.

Back at "headquarters," Eric also met the full editing crew of the film. His name was Pat. That's right. The entire crew was one guy.

Eric said, "Let's go." He was expecting to be filmed in one thirty-second scene.

"Not so fast," said Shane. "We have to go over the scene to make sure we film it right the first time."

Eventually Eric and Shane set off to the first location to shoot. It was a bed and breakfast Shane was using as Detective Watkins' home on the island. As the retired detective, Eric was supposed to meet with the three characters and give them a brief explanation of his involvement as the lead investigator on the murder case many years before.

Three lamps in the parlor were moved closer to a corner chair where Eric would sit to film the scene. Lampshades were skewed at an angle to cast the perfect light on Detective Watkins' face. Makeup and hair? Forget it. "Check yourself in the mirror, comb your mop if you want to, and let's get shooting," was Shane's approach to Detective Watkins' "look." Shane held the one camera to shoot the scene, and Pat, the editor, doubled his participation by holding the sound boom for the scene. Two actors off-camera sat across from Eric to ask the questions Eric would answer.

Shane used an interesting technique here. Instead of writing specific dialogue for Detective Watkins, he asked Eric to think about someone he knew from high school and try to remember a story or two from that relationship. So when the actor seeking information about his long-dead dad asked, "You knew my father since high school—what was he like?" Eric would just sit in the chair and describe a real friend he knew from high school, relating several incidents from those days. The "real stories" became the script for the scene.

## "Just talk"

"Take one." "Okay, do it again." "Again."

"Now you got it, Eric," they told me. "Just talk. Talk like you're remembering that real friend, and you're telling something you already experienced."

"See," Eric said to my Abacrombie guests, "that way you weren't acting, you were just talking. Like I'm talking to you guys right now. About myself. It was easy."

About an hour after they began, the scene was finished. Eric thought his work there was done. Not so, Detective Watkins. "That went well," Shane said. "Maybe you can do a little more."

"Not until I take you all out to dinner," Eric told them. It was then that he found out there were no restaurants open on the island during the week.

"What about a grocery store?" Eric asked. "Surely we can buy some food and take it back to the house." The grocery store stood two doors down from the B&B where Shane and his group were shooting.

When Eric opened the door to the small grocery, he was greeted by the owner, who immediately asked if he was the new movie guy who just came over on the ferry. There are no secrets on a small island. After acquiring some ham, cheese, and bread, the little band headed back to the film headquarters. At least they wouldn't starve.

When we entered the house around 7:30 in the evening, an old man who looked to be in his eighties pulled into the driveway. The movie guys had met the gentleman while conducting interviews before Eric got there. This man had proudly spent fifty-nine years as a waterman, fishing and crabbing for a living. He had glimpsed how meagerly the film folks were living. So he brought over a bushel of steamed crabs. The whole band dove in.

"Ham sandwich, hell," Eric said. "We were in crab Heaven, eating one of Maryland's favorite delicacies caught and prepared by one of its oldest experts."

When the crabs had been devoured, Shane sprang his new idea on Eric. He and Shane would rise at 5:00 AM to shoot another scene involving Detective Watkins. This time Shane would write a real script outline, but Eric was to improvise a conversation with the lead actor.

"Uh-oh. We were crossing into new territory here. But my ego being up to the task, I said 'Let's do it.'"

Early the next morning, Shane outlined the scene, and he and Eric went to a new location to shoot. Again, just one cameraman and one boom operator. The lead actor was great. A professional acting in independent films like this in hopes of being "discovered," he had worked this way many times before.

"Please give me something to work with," Eric deadpanned. "I need motivation, and not that crap you gave me in yesterday's scene."

There was a moment's stunned silence till everybody realized Eric, the nervous one on the set, was kidding.

Once the scene was shot, Eric caught the next ferry and headed back to reality. He thought his movie days were over. Two days later he got a call from Shane. The scenes were terrific. Would he do some more? It seemed Eric was going back to Hollywood by way of Smith Island.

On the second trip, Eric met the lead actress. She had been away shooting a commercial when his earlier scenes were filmed. The only woman in the movie other than locals, she was beautiful. And she was good. In fact, all the young people were very good at their craft.

"All of them were waiting to be discovered. Watching them showed me how the pursuit of the goal is a stairway with many steps. One day Shane may be in Hollywood. Or those actors may be in a major play, movie, or TV show. Appearing in *Hachigame* would be a step along the way."

## Just like the big ones

Several scenes were shot during that second two-day trip to the location. They weren't long scenes, but they got Eric even more deeply immersed in how it all was done. He was fascinated, realizing that the process they were following as they rehearsed, set up a scene, practiced dialogue, did rewrites—even making use of the location's history and people—was the same used in a big-budget film.

"When the movie comes out, I hope Shane's as proud of his effort as I was to share in the passion those young people put into the effort," Eric declared.

As Eric walked onto the ferry, Shane was filming the last scene where Eric would appear: Detective Watkins leaving the island. Eric was saying goodbye on film to the actors he was leaving. He felt as if the spirit of his father, who'd played a bit part on the silver screen over eight decades ago, was watching.

"Shane kept the film rolling until I was safely seated on the boat. As we pulled away from the dock, I said my final line ... *'See you at the Oscars.'*"

# Things You Love: Rick's Tale

Rick put his legs up on the antique chair next to him, then quickly put them back on the floor. He shifted in his seat. He coughed tentatively. We waited.

"You know how sometimes you reach a point in your life when you know you have to change?"

Sounded as if we were going back to confessional mode. "Funny how often this topic comes up at this table," I encouraged him. "I think maybe it's because as we get older, we start to understand that our whole life is just a process of figuring ourselves out."

Tim agreed. "Sometimes I wish we could hit the pause button and think a minute, but we can't. Life rolls along. We're driving the bus, not riding in the back."

He may have mixed his metaphors, but everybody in the room seemed to know from experience what he meant.

## Enough crashes

Rick launched into his tale. After separating from his wife of many years and going through a particularly difficult schedule at work, Rick realized that "it was change or crash." Having already experienced a few crashes, he didn't want any more right now.

"Slow down, I began telling myself. Stop being a wheel. Be a passenger. Enjoy the ride."

While it is true that his family had always begged him to do just that, the simple truth was that he'd had to maintain a thousand-mile-an-hour pace just to keep the wolf from the door. Finally the wolf was gone, or at least far enough away for Rick to live more for himself than for family survival.

"Is that selfish or just being honest?" Rick asked, but he didn't wait for an answer. "My kids wouldn't starve—and the roof over their heads was a damn nice roof. And even though their mother and I were divorced, I took care of the kids *and* her, financially. She didn't have to work."

Rick's business success had finally reached a level that meant he no longer had to climb out of bed every morning and bust a gut all day long, or leap onto a plane or train for a six-hour trip just to spend one hour face-to-face with a client. No longer did he have to spend most nights alone in a second-rate hotel before heading off to yet another battle for money.

Rick talked slowly about how his body had become so tired that his mind finally started to listen. Through a company he owned, he arranged to take a furlough from work for six months. For the first time in almost thirty years, he wouldn't have to "catch the bus." Or punch the clock. Or tote that bale. When he put the plan into effect, his first thought was "Thank God," but his second thoughts were about the "me-ness" of it all.

"Hey," I said, talking to myself as much as him, "isn't it okay to care enough about yourself to be good to yourself?"

"Yeah, maybe so," Rick acknowledged. "At least I hope so, because that's what I tried to do."

## Meeting ladies (make that "the lady")

Because in the past his work had kept him out of town for long periods of time, Rick didn't know many women well enough to ask them out following his divorce. But there was one very attractive lady at his bank whom he eventually got up nerve enough to ask out to dinner. Sure, she said, dinner would be fine.

The first question Sophie asked Rick at dinner was, "So why do all men lie?"

"No way was I going to defend all men! You can tell a man is lying if his lips are moving." Rick laughed. "Sophie didn't keep up the third degree, though. In fact, she was sweet and kind and patient, even though I immediately started to blather my whole life story without her asking."

He continued, "Two things were great about my six months off. The first was spending more time with my kids, going to 'Daddy Day' at their school, stuff like that. Another great thing was that I could take my time getting to know Sophie. Not rush things like I always used to."

Sophie was a pleasure to spend time with. She was beautiful. ("Of course," somebody murmured through a mouthful of pastry). She made no demands whatsoever. She was basically unencumbered. Divorced many years earlier, she had two grown children, one in town and one in Florida. Rick found himself wanting to be with Sophie all the time. Carefree, on extended vacations, he found it idyllic to be able to travel, go to the beach, and do whatever the two of them wanted.

Sophie introduced Rick to the world of "creative scavenging." Together, they scoured estate auctions, antique stores, flea markets, and all sorts of "please buy my junk" sales. Sophie made this kind of shopping seem like a sport. After scoring some old wooden thing or other, Sophie would show Rick how to strip and refinish it, how to make it look beautiful. They began buying and buying and buying. Soon the basement at Sophie's house was full, and they were putting their loot into a barn behind Rick's new house.

"Finally, we had accumulated so much stuff that it was just too much. Sophie made a very wise rule: not to buy anything unless it was a thing we truly loved."

Rick discovered that Sophie was what he truly loved. And the feeling was mutual. Within just a few months, they had become a couple.

Sophie worked at a bank part time. She also had a home-based monogram business. Each Christmas she set up in a kiosk at a local mall. Rick knew nothing about that kind of business. But he went to a mall with Sophie to see how much they would charge for her kiosk that year. One mall wanted ten thousand dollars for ten weeks, mid-

October until the end of the year. For a kiosk, not a store! Another mall was commonly referred to as "Death Valley Mall" because there was very little traffic, but that mall wanted more vendors and offered something unique. Take any open store space they had for two thousand dollars for ten weeks.

How would they possibly fill all that space? Sophie just wanted her ten-foot-square area to set up the sewing equipment, nothing more. Rick had an idea. Get a big space and fill it with the collection of stuff they had bought in their antiquing expeditions. They would work the store together. Since it was to be filled with their purchases, it could have only one name: "Things You Love."

## A labor of love

Sophie was a true merchant. Entrepreneurship was in her blood. Her grandfather had owned the small market on his farm where people from all over the area shopped for bread, milk, cigarettes, and gas. Sophie grew up selling penny candy and ice cream cones. She had worked the farm as well.

"I never met anyone, ever, who works as hard as Sophie," Rick declared.

Together they worked at the store through the holidays. The store looked beautiful, especially with Sophie there monogramming shirts and stockings and towels. Rick lugged furniture from auctions to the store and then on deliveries to customers. The store provided a great foundation for their relationship. Being together, they didn't mind the long days or the off-nights chasing down furniture at auctions.

Rick and Sophie married seven years after they met, six years after Things You Love first opened. Rick and his girls, Sophie and her two kids blended together and became a new family.

Soon, Things You Love moved from the mall into a 230-year-old building that they renovated together as a combined coffee house and antique shop. After eleven successful years, Sophie is thinking about ending the run.

"That place really brought us together," Rick mused. "Even if we let it go, I'll always love Things You Love."

Of course Rick's six-month bubble of relief had popped long ago, but the Rick who emerged to go back to work was a Rick who had learned to slow down and savor spending that kind of time with Sophie and their blended family.

"I never thought I'd hear myself saying this, but you know what? I'm really looking forward to retiring!"

# The Abacrombie: Herman's Tale

The guests had been talking for a full day. Herman had served breakfast enough for a week, followed by lunch, followed by a remarkable dinner which the chef (likewise marooned) pieced together without benefit of his early morning fresh-food buying trip. The snow was starting to fall again outside. No one could leave.

"So tell us, Herman, how you came to buy this place," Burt asked.

"Yeah, Herman, you haven't given us the Abacrombie story," Rick chimed in.

So, one more time, I freshened the coffee—by now espresso high-test or espresso decaf—for all the troops still standing, and I proceeded to outline how our family bought the place to begin with.

"Before getting into the purchase details, let's talk about how the Inn was founded," I began. "In 1890, long after the Civil War, Colonel Biddle of the Society Hill Biddles of Philadelphia came to Baltimore as the commander of the troops stationed here. This house was where he lived. It's five stories tall and covers seven thousand square feet.

"Fast forward. In 1981, Joseph Meyerhoff donated money to build the Meyerhoff Symphony Center across the street. That's it out the window there. At that same time, the area was undergoing a change. People left Baltimore in the late sixties, and not much was happening in this area. There were no places for people to stay who might come to the symphony and no restaurants for diners, both of which the symphony's benefactors, the Meyerhoffs, recognized as essential. If the Symphony Center was to be successful, that had to change.

"The Baltimore City Fire Department retirement fund loaned money to the original 'modern' owners of this property. They renovated the five stories into four floors of rooms, a total of fifteen bedrooms, and a large restaurant and bar in the basement. It became known as the 'Society Hill Hotel,' with a bar called 'Grill 58.' You probably didn't notice, but this building's address is 58 West Biddle Street, the street named for the original owner of the house.

"The first owners were the absentee variety. They lived out of town. And while the bar was popular—especially the piano player, Mel—the owners never seemed to generate enough revenue from the rooms.

"When a guest arrived, they would check in at the bar. The bartender would collect their money and send them up the back steps to their rooms above. So, when you arrived, the bartender might say, 'A hundred twenty-five dollars, but if you pay cash instead of using a credit card, it's only a hundred bucks.' When the owners called to ask how many rooms rented the previous night, the bartender might say only seven or eight. Why should he report the three who paid cash? Folks, trust me: absentee ownership in a cash business doesn't work.

"And although the place was popular immediately, there wasn't enough revenue getting to the absent owners to pay the bills. And the bartender had started his own little business, renting rooms for less than a full night, as long as you paid cash. Not the right clientele to build a great business.

"After about eight years of building a fine reputation, the place started to slide downhill. By then the beautiful renovations had been trashed by the transient population. Now, mind you, some early guests remember elegant furnishings and wonderful service. But some in-between guests remember being disappointed. And when enough of the regulars who loved the place stopped coming, bankruptcy was inevitable. What had cost almost one and a quarter million to buy and renovate was now auctioned in court for four hundred thousand dollars.

## New wind in the old willows

"The buyers were Paul and Colin, two terrific men who operated a bed and breakfast in nearby Bolton Hill called 'Mr. Mole.' Colin had been a set designer in the theater and was a genius with a swatch of fabric, some lumber, and a paintbrush. Their place in Bolton Hill had five rooms to rent and was very successful. The place was fabulous. Gorgeous rooms with wonderful paint techniques, lavish curtains, four-poster beds with drapes, and stenciled flowers on the walls. Truly one of the most beautiful places where you could hope to stay. And since Colin managed Mr. Mole, the two men took on another property to be run by Paul.

"When they bought Society Hill Hotel at the bankruptcy hearing, they knew it had to be renovated from top to bottom. Colin's skills were put to the test. Together he and Paul changed the once-beautiful interior that had been ravaged by tenants back to its resplendent self. Perhaps even better.

"From the beginning, Paul and Colin knew they didn't want to run the restaurant. A chef from Baltimore's famous Little Italy came along and agreed to rent the space, operating the restaurant as a separate business from the hotel above. Instead of renting out fifteen rooms, Paul rented only twelve, turning two rooms on the first floor into a beautiful sitting parlor and a breakfast room, with the third bedroom on that floor serving as the office. Paul and Colin never called it a hotel again. It was 'The Badger Inn, a Bed and Breakfast.' The restaurant was called 'La Teso Tana.'

"The owners called the place 'The Badger Inn' after the classic children's novel The Wind in the Willows, featuring Mole and Badger. Mr. Mole. The Badger Inn. Get it? But when you advertised with a name starting with a B, others came up first on the Internet sites. So they made up a name for the Badger, starting with A, closely followed by other letters that begin the alphabet. The place became 'The Abacrombie Badger Bed and Breakfast.' And believe it or not, they actually kept a stuffed badger on a shelf above the breakfast eaters. (Look right up there, Tuck, over your head!)

"Paul ran the Abacrombie for almost eight years. He had previously retired from a long career in the Air Force and then had been an innkeeper working long hours. It was time to retire. That was four years ago when our family bought the place. But why was I even looking for a place to buy?

"My wife, Maggie, and I had been together for over seven years by 2002. And her son, Edward, known to all as Sonny, was an accomplished chef at a Ritz-Carlton in Naples, Florida. The young man is a genius with food. Growing up, he had worked for several great chefs, first at the Pimlico Hotel and then at Rudy's with one of the best chefs in the country, Rudy Speckamp.

## And the man can cook

"Sonny attended culinary school at Johnson & Wales in Providence, Rhode Island. After four years there, he went to work in Florida at some of the best hotels, resorts, and restaurants in the country: the Grand Cypress in Orlando, the River Club in Jacksonville, and two Ritz-Carlton hotels, one on Amelia Island and then at their best property in Naples. He went to Washington, D.C., to work with a great chef. He went to Columbus, Ohio, to work with the famous Hartman Henke. Sonny is not driven by money. His passion is food. And the man can cook.

"Chef Sweetman—now we all call him 'Chef'—lives, breathes, and sometimes even eats food. He reads every day to see what others are doing. He goes to other restaurants to cook for one or two weeks at a time to study methods of other great chefs. The Internet has become a medium for young chefs to connect and make progress faster by sharing and not hoarding ideas like so many of the older chefs.

"Chef Sweetman's work ethic is amazing. Forget ten-hour days; great chefs work for twelve to fourteen hours a day, either in research, preparation, or actually 'on the line' plating dinners for their guests. They never calculate their hourly wage, because sometimes the servers make more than they do per hour, even in the finest restaurants. People who eat their wonderful food and taste the flavors provided by the many hours of thinking and caring about the finished product should stop in the kitchen and thank them more often.

"Anyway, I digress, as usual. Seeing the passion Sonny had for his craft was easy. And at a point where I was selling my company and heading into semi-retirement, I offered to invest in a property that Sonny and his wife, Melanie, would operate. Let me introduce you to Melanie. Abacrombie guests have already met her—pretty, unassuming, yet you always knew you were in the hands of somebody who had more knowledge and clout than a waitperson.

"As a child, Melanie grew up in Austria and Germany. Her dad was a businessman who traveled the world. When he returned home, he would tell her of stories from around the globe. Here, there, somewhere.

"'And when you stay *somewhere,* Daddy, which is the best place in the world to stay?' young Melanie had asked.

"Her father always answered, 'The Ritz-Carlton is the best.'

"And so, early on, Melanie decided she would study hard and one day go to work at a Ritz-Carlton hotel. Once out of university, Melanie traveled to Brazil. And then to Denver, Colorado, and on to Florida, where she served at the Ritz-Carlton in its capstone, the one in Naples.

## A story of Melanie and Sonny

"As the dining room manager at the Grille Room, Melanie became acquainted with the new diva in the kitchen, Chef Sonny Sweetman. Now waitpeople in the 'front of the house' always are at war with the 'back of the house' kitchen crew. Timing a dinner between what the kitchen is doing is tough for the servers out front. They face the guests offering drinks, bread, and chat, while they are at the mercy of the kitchen as to when the guests will see their food. And though servers smile when they leave the floor and enter the kitchen to pick up food, there are many harsh words exchanged in the back on a busy night.

"A server has a few tables and maybe a dozen guests. The chef is trying to coordinate dinners for perhaps eighty or more people at once. His agenda and yours do not always mesh. And make no mistake, the chef is god in a restaurant.

"Melanie took another job as manager on the Club level of the hotel. She was a perfect hostess. She was always concerned about meeting a guest's needs. And being seven floors away from Sonny actually made it possible for them to get closer in their relationship. Love blossomed. They planned a wedding. It would take place in Europe in July 2002, while they were looking for a property to start a new business with me.

"Aware of their individual preferences, talents, and backgrounds, they wanted a combo: an inn for Melanie to run and a restaurant for Sonny. And while there are hundreds of such places around, I had to be sure they would make enough money to live on, and most importantly, pay me my rent!

"As the investor, I talked with several owners of B&Bs that were for sale for in excess of one million dollars. The owners were cordial people. But when I asked about the cash flow, I was stunned. Some said as little as thirty thousand to fifty thousand dollars a year. How would that pay back a million-dollar investment and allow Sonny and Melanie to make a living?

"'You are not buying a business, Herman,' the owners would reply, 'you are buying a lifestyle.'

"You see, merely living in that beautiful home was considered a 'lifestyle' by the owners. Well, damn if I would give Sonny the million dollars just so he could have a grand lifestyle—without working at all!

"We talked about Maine, the Carolinas, Colorado, maybe Phoenix or California. But one day Sonny called home to tell me and his mom that while searching on the Internet, he had found the perfect place, right here at home.

"Maggie and I had lived in Baltimore all of our lives. Neither of us had ever been to this place. We drove down to see the property, just twenty minutes from our home, and we fell in love with it in half an hour. Look around, folks, you can see how beautiful it is here. Paul and Colin had made it warm and inviting when you walked in the small lobby. It is elegant, charming. The furnishings are beautiful. Some of the chandeliers around the place are exquisite. Maggie and I asked the kids to fly home to see it, and we made an offer. It was the end of June in 2002. Closing would take place in early September. Then we would take over the property.

"But first we had a wedding to attend. In Austria. Forget *The Sound of Music* and any other vision you have from Hollywood of what it is like there. None of those visions is as beautiful as it really is. Merely walking into the lobby of our B&B in Portschach, Austria, made you breathless. You are across the street from the Worthersee, a beautiful huge lake, and the inn is housed in a five-hundred-year-old former monastery. Gorgeous old stone walls. A courtyard with a fountain Maggie and I plan to duplicate one day in our yard (right!). A quaint bar with windows that are perpetually open to the breeze from the lake. The small curly main street of the town lined with shops and restaurants, and boasting the train station displayed in every American movie with a European setting made in the forties and fifties.

"You cannot imagine how beautiful this place is in July. Or any month, I'm sure. Maggie and I took my three daughters, my son-in-law, James, and of course her daughter, Julie, with us on the trip. Melanie's mother and father had arranged the wedding plans. About fifty people stayed at the inn for the wedding. The civil ceremony took place with the bride and groom in traditional Austrian garb, Sonny in lederhosen and Melanie in a dress native to her homeland. The Public Official pronounced them bride and groom in the courtyard. One of the most wonderful dinners ever served followed. But they weren't married yet. Not in the church.

"The morning after the civil ceremony was better than any wedding in any movie you have ever seen. Picture the sun beaming down on the lake. Crystal blue sky. Even more blue than you are now thinking. And as the guests walk across the street and over a green lush carpet of grass to the dock, you see before you a large gondola boat that would easily hold all of the guests. We were going out on the lake.

"After about thirty minutes, we came to a peninsula with a large rock hill jutting out to the sea. All disembarked and started climbing the stairs. At the top of this piece of Earth that only God could make was a Catholic church, approximately a thousand years old. You were already breathless, but this took your last breath away.

"As the organ began playing, and the priest walked to the altar, nobody could help crying. It was too much. And yet it was simple and elegant. It probably illustrated every girl's dream wedding. After that ceremony, Melanie and Sonny were truly married.

"Back on the boat and back to America? Not yet. While Maggie and I wanted to take the kids to Salzburg, Melanie's parents had other plans. We were going to see the family home, the one that had been in the family for five hundred years.

"Again, the place looked like a movie set come to life. The 'willage,' as our hosts called it, was surrounded by the large stone wall of a fortress. Two drawbridges crossed the moat for access. Up on the highest point, looking down on the town, was the castle where the King had lived. Cobblestone streets. Buildings a millennium old.

"In the center stood what was once a small hotel owned by Melanie's ancestors. And then we knew where the innkeeper-blood flowing through Melanie had come from. For five hundred years, the property has passed down from generation to generation. It was never for sale. A family in the village cares for the property, now vacant. Perhaps a baker will set up shop on the first floor, and above that three apartments await the family, should they want to spend time there. And Charlie and Vera, her parents, announced that now it would be in Melanie and Sonny's hands to pass down in another fifty years. Amazing. Sonny turned to me and shrugged. 'Who knew. It's quite something, isn't it?'

"Back in America from this storybook setting, this dream, we were about to take over a bed and breakfast with a restaurant operator in the basement. His lease would expire in a year, so we were not expecting to operate the restaurant right away. Sonny and Melanie would run the Inn, while Sonny prepared his plans for his first restaurant. Maggie and I would collect rent and pay the mortgage we had taken out to buy the place.

"For months, the kids ran the place by themselves. And they quickly learned that things were different when you owned the place. Where was Human Resources to help send in another employee? What was the phone number of the maintenance department to fix that sink? Who does these books? How do you know which bills to pay first? What does owning this place have to with helping a guest or cooking a great meal? And how come Melanie keeps getting sick every morning?

"So, six months after taking on the Abacrombie, Sonny was going nuts. He was not cooking, and Melanie was pregnant. What business plan were they reading? Maggie and I jumped in to help. First I cut a deal with the restaurant tenant to vacate right away, so we could begin renovating the place. And, in my retirement, I became an innkeeper—when I had thought, with delight, that I was going to become a bum.

"Everything in the restaurant was gutted. The bar was taken apart piece by piece from the main room and moved to the front room of the lower level. That meant the ceiling had to be taken out and the ductwork moved to accommodate the high old wooden bar back and mirrors. And a new tile floor was put in the new bar area. Who did all the work? We did. This was a family project. Save some money and do it yourself. Of course professional plumbers and electricians did their jobs, but anything the family could do, we did.

## Countdown to the menu

"Charlie, Melanie's father is an artist. He left Paradise and crossed the Atlantic to come to Baltimore and cover all the chairs. Julie and Maggie painted the brick walls, ceilings, and hallways. Sonny tore the kitchen apart. He needed a window from the kitchen into the dining room to send cold food through. No problem. I started cutting the brick with a rental saw. The plumber working a few feet away cried, 'Stop, what are you doing? How do you know you won't hit any pipes or wires in those walls?'

"'Hey, I need a window here—so there can't be anything inside,' was my response.

"The 'tunnel' is lined with copper and set off by a gilt-edged painted frame that Julie created. Looks like it was put there in 1890 when they built the place. And now every dessert goes through that window.

"Working against our own deadline, food would start being served on March 21, 2002. As in 3/21. Like three, two, one, blast off! On that date, Sonny gave the kitchen a shakedown cruise. Potatoes boiled, fish prepped, beef marinated, and whatever it takes to make an Apple Tart Tatain readied by Chef Sweetman and his staff.

"The first night's menu was to be simple, and yet show the chef if his equipment and staff were ready for paying guests. The people coming to eat that maiden voyage meal were friends and family. What was he going to serve?

*Oven Roasted Tomato Soup with*
*Prosciutto & Mozzarella Tea Sandwich*

*Young Lettuce Salad with*
*Wild Mushroom Strudel*

*Poached Halibut with*
*Sauteed Potatoes and Olives in a Parsley Sauce*

*Oven Roasted Petite Chicken with*
*English Peas, Rosemary Bread Pudding, and Chicken Jus*

*Beef Tenderloin with*
*Cumin-Roasted Carrots and Chive-Scented Mashed Potatoes*

*Grilled Colorado Rack of Lamb with*
*Eggplant and Potato Gratin with Balsamic Jus*

*Vanilla Bean Crème Brulee with*
*Caramelized Bananas and Grand Marnier Marinated Strawberries*

*Apple Tart Tatain with*
*Vanilla Ice Cream and Caramel Sauce*

"That morning it seemed impossible that people could eat there that night. But they would.

"During the weeks when everybody was busy making the restaurant beautiful, my daughter Kelly was busy making a baby. Apparently the kid was a gourmet and wanted to be at the first dinner.

"At four o'clock in the afternoon, Kelly called and said, 'Dad, if you want to see your grandchild born, you better hurry to the hospital.' In two hours, the guests would arrive. Did they need me? I wasn't cooking, making drinks, or serving the tables. So I went to the hospital and was there for the arrival of another bright light in my life.

"Tyler Herman Lochte arrived as guests were being served their first course. Holding that little bundle was thrilling. But I couldn't give him the kind of milk he wanted, so I hurried back to the restaurant to celebrate Tyler's arrival over dessert with my friends.

"Soon the day-to-day grind became the norm. You are all guests here at the Inn. You're good people who travel about and love your creature comforts. And thank God, most of you show your appreciation with a thank you or a compliment about the service, or the flowers, or the nice rooms we have. And the restaurant guests absolutely love the place. The food amazes them. I'm not the one saying that. The professional food critics have constantly acknowledged and appreciated Chef Sonny Sweetman's efforts. Being named Best Restaurant by one local paper in his first year was quite an accomplishment, and shortly Abacrombie was featured in magazines and other papers as one of the top restaurants in the city. The highlight may have been the feature in *Bon Appetit*, a bible in Sonny's world.

"And now you know how we came to buy the place. And as we end the fourth year here, new accolades keep coming. Even as this is being typed, the Inn will be featured in the Rachael Ray magazine, as well as on her syndicated television show. Rachael Ray, as lovely in person as she is on the air, filmed a spot with Chef Sweetman, which played nationally on the Food Network.

"Those of you who have stayed with us often know it is not an easy life. Melanie has Alisa, now turning three, and Sonny works ungodly hours in a tiny kitchen putting out meals for a price far less than they are worth. Most guests realize that. But it snows in the winter here, and it can stay cold for months. Chef Sweetman gets calls every week to go elsewhere to cook in a warm climate where someone else will tend the business and he can just be a chef.

## Make me an offer

"As his original backers, Maggie and I would love to see Sonny stay home forever. We love having his family with us. But even when we first launched this project, we knew it might not last forever. So which one of you wants to indulge your fantasy of being an innkeeper, give up your life, and write me a check?

"An ophthalmological surgeon stayed with us recently while attending to patients at Johns Hopkins Hospital. He said he was tired of the tedious and nerve-wracking task repeated hundreds of times over the years to save his patients' eyesight. Despite being rewarding, the stress took its toll on him. He would come down here each morning to have breakfast with me while his wife slept. Every day he would question me about the day-to-day life of an innkeeper. It seemed idyllic to him. Serving nice people in a leisurely way. Cutting the bagels and putting out the fruit. Getting people that second or even third cup of coffee. No pressure. And listening to their stories.

"'Tell me, Herman,' he asked me, 'how much would you want for selling this place?'

"'Doc, your wife would kill you if she heard you ask me that.'

"Sure enough, later, the doctor's wife came down for her breakfast. She seemed a little worried. She kept fidgeting about her cereal and yogurt. I asked her what was up.

"'My husband didn't come down here and make you an offer, did he?' she wanted to know.

"I laughed out loud. He was at least the tenth person in the last four years who had asked how much, and asked seriously, with a big check available. Everyone thinks it would be great to be the innkeeper. Meet the nicest people in the world. Be around beautiful rooms all day.

"Thank God they feel that way. One day soon, this place just might be for sale."

# Revelations: The poor naked guy, and other exposures

As I have said earlier, the Abacrombie embraces the diversity of life. It's a place where everybody feels comfortable and at home. That point is proved in many ways, both in and out of these Tales. One no-longer-young gay couple who stayed here provided further proof in a funny little incident that may be worth repeating now.

One of the two gentlemen wanted to take a walk while his partner stayed behind to soak in the tub. "I'm going to go explore Mount Vernon [the Baltimore area surrounding the Abacrombie]. I'll be back in a few hours," said the walker. And he left.

As the tub soaker pulled the door shut on entering the bathroom, he heard a noise on the other side. It sounded as if something had fallen on the floor. Oh well. The bath was ready. He enjoyed a long soak. When his body had turned into a prune, he stepped out of the tub. Oops, all the towels had been taken from the bathroom and laid out at the foot of the bed. The robes usually hanging on the door were also on the bed. And as he turned the doorknob to exit the bathroom, he discovered what that noise was: as he shut the door, the doorknob on the other side had fallen off. And the knob on his side didn't open the door anymore. Uh-oh.

Naked, and with not even a towel to cover himself. And now locked inside the bathroom. Knowing his partner would not be coming back soon. An hour passed and no one came. Then a second hour. Suddenly he heard a noise. Yes, it must be his partner.

"Housekeeping," Theresa called as she opened the door to the room. A small squeaky voice begging, "Help me please," emanated from the bathroom.

"Are you all right?" Theresa picked up the doorknob and realized what had happened. She put the knob back in place and began opening the door.

"No, no, no, don't open it, I'm naked in here!" the little man's little voice shrieked.

Theresa grabbed a robe, opened the door, and handed the man hiding behind the door something to put on. While it was sad that he had spent a couple of hours naked in the bathroom, it was also just plain funny. The next day the trapped man laughed about it with other breakfasters. What a way to start their union! You see, they had just celebrated their commitment ceremony, and this was their honeymoon.

A year later, they returned to the Inn for their anniversary. With the room full of breakfast eaters, I remembered the incident and felt that it needed to be commemorated. I took a breakfast muffin and placed one candle in its center. As I walked out to the room full of people, the two men were delighted to have me remember their anniversary.

"Yes," I told the whole room. "It has been one year since one of you was locked naked in the bathroom!"

The little man asked if everyone at the Inn knew of that incident.

"Hell," I said, "You are a legend here because of that!"

Being a good sport, he took it very well.

## Stress leads you to high places

When you audition for a world-class orchestra, no one doubts that you're under stress. Many of those who try out for the Baltimore Symphony Orchestra stay at the Abacrombie. We are literally one hundred feet from the stage door they must enter to try to prove they're fit to "join the band."

Violinists, oboe players, percussionists, pianists, harpists, and hopeful conductors have all stayed with us for the multiple-day auditions across the street. Day One may include three, four, or even five musicians from all over the world who have traveled to play their piece in an effort to get a job with the BSO. This makes the house sound wonderful, as they always practice in their rooms before heading over to face the judges.

One woman loved playing downstairs in the restaurant before it opened at night. She said the acoustics were remarkable, and she could easily tell when she was making mistakes. As she played and played, the staff and I were one flight up checking in newly arriving guests. As you must've noticed, the lobby and parlor room look strikingly beautiful when you enter the building. As I was explaining to the guest the codes to enter the door, the music from the violinist soared about us. The guest checking in said it was the most elegant B&B he had ever visited. "Why, you have even hired a violinist to make it feel inviting!" Why can't auditions happen every day?

Those who are trying out play no more than an hour or two on Day One or Two. If they "make the cut," they come back the next day. Some go home after just one effort, others stay to compete again Day Two. Sometimes it isn't pretty. Nerves get a little edgy—as if world-class young musicians aren't high-strung enough.

One night I got a call from the burglar alarm company at two in the morning telling me the alarm was going off and the police had been dispatched. When I arrived at the Inn, the place was surrounded by police cars, with officers standing at the ready. The person in charge told me someone was in the restaurant's bar. Though the place was dark, they had seen a figure lurking in there. They wanted me to open the door so they could send in the accompanying police dog to capture the intruder.

As I unlocked the door to the restaurant, the officer used the bullhorn to announce that they were sending in a dog in thirty seconds unless the person came out with his hands up, now. The figure scurried down the hall and disappeared into the kitchen. The dog was right behind him. The intruder moved fast as lightning, running through the kitchen and up the back "tower steps" four floors to the roof. Blasting through the roof door, the intruder climbed a ladder left there to use in fixing the equipment on the roof.

Dogs can't climb ladders.

Floodlights from the parking lot below illuminated the huge, twelve-foot-high air conditioning tower with a small woman dressed in a white bathrobe perched on top of the AC unit, five floors above the street. I hoped she didn't plan on trying to fly. The dog handler was at the base of the ladder now, gun drawn, staring at the woman sitting above her. I could see who she was from the parking lot below.

"Stop," I told the police, "she's a guest here." And sitting next to the almost-naked guest, perched in her lofty place, was the object of the search that had made her set off the alarms in the bar: a bottle of Chivas Regal. Apparently the bar where she had gotten drunk earlier had closed. She told the upward-staring throng that she simply wanted to be "near Heaven and have a drink in peace."

The police retrieved her from the roof and brought her down to the front steps. "Should we book her?" they asked. The dog handler mused that she had agitated her dog badly, and it would be nice if the dog could at least take a bite out of her. I myself was thrilled that she didn't fall off the damn roof and make a front-page headline in the next day's *Baltimore Sun*.

As the police pulled away from the building and I escorted the woman to her room, she asked if I could do just one thing for her before she closed her eyes to rest. "Would you have a drink with me?"

I declined.

## Time for full disclosure

Now I guess it's time for *me* to strip down. By now you have read about a group of diverse characters and are probably wondering if any of these stories is true. You heard various characters insist that you can't make this stuff up—but really, now, did these people really exist?

Did a dishwasher really admit his humble entry into the working life? Are those pilot stories "just the facts"? Come on, Tony, or whoever you are, nobody owns that many cars. And those business tales by Randy—can you really believe they happened, or were the things "he" described just a bunch of hot air, the combined bragging or wishful thinking of a couple of guests who just wanted to make themselves feel good and entertain the others?

Every word of the book is true.

You heard what I said about not making that stuff up. That's right, you heard *me* say it. Every one of the events happened. All of them. How can I be so sure? *Because they were all my own tales.*

Enzo, Ben, Jeff, Tuck, Danny, and so on—they are the names of my best friends. Friends who helped me through, around, and over the pits and peaks of a lifetime. They lent me their names to use in this book. But their tales are mine. I used their names as a way of immortalizing them. They have been with me throughout the events "they" recount. These people have already shared the events—while they were happening to me.

You have now read a version of my life. A very incomplete one, without some of the intimate details of love and relationships and marriage. We spoke nothing of my religious beliefs here. You wouldn't expect me to confess to all my sins at once, would you? And by the way, to my children and grandchildren reading this, be assured that the "Alpha Male" stories are not about me! As my editor said on reading that section, "You may have the world's most Type A personality, but you are *nothing* like those Alpha schmucks." When it comes to that side of my life, kids, I am not telling you anything.

I shared this journey to make you think about yours. Countless failures and mistakes occurred along the way. So what? I tell my kids that if you do a lot of things, you will do a lot of things wrong. But you will also do a lot of things right. The "rush" of accomplishment and the happiness your efforts bring to those around you, along with the sheer joy of watching your kids grow, is the magic of life.

When my children were young, we didn't tell fairy tales at night when they climbed in bed. They asked about my many jobs, houses, cars. And goof-ups. They wanted reality TV long before it became popular. Now they are grown and are facing the challenges of adulthood. And there are now four wonderful grandchildren. Clayton lives in Richmond. He's my buddy. Tyler has a brother now named Morrissey, and the little guy melts your heart with his smile. Little princess Alisa took me to the fair yesterday and showed me all the farm animals. And more will come, we hope, and fill their parents' lives with the joys our children have given me and their mother.

What will I do now? I wrote the book to catch up with myself. After years of being different and following paths others seemed to stay away from, I know it's okay not to be like everyone else. Hell, I have made my troubles and triumphs fodder for conversation with all of you. I hope you enjoyed them.

Perhaps I will teach a class. Or open an ice cream shop. It really doesn't matter what I do—or what you do. Serving guests bagels can be as satisfying as closing a major deal. It just doesn't pay as much.

# Index: Business Topics